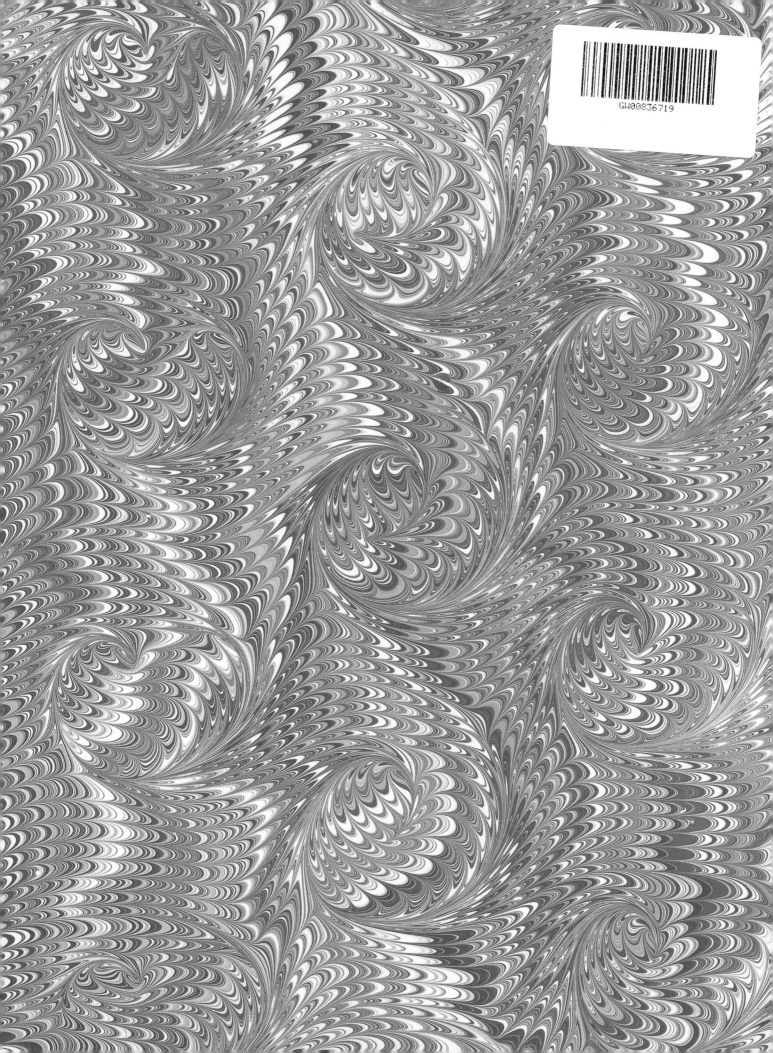

Arnhem:
Defeat and Glory

Arnhem:
Defeat and Glory
A Miniaturist Perspective

G.S.W. DeLillio

Schiffer Military History
Atglen, PA

Dedication

To my wife, Nina, and daughter, Kathryn....

...and Private Jack Allen, 3rd Parachute Battalion, the Parachute Regiment

Book Design by Ian Robertson.

Printed in China.
ISBN: 0-7643-1443-2

We are interested in hearing from authors with book ideas on related topics.

Published by Schiffer Publishing Ltd.
4880 Lower Valley Road
Atglen, PA 19310
Phone: (610) 593-1777
FAX: (610) 593-2002
E-mail: Schifferbk@aol.com.
Visit our web site at: www.schifferbooks.com
Please write for a free catalog.
This book may be purchased from the publisher.
Please include $3.95 postage.
Try your bookstore first.

In Europe, Schiffer books are distributed by:
Bushwood Books
6 Marksbury Avenue
Kew Gardens
Surrey TW9 4JF
England
Phone: 44 (0) 20 8392-8585
FAX: 44 (0) 20 8392-9876
E-mail: Bushwd@aol.com.
Free postage in the UK. Europe: air mail at cost.
Try your bookstore first.

Contents

Acknowledgments

Many options are available to the serious student of military history concerning a plethora of well-written and documented descriptions of the ill-fated Operation Market Garden. Best known perhaps are Cornelius Ryan's epic histora-drama "A Bridge Too Far," Martin Middlebrook's "Arnhem 1944," Robert Kershaw's "It Never Snows in September," and Cornelius Bauer's "The Battle of Arnhem—The Betrayal Myth Refuted."

These masterworks are essential reading and certainly provide anecdotal as well as sufficient amplification of the sweeping Ryan work. Middlebrook's "Arnhem 1944" solemnly infuses First Airborne Division facts and figures with first hand accounts, and expertly draws the reader into the haze and tragedy of war. Robert Kershaw's "It Never Snows in September" masterfully documents the German perspective, and provides a comprehensive overview, high quality reference tables, and superb tactical maps. Finally, the "foundation" work and truly required reading is Cornelius Bauer's "The Battle of Arnhem—The Betrayal Myth Refuted."

The primary purpose of this work, though, is to generate a most unique perspective through a combination of historical research and interpretation through essentially 20mm miniature portraiture.

The author has been most fortunate in receiving support from the following:

Colonel John L. Waddy, for his clear and concise amplification of the battle and permission granted to use the bridge perimeter scene sketched by Michael White. Geert Maasen, Chief Archivist at Renkum, for his insightful comments. Lt. Colonel Anthony Cirillo (retired), for his limitless knowledge of contemporary European warfare. Dennison Hatch, III, for his creativity in improving the overall quality of the maps and illustrations. Joe and Lynne Cherico for their superior photographic enhancements. Robert Coffey, for the many challenging photographic perspectives required by the author. Ian Robertson, a most patient and flexible editor, and Bob Biondi, both at Schiffer Publishing. Professor Ray Callahan of the University of Delaware, for his historical inspiration. Laurie Milner of the Imperial War Museum, for his direction and candor. Alan Myers, Doctoral Candidate in History at the University of Delaware for his painstaking editorial support.

The author assumes the reader fully appreciates that war remains a horrific experience. Hopefully this work in some way conveys the pathos inherent in the Arnhem tragedy itself.

G.S.W.DeLillio

The author is grateful to the following for their permission to reproduce maps and drawings appearing in the following chapters:

"Pursuit to the German Border" – Office of the Chief of Military History, Chapter I

"Execution of Market Garden" – Office of the Chief of Military History, Chapter VI

"Hells Highway" – Office of the Chief of Military History (enhanced by Dennison Hatch), Chapter VI

"Disposition of the 1st Para.Brigade Group at Arnhem" – Colonel John Waddy (sketch by M. White), Chapter VII.

"Landing on a Hornets Nest" - Estate of C. Bauer and Theodore A. Boeree, Chapter VIII

"Execution of Market Garden" - Office of the Chief of Military History, Chapter VI

"Execution of Market Garden" - Office of the Chief of Military History, Chapter VI

"Airlanding Maps" - Martin Middlebrook, Chapters I, V, VII, and IX

The Charge of the Light Brigade[1]

Alfred, Lord Tennyson

1.

Half a league, half a league,
Half a league onward,
All in the valley of Death
Rode the six hundred.
"Forward, the Light Brigade!
"Charge for the guns!" he said:
Into the valley of Death
Rode the six hundred.

2.

"Forward, the Light Brigade!"
Was there a man dismay'd?
Not tho' the soldier knew
Someone had blunder'd:
Their's not to make reply,
Their's not to reason why,
Their's but to do and die:
Into the valley of Death
Rode the six hundred.

3.

Cannon to right of them
Cannon to left of them,
Cannon in front of them
Volley'd and thunder'd;
Storm'd at with shot and shell,
Bodly they rode and well,
Into the jaws of Death,
Into the mouth of Hell
Rode the six hundred.

4.

Flash'd all their sabres bare,
Flash'd as they turn'd in air,
Sabring the gunners there,
Charging an army, while
All the world wonder'd:
Plunged in the battery-smoke
Right thro' the line they broke;
Cossack and Russian
Reel'd from the Sabre stroke
Shatter'd and sunder'd.
Then they rode back, but not
Not the six hundred.

5.

Cannon to right of them,
Cannon to left of them,
Cannon behind them
Volley'd and thunder'd;
Storm at with shot and shell,
While horse and hero fell,
They that had fought so well
Came thro' the jaws of Death
Back from the mouth of Hell,
All that was left of them,
Left of six hundred.

6.

When can their glory fade?
O the wild charge they made!
All the world wondered.
Honor the charge they made,
Honor the Light brigade,
Noble six hundred.

[1] Copied from *Poems of Alfred Tennyson,* J.E. Tilton and Company, Boston, 1870. Published by the English Server at CMU, a non-profit collective of students and faculty at Carnegie Mellon University.

Arnhem

The Germans named the Red Devil redoubt *Der Hexenkessel*, or "Witches Cauldron." Its nexus was the shell-scarred Hartenstein Hotel, which would symbolize British heroism and defiance reminiscent of Hougoumont and Rorke's Drift. Unlike these grandiloquent last stands, the killing grounds at Arnhem would be uncharacteristically relinquished on September 25, 1944.

The fateful charge of Haupsturmführer Victor Gräbner.

1

The Allies:
"Unbridled Optimism"

"The process of final military defeat leading to the cessation of organized resistance has begun…"

Optimism among the Joint Chiefs of Staff and SHEAF

During the opening week of September 1944, the British Joint Chiefs of Staff concluded "the process of final military defeat leading to the cessation of organized resistance has begun."[1] On the left wing of the Allied advance, the British 21st Army Group, commanded by Field Marshal Bernard Montgomery, had swept hundreds of miles across the northern plains of France and Belgium, opening a 75-mile gap in the enemy's front stretching from the North Sea to the city of Maastricht.[2] In the Allied center, the American 12th Army Group, commanded by Lt.-General Omar Bradley, reached the Meuse River in force, less than sixty miles from the German border.[3] The Allies were now seven months ahead of the land-battle schedule.

Unbridled optimism circulated among the Allies, culminating with SHAEF (Supreme Headquarters Allied Expeditionary Force) predictions that "the enemy has lost the war and the defeat of the German Seventh Army and Panzer Gruppe West will hasten the end of the European conflict."[4] French and American armored columns swept into Paris "amid scenes of wild excitement," and the Russians were at the outskirts of Warsaw after capturing the Ploesti oilfields.[5]

German losses during the Battle of Normandy were 400,000 troops, over 1,300 armored fighting vehicles, nearly 3,500 heavy guns, twenty senior commanders killed or captured, and forty-five divisions destroyed or severely mauled. The German Army appeared to lack any coherent order of battle or strategy outside the West Wall, and was considered "bankrupt" in terms of overall fighting strength. SHAEF intelligence estimated that by September 9, after allowing for reinforcements and reorganization of troops cut off in Belgium and southern France, Germany could only muster a mere fifteen divisions, including four panzer divisions.[6]

Reinforcing Success

During the late summer of 1944, the British War Cabinet and Joint Chiefs of Staff informed Prime Minister Winston Churchill that while it was remotely possible that Germany could prolong the war into the winter of 1945, there remained a serious opportunity to end the campaign in northwest Europe by year's end. Prime Minister Churchill challenged this growing optimism, reminding his generals that the Allies had yet to secure a major port other than Cherbourg, France. Earlier attempts to capture German occupied port "fortresses" were unsuccessful and had consumed nearly one-third of Field Marshal Montgomery's British 21st Army Group.[7]

Despite Churchill's misgivings and stiffening resistance along an already over-stretched Allied front, Field Marshal Montgomery demanded a concentrated left wing assault, employing the British 21st Army Group as the lead Allied assault force. Montgomery believed the time was right for a major thrust across the Belgium-Dutch frontier, north of the Siegfried Line into the heart of Germany's industrial Ruhr Valley.

Field Marshal Montgomery presented his commander, General Eisenhower, with three major demands:

1   Restore ground control to Montgomery, including nine American divisions from Lt.-General Omar Bradley's 12th Army Group located on British Lt.-General Dempsey's Second Army right flank.
2   Redirect the majority of transport and supplies arriving in captured French ports to Montgomery's forces.
3   Suspend First and Third American Army advances in central and southern Europe.

The recently anointed British Field Marshal strongly believed that only *his* unparalleled generalship could lead the Allies to final victory before the close of 1944. General Eisenhower eventually capitulated to Montgomery's demands, easing pressure on his subordinate to open the port of Antwerp and redirecting logistical efforts behind the Field Marshal's "final drive" across the Lower Rhine at Arnhem.[8]

Eisenhower's logic for allowing Montgomery's left wing advance appeared well founded. Throughout every major Allied campaign in Africa, Italy, and Normandy, Field Marshal Montgomery remained one of few commanders to clearly demonstrate an aggressive willingness to hasten the ending of the war. In July 1944, the British 21st Army Group successfully drew the bulk of the German armor near Caen while the highly mechanized Americans swept deeply into enemy supply lines. To the Supreme Commander, it appeared an opportune moment to delegate Montgomery command of the next major phase of attack towards the industrial Ruhr Valley, which fortuitously lay ahead of the British 21ˢᵗ Army Group. Another benefit would be the destruction of recently discovered V-2 weapon sites attacking London from the coast of Holland.[9]

Field Marshal Montgomery's focus on the Ruhr Valley overlooked several fundamental difficulties inherent in clearing the northern banks of the Schelde approaching the port of Antwerp. Holland was canal country, much of which lay below sea level, and had already been flooded on Adolf Hitler's personal order to slow the Allies' northerly advance. Montgomery incorrectly assumed that the Second Canadian Army would, in addition to clearing the northern banks of the Schelde, be able to overcome difficult terrain and support the surging left wing of the British 21st Army Group. This costly error would eventually allow nearly 80,000 troops of General von Zangen's 15ᵗʰ Army to escape, thus weakening the left flank of the British Second Army advancing towards the Lower Rhine at Arnhem.

Allied Airborne Reserve: "Coins Burning Holes in SHAEF's Pocket"[10]

In addition to the ongoing debates with his ground commanders, General Eisenhower also faced the twin challenges posed by his superiors in Washington D.C. and the British Chiefs of Staff. On August 22, General Eisenhower presented the final Allied command structure for the European Theater to the Allied Joint Chiefs of Staff. The new command arrangements retained the Tactical Air Force, the United States Strategic Air Force, and Bomber Command as independent formations reporting directly to General Eisenhower, Supreme Commander of SHAEF. This decision would become a deleterious distraction between SHAEF and British 21ˢᵗ Army Group Headquarters. Field Marshal Montgomery's removal as overall ground commander of both the 21ˢᵗ Army Group and American 12ᵗʰ Army Group escalated into a series of fractious debates over which group commander controlled the ground war, and would adversely impact Allied ground and air support for Operation Market Garden. Elevating Montgomery to Field Marshal and offering him the entire SHAEF reserves of airborne forces failed to restore a collective focus on the mounting evidence that Germany was *not* prepared to surrender in September 1944.[11]

"This is a tale you will tell your children." Horrocks' XXX Corps moving beyond the Neerpelt Bridgehead amid destroyed Irish Guards armor.

Allied Order of Battle

Supreme Headquarters Allied Expeditionary Forces (SHAEF)
Supreme Commander: General Dwight D. Eisenhower
Deputy Commander: Air Chief Sir Arthur Tedder
Chief of Staff: Major General Walter Bedell Smith

Air Forces

RAF SECOND TACTICAL AIRFORCE
Air Marshal Sir Arthur N. Coningham

RAF 83 GROUP
Air Vice Marshal H. Broadhurst

RAF 2 GROUP
Air Vice Marshal B.E. Embry

RAF 84 GROUP
Air Vice Marshal E.O. Brown

**RAF AIR DEFENSE of Great Britain
(FIGHTER COMMAND)**
Air Marshal Sir Roderic Hill

RAF BOMBER COMMAND
Air Chief Marshal Sir Arthur Harris

RAF COASTAL COMMAND
Air Chief Marshal Sir Sholto Douglas

USAAF 9TH AIR FORCE
Lt.-Gen. H. S. Vandenberg

USAAF 8TH AIR FORCE
Lt.-Gen. J. H. Doolittle

21st Army Group

Commander: Field Marshal Bernard L. Montgomery
Chief of Staff: Major Gen. F. de Guingand
Second British Army: Lt.-Gen. Sir Miles Dempsey

XII Corps: Lt.-Gen. N.M. Ritchie
7th Armored Division - Major Gen. G.L. Verney
15th Scottish Division - Major Gen. C.M. Barber
53rd Welsh Division - Major Gen. R.K. Ross

VIII Corps: Lt.-Gen. Sir Richard O'Conner
11th Armored Division - Maj.Gen. G.P.B. Roberts
4th Armored Brigade- Maj. Gen. R.M.P. Carver
3rd Infantry Division - Maj. Gen.L.G. Whistler
1st Belgian Brigade - Colonel B. Piron

XXX Corps: Lt.-Gen. B. G. Horrocks
2nd Household Cavalry Regiment
Guards Armor Division - Maj.Gen. A.H.S. Adair
5th Guard Brigade (Irish/Grenadier)
32nd Guards Brigade(Coldstream/Welsh)
43rd Wessex Division - Maj. Gen. G.I. Thomas
50th Northumbrian - Maj.Gen.D.A.H. Graham
8th Armored Brigade - Brig. E.G. Prior-Palmer
Royal Netherlands Brigade "Prinses Irene"
- Col. A. de Ruyter van Steveninck

12th Army Group

Commander: Lt.-Gen. Omar Bradley
First US Army: Lt.-Gen. C. Hodges
XIX US Corps: Major Gen. C.H. Corlett

FIRST ALLIED AIRBORNE ARMY
Commander: Lt.-Gen. L. H. Brereton
Deputy Commander: Lt.-Gen. F.A. M. Browning
USAAF IX Troop Carrier Command
Commander: Major Gen. P. L. Williams

RAF 38 Group
Commander: Air Marshal L.N. Hollinghurst
RAF 46 Group
Commander: Air Cmdr. A.L. Fiddament (9/15/44)
Air Cmdr. L. Darvall

XVIII US AIRBORNE CORPS
Commander: Major Gen. M. B. Ridgway
82nd Airborne Division - Brig. Gen. J. Gavin
101st Airborne Division - Major Gen. M.Taylor

1ST BRITISH AIRBORNE CORPS
Commander: Lt.-Gen. F.A. M. Browning
1st British Airborne Division - Maj. Gen.R. Urquhart
1st Polish Independent Para. Brigade Group -
Maj.Gen. S. Sosabowski
52nd Lowland Division - Major Gen. E.Hakewell-Smith

Only weeks following the Normandy landings, Army General George C. Marshall and General Hap Arnold, chief of the Army Air Forces, urged Eisenhower to reinforce the July breakout and pursuit of the retreating German Army with the largely underutilized Allied airborne forces and transports. General Arnold wanted reassurances that Army Air Force transport resources, which he considered misdirected assets from strategic bombing campaigns, would be utilized before the end of the war in Europe. General Marshall supported strategic airborne envelopment because of his firm belief that airborne forces remained the sole means to prevent tactical deadlocks reminiscent to those he had personally witnessed during World War I. In Great Britain, Field Marshal Viscount Alanbrooke, Chairman of the British Chiefs of Staff, urged Eisenhower that the early weeks of September were "the opportunity for delivering the *coup de grace* by rushing the Ruhr."[12]

To satisfy everyone's wishes, Eisenhower approved the formation of the First Allied Airborne Army (FAAA) on August 8, 1944, with Lt.-General Lewis Hyde Brereton assigned overall commander. Brereton was former Commander of the Far and Middle East Air Force, and previously commanded the American Ninth Tactical Air Force during the Normandy invasion. Brereton assumed operational command of the following Airborne Army formations:

XVIII Airborne Corps – Major General Matthew B. Ridgway
First British Airborne Corps – Lt.-General F.A.M. Browning,
IX Troop Carrier Command – Major General Paul L. Williams
British 38th and 46th Royal Troop Carrier Groups - Air Vice-
  Marshal A.V.M. Hollinghurst.[13]

As commander of the First Allied Airborne Army, Brereton would oversee planning and coordination of five airborne divisions composed of nearly 3,500 gliders, tugs, and transport aircraft.[14] Despite Brereton's inexperience with combined airborne operations, battle-seasoned Corps, Divisional, Regimental, and Battalion commanders surrounded him. Throughout its first forty days, the newly formed First Allied Airborne Army would plan seventeen missions, with all but the final canceled by the rapid rate of Allied thrusts across France and Belgium.

The Final Plan: "Operation Market Garden"

On August 10, Brereton's First Allied Airborne Army was reassigned from SHAEF reserves to Montgomery's 21st Army Group for the northeast drive to the Ruhr.[15] That same day Field Marshal Montgomery proposed a seventeenth plan, code-named Operation Market Garden, to utilize the First Allied Airborne Army.[16]

Market

Market was the airborne phase in which three and a half-airborne divisions were to be dropped or airlanded in the general vicinity of Grave, Nijmegen, and Arnhem. The airborne attack phase would require three days to complete because of limited air transport capacity and ground maintenance. Despite suggestions to the contrary by Air Vice-Marshal A.V.M. Hollinghurst, Air Operations commander Major General Paul L. Williams permitted only one full-scale flight each day.

The veteran American "Screaming Eagles" 101st Airborne Division, commanded by Major General Maxwell Taylor, would land all three parachute regiments, plus light artillery, in the southern sector of the XXX Corps attack corridor between Eindhoven and Veghel. The 101st Airborne Division was to secure a sixteen-mile path across the Dommel River at Eindhoven and St. Oedenrode, the Wilhelmina Canal at the town of Son, and the Willems Canal and Aa River at Veghel. The battle-seasoned "All American" 82nd Airborne Division, commanded by Brigadier General James M. Gavin, would land three parachute regiments plus light artillery in the middle sector between the town of Grave and the Groesbeek Heights. From there, the 82nd Airborne Division was to seize the Maas crossing at Grave, the Waal bridges at Nijmegen, and capture five crossings along the Maas-Waal Canal. Both divisions were expected to land within three miles of their objectives and seize all key positions on D-Day, September 17, 1944.

The "prize" of Operation Market Garden, the Arnhem rail and road bridges, were the key objectives of the British First Airborne Division, landing over six miles west of Arnhem near the towns of Wolfheze and Renkum. On D-Day only two British airborne brigades would arrive, and a single company of specially fitted jeeps was expected to storm ahead and seize the distant Arnhem High-

Only two reconnaissance squadrons were available to support the Second British Army.

way Bridge. The 1st Parachute Brigade, which included three oversized assault battalions, would march several hours later via separate roads to reinforce the expected jeep borne *coup de main*. The 1st Airlanding Brigade, plus a preponderance of headquarters personnel, would remain at the airhead to establish a firm defensive base until the transport phase was completed by D+2, then proceed to Arnhem with the recently arrived 4th Parachute Brigade. On the third day, the First Polish Parachute Brigade Group would arrive southwest of the Arnhem Highway Bridge and seal off expected enemy counterattacks. Following the completion of landing strips near Arnhem, the British 52nd Lowlands Division (air transportable) would arrive by glider to reinforce the British First Airborne Division. The airborne support tail would arrive in Arnhem several days later with XXX Corps.

Garden

Following a massive artillery barrage, the ground attack phase *Garden* would commence at the Neerpelt bridgehead with a rapid advance northeast over sixty miles along a two lane highway. According to the plan, the ground forces would reach Arnhem in *just three to four days*. This roadway-restricted ground attack would consist of a British three corps front, commanded by Lt.-General Miles Dempsey. Lt.-General Brian Horrocks' mobile 20,000 vehicle XXX Corps would spearhead the main drive beyond Arnhem to the IJsselmeer (Zuider Zee) and into the industrial Ruhr.[17] The British XII and VIII Corps were to provide flanking protection.

Field Marshal Montgomery ordered British ground force commanders to conduct "violent" attacks along the invasion corridor and quickly relieve the thinly laid carpet of First Allied Airborne Forces. Since the river and canal obstacles varied from 200 to 400 meters in width, speed and mobility were the key to capturing the objectives. British XXX Corps was to reinforce the three pockets of airborne forces before Army Group B formations counter-attacked and overpowered the lightly armed troops.

Unfortunately the Garden phase appeared far less aggressive than most planners realized. Lt.-General Horrocks' XXX Corps would advance one hour following the first wave of airborne drops, then proceed only six miles north to the town of Valkensward before resting for the night. Prior to September 17, Horrocks spoke only informally of reaching Eindhoven to relieve the American 101st Airborne Division during the first critical hours, instead of incorporating a more rigorous timeline into the already tactically demanding schedule.[18]

In summary, Operation Market Garden was expected to push the Allied forces across the Rhine and ultimately capture the Ruhr industrial region. To support this objective, General Eisenhower

What the Allies failed to grasp was the nascent stages of a major recovery of the German Army in the West.

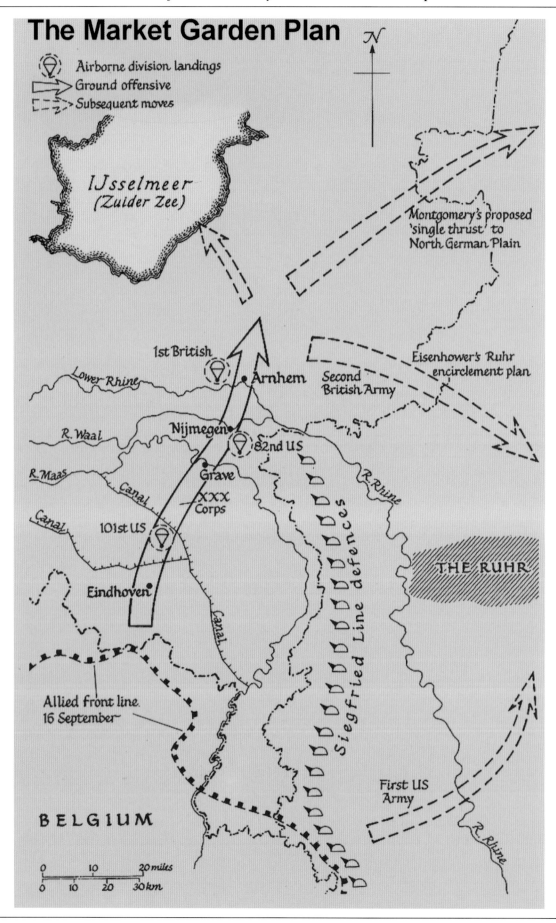

The Market Garden Plan

- Airborne division landings
- Ground offensive
- Subsequent moves

N

IJsselmeer
(Zuider Zee)

Montgomery's proposed
'single thrust' to
North German Plain

1st British

Lower Rhine

Arnhem

Second
British Army

Eisenhower's Ruhr
encirclement plan

R. Waal

Nijmegen

82nd US

R. Maas

Grave

Canal

R. Rhine

XXX
Corps

Canal

101st US

THE RUHR

Eindhoven

Canal

Siegfried Line defences

Allied front line.
16 September

First US
Army

BELGIUM

R. Rhine

0   10   20 miles
0   10   20   30 km

ordered Lt.-General Patton to halt his Saar offensive and reallocate the bulk of Lt.-General Bradley's 12th Army Group logistical support to Lt.-General Courtney Hodges' eight-division First Army, positioned on Montgomery's right flank. Ground transportation belonging to three American Divisions would be transferred to the British 21st Army Group, and nearly 1,000 tons of supplies would arrive daily via ground and air. The plan now conformed to General Arnold's and General Marshall's recommendations to utilize idle airborne reserves for an operation behind the enemy's forward positions. Field Marshal Montgomery would secure his wish to command what could be the last great drive across the Rhine while the enemy remained disorganized.

However, by mid-September a number of seemingly isolated problems began to coalesce: Allied division-level logistics remained keenly strained; German ground resistance had intensified along the Albert Canal; European weather was becoming more unpredictable; and Lt.-General Patton's forces continued to draw vital supplies while attacking the Saar.[19] Finally, Air Chief Marshal Sir Trafford Leigh-Mallory's closing of the successful joint Allied Expeditionary Air Force (AEAF) Headquarters in mid-August had split tactical and strategic Allied air support along national lines.[20]

The Overall Strength of the British 21st Army Group

By the end of August 1944, Field Marshal Montgomery's 21st Group included the First Canadian Army, commanded by Lt.-General Henry Crerar; the Second British Army, commanded by Lt.-General Miles Dempsey; and the First Allied Airborne Army, commanded by Lt.-General Louis Brereton.[21] The First Canadian Army was ordered to capture at least two major channel ports and simultaneously protect the left wing of Dempsey's Second British Army. The First Canadian Army included two corps of six divisions each, but possessed neither the strength nor the logistics to fulfill its dual role. Lt.-General Crerar's forces would suffer several key setbacks days prior to Market Garden while attempting to sever the escape route of the German 15th Army east of the Schelde.[22] Despite an already overburdened left wing, responsibility for opening the port of Antwerp shifted to the now embattled First Canadian Army on September 16 as Dempsey's Second Army prepared to attack beyond the Albert Canal.

To sustain a concerted British Second Army drive of seven and a half divisions, only Lt.-General N.M. Ritchie's XII Corps on the left and Horrocks' XXX Corps in the center possessed the mobility to advance with any rapidity. Major General Sir Richard O'Conner's VIII Corps had been previously stripped of most first and second line transportation, resulting in a slower pace of advance on the right wing.[23] Lt.-General Bradley, commander of the 12th American Army Group, ordered the First U.S. Army to protect Dempsey's right flank with eight divisions.

In total, Montgomery's overall ground force was comprised of twenty-two and a half divisions, with an additional 200,000 air force, airborne, and troop transport personnel.[24] A few days later, Horrocks' XXX Corp would spearhead the Market Garden attack with orders to ignore his flanks and trundle up the entire corridor in three to four days.

Issuance of Market Garden Operating Directives

On September 14, after Field Marshal Montgomery issued formal directives identifying the Ruhr industrial area as the primary objective, Operation Market Garden was set in motion. Montgomery added that the British 21st Group would advance to Berlin without opening the port of Antwerp, since the smaller ports of Dieppe, Boulogne, Dunkirk, Calais, and Le Harve could provide nearly 3,000 tons per day, supplemented by an additional 1,000 tons by air.[25] Lt.-General Brereton and FAAA Deputy Commander Lt.-General F.A.M. Browning also issued orders for 35,000 Allied airborne troops to seize key bridges along the Market Garden corridor. Horrocks would lead XXX Corps, which now included 300,000 troops and 20,000 vehicles positioned south of the Meuse-Escaut Canal. Horrocks' forces were to relieve each airborne division *en route* and cross the Arnhem Bridge sixty-four miles away. The British VIII and XII Corps were to support XXX Corps with flanking protection along the "Club Route," later renamed "Hell's Highway" by the American 101st Airborne Division.

However, a key facet of the plan remained unclear concerning the role of 2nd Tactical Royal Air Force (TAF), located at forward fighter-bomber bases in Belgium. The 2nd TAF planning staff were not present during the closing air support conference called by Air Marshal Leigh-Mallory at Stanmore, England. Lt.-General Brereton's orders to ground the 2nd TAF throughout the opening airborne phase, issued on September 17 1944, further complicated the situation.[26]

Air reconnaissance remained weak, as multiple tasks were demanded of No. 35 (Recce) Wing of No. 84 Group and No. 39 (Recce) Wing of No. 83 Group. Each wing was expected to maintain a constant watch for German troop formations along the Scheldt and proposed drop zones, and also search for V-2 rocket launching sites in Holland.[27] Only two squadrons were available to support the entire British Second Army. As a result, fewer than ten reconnaissance missions were flown between September 12 and 16, 1944.[28]

The Closing Errors: Waving Intelligence Warnings Aside

Operation Market Garden was now set in motion, despite increasing ground intelligence intercepts confirming the recent arrival of German units along the canal bridgeheads, including the 3rd, 5th, and 6th Fallshirmjaegers, 719th and 344th Infantry Divisions, numerous battle groups, training regiments, Flak battalions, and elements of von Zangen's 15th Army. ULTRA decrypts continued to reveal the presence of the II SS Panzer Corps in the vicinity of Arnhem, including the battered 9th SS "Hohenstaufen" and 10th SS "Frundsberg" Divisions and the Independent Heavy Assault Gun Abteilung 217.[29] British Second Army and XXX Corps intelligence had previously concluded that the armored divisions now located several miles north and northeast of Arnhem were essentially "unfit" for action and in possession of little armor.

Less than forty-eight hours before Operation Market Garden H-Hour, SHAEF's intelligence chief, British Major General Kenneth W. Strong, concluded that German forces were significantly stronger than previous British and American estimates. General Eisenhower's Chief of Staff, Lt.-General Walter Bedell Smith, also believed that the airborne plan should be modified to reinforce the

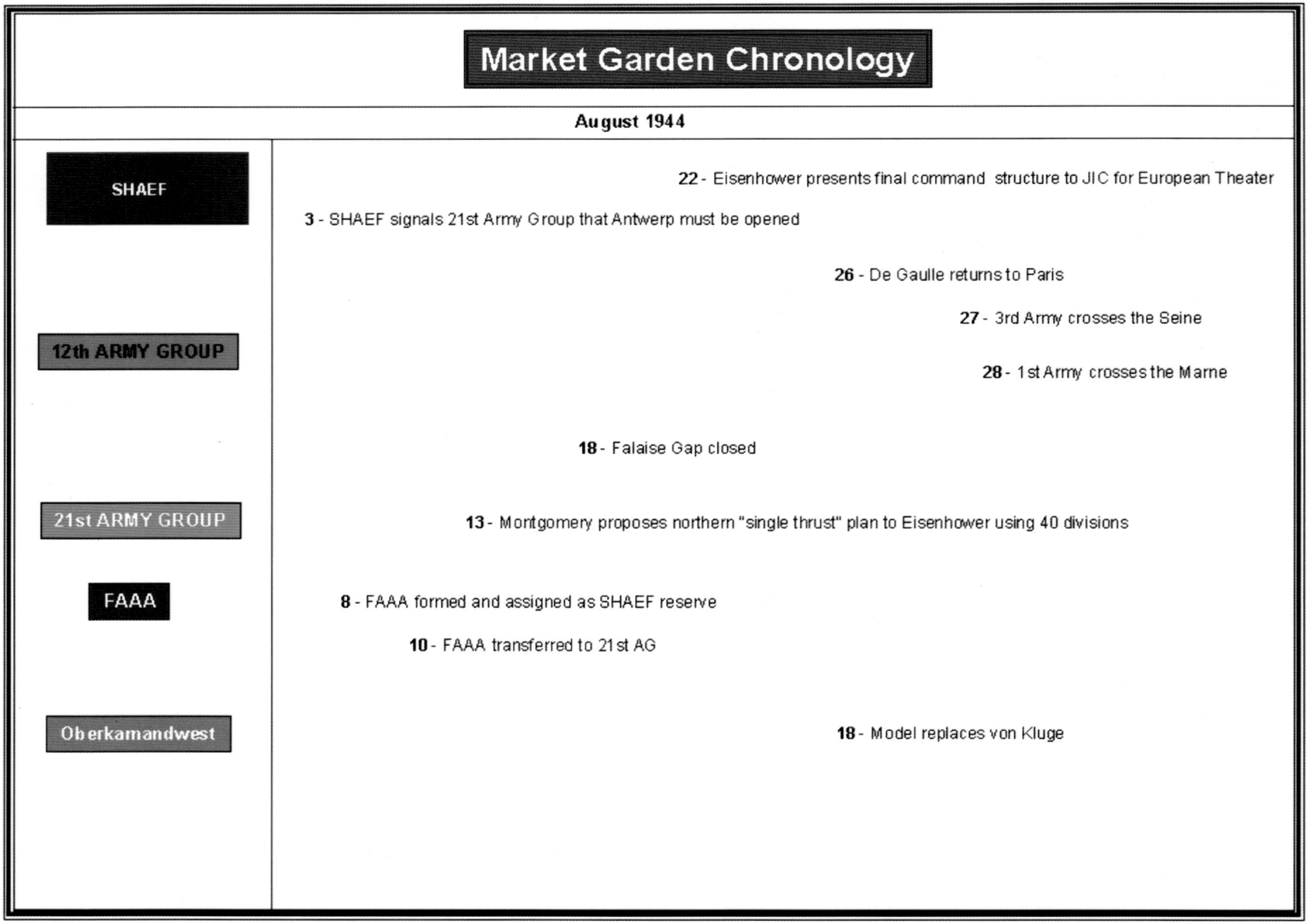

Market Garden Chronology

August 1944

SHAEF

22 - Eisenhower presents final command structure to JIC for European Theater

12th ARMY GROUP

3 - SHAEF signals 21st Army Group that Antwerp must be opened

26 - De Gaulle returns to Paris

27 - 3rd Army crosses the Seine

28 - 1st Army crosses the Marne

21st ARMY GROUP

18 - Falaise Gap closed

13 - Montgomery proposes northern "single thrust" plan to Eisenhower using 40 divisions

FAAA

8 - FAAA formed and assigned as SHAEF reserve

10 - FAAA transferred to 21st AG

Oberkamandwest

18 - Model replaces von Kluge

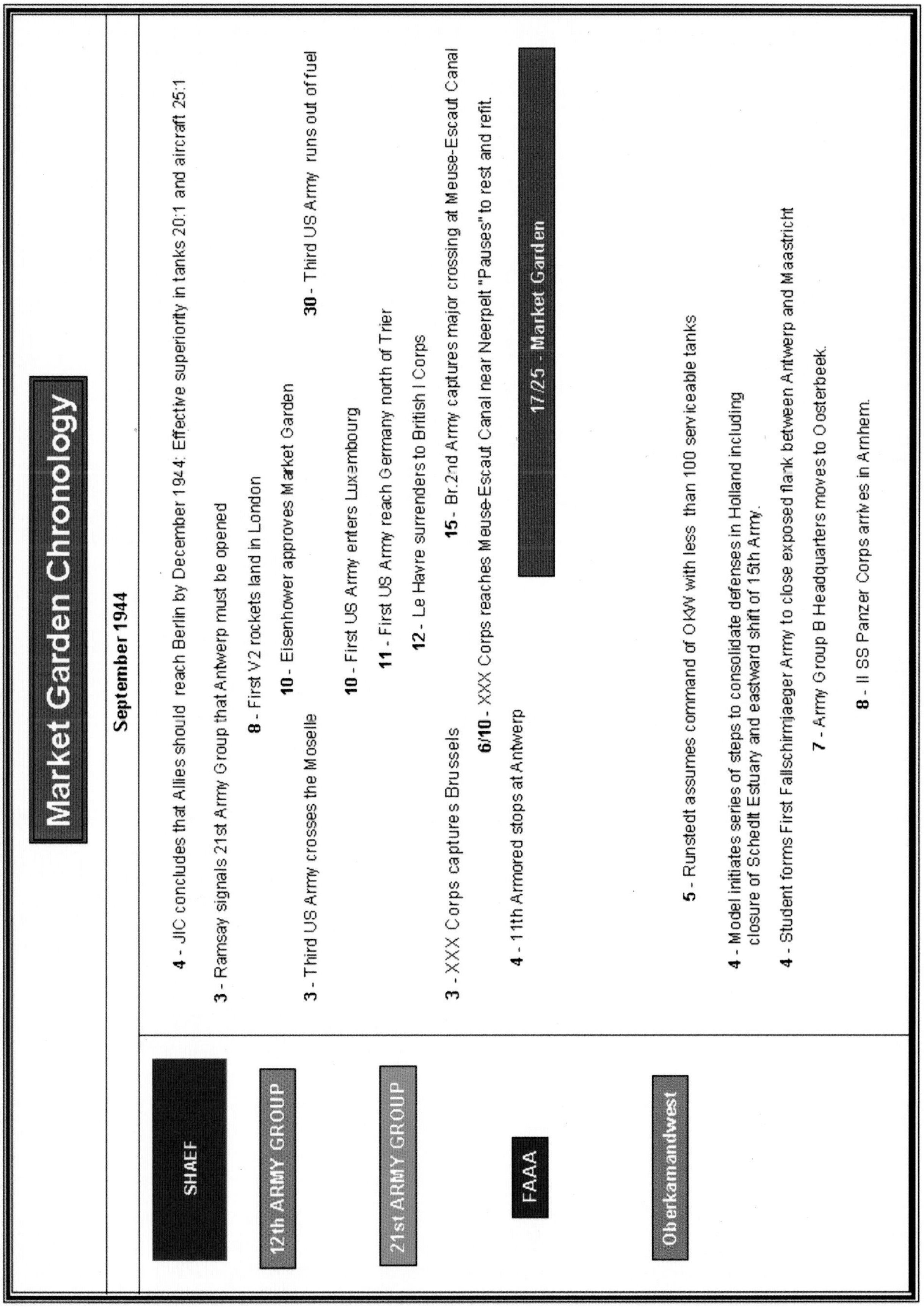

Market Garden Chronology

September 1944

SHAEF
- 4 - JIC concludes that Allies should reach Berlin by December 1944: Effective superiority in tanks 20:1 and aircraft 25:1
- 3 - Ramsay signals 21st Army Group that Antwerp must be opened
- 8 - First V2 rockets land in London
- 10 - Eisenhower approves Market Garden
- 30 - Third US Army runs out of fuel

12th ARMY GROUP
- 3 - Third US Army crosses the Moselle
- 10 - First US Army enters Luxembourg
- 11 - First US Army reach Germany north of Trier
- 12 - Le Havre surrenders to British I Corps

21st ARMY GROUP
- 3 - XXX Corps captures Brussels
- 15 - Br.2nd Army captures major crossing at Meuse-Escaut Canal
- 6/10 - XXX Corps reaches Meuse-Escaut Canal near Neerpelt "Pauses" to rest and refit.
- 4 - 11th Armored stops at Antwerp

17/25 - Market Garden

FAAA

Oberkamandwest
- 5 - Runstedt assumes command of OKW with less than 100 serviceable tanks
- 4 - Model initiates series of steps to consolidate defenses in Holland including closure of Schedlt Estuary and eastward shift of 15th Army.
- 4 - Student forms First Fallschirmjaeger Army to close exposed flank between Antwerp and Maastricht
- 7 - Army Group B Headquarters moves to Oosterbeek.
- 8 - II SS Panzer Corps arrives in Arnhem.

British First Airborne with either the American 82nd or the idle British 6th Airborne Divisions. However, General Eisenhower refused to consider overriding Montgomery's Market Garden plans, either by proposing further reinforcements or by canceling airborne operations altogether for the seventeenth time. A combination of factors—pressures from superiors in Washington, potentially adverse British criticism for challenging Montgomery's generalship, and the difficulties of maintaining an already delicate balance of command—led General Eisenhower to take no action beyond issuing a warning. Eisenhower sent his Chief of Staff to personally communicate a *strongly worded suggestion* that Field Marshal Montgomery alter plans rather than allow the lightly armed British First Airborne to confront a refitted and potentially formidable II SS Panzer Corps. Field Marshal Montgomery would ridicule Lt.-General Smith's ideas, and "[he] simply waved my [Smith's] objections airily aside."[30]

Despite Montgomery's aversion to unfavorable intelligence estimates, lower echelons within British First Airborne Corps continued to receive startling RAF photo reconnaissance information from British Second Army Intelligence. When conclusive aerial photographs of German armor near proposed landing and drop sites arrived at FAAA Corps Headquarters, Browning simply disregarded the mounting evidence.[31]

The British 21st Army Group would eventually receive little support from American ground forces in the south, as Hodges's First American Army on Montgomery's right flank bogged down among the fortified defensive belts surrounding the city of Aachen. Bradley's 12th Army Group would provide minimal flanking support as Patton's forces continued attacking towards Metz, drawing supplies vitally needed to sustain Montgomery's left hook into the Ruhr.

In a matter of hours the largest airborne operation to date in World War II would transport nearly 35,000 airborne troops behind enemy lines with the entire British Second Army prepared to reach the Zuider Zee within three to four days.

Notes:

1. F.H.Hinsley,ed., *British Intelligence in the Second World War,III Volumes* (London: HMSO, 1988), Vol.III, Part 2, pp.367-368.
2. Robert J. Kershaw, *It Never Snows in September* (Ramsbury: Crowood Press, 1990), p.21.
3. Clay Blair and Omar Bradley, *A General's Life* (New York: Simon and Shuster, 1983), p.318.
4. Kershaw, op.cit., p.368.
5. Geoffrey Powell, *The Devil's Birthday: The Bridges to Arnhem 1944* (London: Leo Cooper, 1992), pp.16-17. *First printed by Buchan and Enright, Publishers Ltd. in 1984.*
6. Ibid., p.368.
7. General Walter Warlimont, *Inside Hitler's Headquarters 1939-45* (Novato, CA,Presidio Press, 1964), p.478. *First published in Germany under the title Im Hauptquartier der deutschen Wehrmacht 1939-1945.*
8. Charles MacDonald, *The Siegfried Line Campaign* (Washington DC: U.S. Military Institute, 1993), p.209.
9. Tieke, Wilhelm, *In the Firestorm of the Last Years of the War: II SS-Panzerkorps with the 9.and 10. SS-Division "Hohenstauffen" and "Frundsberg"* (Winnepeg, J.J. Fedoricz, 1999), p.227.
10. MacDonald, op.cit., p.368.
11. Alfred D. Chandler Jr.,ed., Stephen E. Ambrose, assoc.ed., et.al., *The Papers of Dwight David Eisenhower: The War Years* (5 Volumes, Baltimore: Johns Hopkins Press, 1970), Volume IV, pp.2087-2088.
12. Arthur Bryant, *Triumph in the West: Completing the War Diaries of Field Marshal Viscount Alanbrooke* (London: Collins, 1959), p.284.
13. Powell, op.cit., p.14.
14. *American 82nd, 101st, and 17th Airborne, British First Airborne, 52nd Lowland (Air Tranportable), and Polish First Independent Parachute Brigade.*
15. Russell F. Weigley, *Eisenhower's Lieutenants* (Indiana: Indiana University Press, 1981), pp. 287-289.
16. McDonald, op.cit., p.120.
17. Ibid., p.120.
18. Weigley, op.cit. , pp.292-294.
19. B.H.Liddell Hart, *History of the Second World War* (New York: G.P. Putnam's Sons, 1970), p.565. *In postwar interviews General Blumentritt, Von Rundstedt's chief planner, considered the Allied forces too widely spread and the attack towards the Metz fortresses south of the Saar by Patton as unnecessary.*
20. Stephen Badsey, *Operation Market Garden* (London: Osprey Publishing, 1993), p.9.
21. *First Allied Airborne was tranferred by SHAEF to Field Marshal Montgomery on September 12, 1944.*
22. MacDonald, op.cit., p.209.
23. B.H. Liddell Hart, op.cit., pp.563-564. Compounding Montgomery's logistical problems was the discovery that 1,400 British built three-ton lorries were found to have faulty pistons. These vehicles could have provided an additional 800 tons of supplies equal to supplying additional two divisions.
24. Clay Blair and Omar Bradley, *A General's Life* (Simon and Shuster: New York 1983), pp.318-319.
25. Hinsley, op.cit., p.381.
26. Robert Jackson, *Arnhem: The Battle Remembered* (Shrewsbury: Airlife Publishing, 1994), pp.34-35.
27. Ibid., p.25.
28. F.H.Hinsley, op.cit., p.385.
29. Ibid., pp.382-383.
30. Cornelius Ryan, *A Bridge Too Far* (New York :Simon and Shuster, 1974), pp.157-158.
31. Ibid., p.159. Lt.-General Browning is remembered for his rather fatuous response to intelligence warnings of German armor. "I wouldn't trouble myself about these if I were you"…"*They're probably not serviceable at any rate.*"

2

The German "Miracle" in the West

"My Führer, whatever you order, I shall do to my last breath...."
- Field Marshall Gerd von Rundstedt.

An Open Road to the Ruhr?

By mid-September 1944, British XXX Corps had advanced an additional twenty miles to the Meus-Escaut canal. The Irish Guards Group, commanded by Lt.-Colonel J.O.E. Vandeleur and his cousin, Lt.-Colonel G.A.D.Vandeleur, completed a successful nighttime dash towards a temporary wooden trestle over the Meuse-Escaut canal.[2] Several days later, the British 43rd Wessex Division seized the Lommel crossing located just a few miles west of the main canal bridge. The advance was costly and significantly slower than the previous week, when XXX Corps had covered a distance of nearly 250 miles.[3]

The capture of the DeGroote Barrier positioned XXX Corps within 14 miles of the Dutch City of Eindhoven. From there it was just thirty miles to Nijmegan, then less than ten miles to Arnhem. The "short distance" to the gateway of Germany's industrial Ruhr Valley provided the added impetus to propel the Second British Army towards Arnhem. However, the road to the Ruhr was fraught with a number of strategic and tactical obstacles in the battle for Northwest Europe.

Strategic Underestimation of German Leadership, Initiative, and Staff Effectiveness

Bomb Plot Aftermath

Following the failed assassination attempt at Hitler's headquarters on July 20, 1944, many German generals considered contacting the Allies. Several key reasons probably prevented them from doing so:

1) Their oath of loyalty.
2) They believed that the people of Germany would not understand any action taken towards making peace.
3) The troops fighting on the Eastern Front would "reproach" the Western military leaders for failing to uphold their responsibilities.
4) An innate fear of being remembered in German history as traitors to their country.[4]

By late summer 1944, the German generals' views and judgements in the field were increasingly brushed aside by *Der Führer*, and protestors quickly dispatched. The Waffen SS assumed greater influence as Wermacht units were decimated in battle, and Nazi spies proliferated in Wermacht headquarters following the attempted assassination and coup. High grade decryption of Army Group B Headquarters dispatches indicated that despite the Allied breakthrough, the Germans considered it decisively important to hold onto the critical ports of Bologne, Dunkirk, and key estuaries leading to Antwerp. They believed this would strain Allied supply lines and slow the advance. Hitler personally ordered on September 8 that all waterways leading to Antwerp were to be obstructed by any means, including laying mines. Allied intelligence also gathered increasing evidence of stiffening German defenses along the Belgium-Dutch border, but the British Chiefs of Staff concluded it was "unnecessary" to surface the matter with SHAEF Headquarters. The British Chiefs of Staff assumed that SHAEF had already recognized the importance of isolating Antwerp and its key tributaries.[5]

What the Allies failed to grasp during the opening weeks of September 1944 were the nascent stages of a major recovery of the German Army in the West. As early as July, Hitler had ordered preparations for a large scale offensive against the Allies in the fall. To achieve this objective, Field Marshal Gerd von Rundstedt was restored as Commander in Chief of the West to reinvigorate a much needed strategy for the western front. Field Marshal Von Rundstedt's return had afforded Field Marshal Walter Model the time necessary to rebuild the shattered remnants of Army Group B and strengthen defenses in Holland and along the Westwall.[6]

Field Marshal Gerd von Rundstedt

Hitler's reinstatement of Field Marshal Gerd von Rundstedt to the political and administrative role Oberkommando der Wehrmacht (High Command of the German Armed Forces, or OKW) symbolized a return to traditional old German military leadership.[7] The seventy-year-old leader was considered far more capable in executing the land battle than the World War I heroes Hindenburg or Ludendorff. Field Marshal von Rundstedt was ordered to rebuild the entire Western Front. This included restoring the nearly aban-

German Order of Battle
OB WEST
Generalfeldmarschall Gerd von Rundstedt

LUFTWAFFE WEST
(directly under Luftflotte Reich)

WEHRKREIS IV

ARMY GROUP B
Generalfeldmarschall Walther Model

ARMED FORCES Command (Nederlands)
Commander: General der Flieger Friedrich Christiansen

Corps "Feldt"
General der Kavalrei Kurt Feldt

406th Landesschutzen Division
Generalleutnant Scherbening

II SS Panzer Corps (transferred to Model 9/17/44)
Obergruppenfuhrer Willi Bittrich

9th SS Kampfgruppe "Hohenstaufen" - Obersturmbahnfuhrer W. Harzer
10th SS Kampfgruppe "Frundsberg" - Brigadfuhrer H.Harmel

"Herman Goering Division " Training Regiment
Oberleutnant F.Fullreide

Kampfgruppe "von Tettau"
Generalleutnant Hans von Tettau

FIFTEENTH ARMY
Commander: General der Infanterie Gustav von Zangen

LXVII Corps
General der Infanterie Otto Sponheimer

346th Infantry Division - Generalleutnant E. Diester
711th Infantry Division - Generalleutnant J. Reichert
719th Infantry Division - Generalleutnant K. Sievers

LXXXVIII Corps
General der Infanterie Hans Reinhard

Kampfgruppe "Chill"
Commander : Generalleutnant Kurt Chill

59th Infantry Division - Generalleutnant W. Poppe
245th Infantry Division - Oberst Gerhard Kegler
712th Infantry Division - Generalleutnant F.W. Neuman

FIRST PARACHUTE ARMY
Commander: General der Fallschirmstruppen Kurt Student

LXXXVI Corps
General der Infanterie Hans von Obstfelder

176th Infantry Division - Oberst C. Landau

KAMPFGRUPPE "WALTHER"
6th Para. Regiment- Oberstleutnent F.F. von der Hydte
107th Panzer Brigade - Major F. von Maltzahn
Division "Erdman" - Generalleutnant Wolfgang Erdman

II Parachute Corps
General der Fallschirmtruppen E. Meindl

doned Siegfreid Line (or Westwall), as well as reorganizing forty-eight "paper" divisions equal in strength to just twenty-seven combat ready divisions. The German front lay exposed to nearly fifty fully equipped Allied ground divisions, including two thousand tanks and nearly ten thousand planes. The Luftwaffe was nearly non-existent, and the only available combat quality formations were committed to fighting Patton's 3rd Army, which was fast approaching the Metz fortresses.[8]

The Chief of OKW was concerned with a major Allied thrust somewhere across the Rhine into the industrial Ruhr and Saar regions. Throughout the late summer of 1944, OKW intelligence noted the disappearance of Allied airborne forces from Europe, leading to speculation that a large scale operation behind the Siegfreid Line or east of the Rhine was imminent. Ground intelligence also observed the diminishing speed of the advancing British 21st Army Group in the north near Antwerp and the American 12th Army Group in the south towards Aachen. The Chief of OKW concluded that the loss of Allied momentum might allow German forces—including hundreds of thousands of troops scattered along the Channel Coast and Westwall—sufficient time to regroup before the next major enemy offensive.[9] Despite heavy front line troop losses, many senior German officers had survived the battle for Normandy, and

the German home front had not reached total mobilization before the fall of 1944.[10]

Field Marshal Walther Model - Revitalization of Army Group B

The commander of Army Group B, Field Marshal General Walther Model, was twenty years younger than von Rundstedt and considered an outsider to the traditionally Prussian dominated High Command. Model previously served as temporary commander of OB West until von Rundstedt assumed command, but retained control of Army Group B thereafter. Model was a defensive specialist, exhibiting rapid front line adaptability and ruthless defensive fighting skills, especially on the Eastern Front, where he earned a reputation as the "Führer's Fireman." Model had personally assured Hitler in the summer of 1944 that he would establish a stabilized front in the west.[11]

Throughout the opening weeks of September, Army Group B staff work and senior officer improvisation reorganized the entire front facing the British 21st Army Group and American 12th Army Group. The revitalized German forces would include three major formations: General der Infanterie Gustaf von Zangen's 15th Army on the right; General der Fallshirstruppen Kurt Student's First

Further decrypts revealed the presence of the II SS Panzer Corps composed of the 9th SS Hohenstaufen and 10th SS Frundsberg Panzer Divisions.

Fallschirmjäger Army in the center; and General der Panzertruppen Erich Brandenberger's Seventh Army on the left. The rear supply zones were commanded by General der Flieger Friedrich Christiansen in Holland and Generalleutnant Feldt east of the Reichswald.[12]

By the close of the second week of September, Model—still certain of an Allied thrust against the southern right flank of Army Group B—moved his headquarters nearly sixty miles to the northeast at Oosterbeek, Holland.[13] Model's decision to relocate group headquarters within several miles of the proposed British First Airborne Division landing sites would later lead a number of popular historians to conclude that German forces were pre-positioned near Arnhem because of an alleged Market Garden security leak. Model was indeed warned of potential landings in Holland, but he had discounted any such suggestions as being operationally impractical.[14] Despite this miscalculation, Field Marshal Model's timely appearance at the sharp end of the fighting would contribute to the eventual destruction of the British First Airborne Division at Arnhem and stoppage of British XXX Corps along the Market Garden attack corridor.

General der Infanterie Gustav von Zangen –
The 15th German Army

By late August 1944, General der Infanterie Gustav von Zangen's 15th Army remained the largest organized formation in Army Group B, yet the British 21st Army Group had trapped the nearly 100,000 German troops against the Channel coast. As the British advance from the south lost momentum in early September, Field Marshal Model ordered von Zangen to conduct a fighting withdrawal across the Scheldt Estuary to Walcheren and South Beveland.[15]

The 15th Army included nine weak infantry divisions: the 59th; 70th; 245th; 331st; 334th; 17th Luftwaffe Field; 346th; 711th; and 712th. Several rearguard units remained along the southern banks of the Scheldt while the bulk of the relatively mobile 15th Army moved eastwards across the estuary. Many units were ferried across the Scheldt at night and then redistributed along numerous points behind the western wing of the First Parachute Army, which occupied the northern banks of the Albert Canal. By September 22, General von Zangen would evacuate nearly 86,000 troops, 600 guns, and 6,000 trucks and horses.[16] The 15th Army escape to the east preempted another large scale destruction similar to the encirclement of the German Fifth Panzer and Seventh Army in the Falaise Pocket. One division, the 59th Infantry Division commanded by Generalleutnant Walter Poppe, retained a formidable force of infantry and anti-tank guns.[17]

Lt.-General Horrocks and Lt.-General Crerar failed to intercept von Zangen's troops, which eventually weakened the left flank of XXX Corps as it advanced towards Arnhem. Horrocks would regretfully state in his memoirs that "My eyes were fixed entirely on the Rhine, and everything seemed of subsidiary importance."[18]

The 9th SS Hohenstaufen was ordered to hand its heavy equipment over to the 10th SS Frundsberg.

The Newly Formed Defensive Crust - The First Parachute Army
Almost immediately following the fall of Antwerp on September 4, General der Fallshirstruppen Kurt Student, Commander of the First German Parachute (Fallschirmjäger) Army, received orders directly from Generaloberst Alfred Jodl, Chief of Wehrmacht Operations at Hitler's headquarters, to build a new 30,000 parachute army.[19] Student's commander, Reichmarschall Hermann Göring, had informed Hitler that he possessed a readily available "army" reserve of Fallschirmjägers, which could support Army Group B in the West. The First Fallschirmjäger Army, however, was a mere shell of former Luftwaffe personnel and battle exhausted parachute regiments spread over the entire western front and Germany.[20] Throughout the next several weeks, Student would establish headquarters at 's-Hertogenbosch in central Holland and reorganize the tattered remains of three infantry divisions, along with numerous Fallschirmjäger and untested smaller units, into a cohesive defensive barrier along the Albert Canal between Brussels and Maastricht.[21]

By September 5, Model reinforced the First Fallschirmjäger Army with Lt.-Colonel Friedrich von der Heydte's Fallschirmjäger Regiment 6 returning from Normandy, the First Battalion of Fallschirmjäger Regiment 2, and five additional but newly formed parachute regiments. Generalleutnant Wolfgang Erdmann would eventually combine three of the new parachute regiments into the 7th Fallschirmjäger Division. Twenty anti-aircraft batteries of various calibers, self-propelled assault guns, and tank destroyers would augment the defensive firepower of Student's foot and bicycle borne "army."[22] However, the only field formation under Student's command during the first week of September was General der Infantrie Hans Reinhard's LXXXVIII Corps, which was concentrated west of the port of Antwerp.

Scraping the Barrel
On September 4, Student had assumed command of General der Infantrie Hans Reinhard's LXXXVIII Corps, which included only one weak "fortress" infantry division. The 719th Infantry Division, commanded by Generalleutnant Karl Sievers, was already thinly stretched across a corps-wide front from Antwerp to Hasselt. These troops were mostly elderly "B" soldiers unfit for combat and previously assigned to guard the Dutch coast since 1940. Over the next several days, improvisation reigned as several additional formations arrived to reinforce Reinhard's understrength formation. These included the 176th, 84th, 85th, and 89th Infantry Divisions. The 176th "Kranken" Division, commanded by Oberst (Colonel) Christian Landau, arrived from Aachen. Its units, made up of soldiers afflicted with common physical disorders, were known as "eyes and ears battalions."[23]

Generalleutnant Kurt Chill, commander of the 85th Division, had fortuitously reorganized his "crazy quilt mob" of D-Day survivors, mixed among the badly mauled 84th, 85th, and 89th Infantry Divisions, into a cohesive "battlegroup" known as "Kampfgruppe Chill."[24] Like many battle seasoned German commanders, Chill coupled initiative with effective staff planning, and reorganized a defensive crust along the Albert Canal between Massenhoven and Kwaadmechelen.[25] "Acting with independence and dispatch," Chill

set up collection points along the Albert Canal and gathered a miscellany of troops, including Kreigsmarine, Luftwaffe, and military government, as well as Wehrmacht stragglers. In a matter of days Chill had established a sufficient defense to repulse British probes beyond the Albert Canal.[26] On September 6 General Chill reported to LXXXVIII Corps and linked up with the right flank of Sievers' 719th Division just in time to halt the British penetration of the Beeringen bridgehead.[27]

By September 7, General Student's unbroken line was stabilized with a series of thirty-two interlocking battalions. This defensive crust was further reinforced by the arrival of General Student's Fallschirmjägers, under the command of Colonel Walther, and several detachments from Bittrich's II SS Panzer Corps.[28]

"Kampfgruppe" Walther
A second major formation to hastily emerge, Kampfgruppe Walther, was attached to General Reinhard's LXXXVIII Corps. Walther's command also faced numerous challenges as urgently needed equipment and combat ready troops arrived, mostly on foot, to fill critical gaps along the defensive front. Walther's forces expanded to include Fallschirmjäger Regiment 2, commanded by Colonel von Hoffman; Fallschirmjäger Regiment 6, commanded by Lt.-Colonel von der Heydte; Parachute Training Division, commanded by Generalleutnant Wolfgang Erdman; two SS Panzergrenadier battalions from the 9th and 10th SS Panzer Divisions; fifteen Jagdpanzer IVs from SS Tank Destroyer Abteilung 10; a motorized battery of 105mm from the 10th SS Panzer Division; Luftwaffe Penal Battalion 6 from Italy (still wearing tropical uniforms); and an odd assortment of heavy weapons ranging from 20mm to 125mm guns.[29]

Student ordered Walther to hold the British Guards Armored Division at the Mass Scheldt Canal, then counterattack near Neerpelt during early September. A series of desperate company level battles ensued, while the bulk of Walther's and Chill's forces repositioned heavy concentrations of troops along the key two lane Garden route leading to Eindhoven.[30] By the second week of September, the First Parachute Army had hardened into a formidable "crust" facing the British 21st Army Group from Antwerp to the juncture of the Albert and Meuse-Escaut Canals.[31] On September 15, British forces defeated a surprise counterattack against the Neerpelt bridgehead by von der Heydte's 6 Fallschirmjäger Regiment. In two days Lt.-General Horrocks' XXX Corps would fight a much stronger force than British Second Army intelligence had optimistically described in its situation reports.

II SS Panzer Corps – The Ready Reserve
By September 8, the last elements of two battered panzer divisions, reduced to "kampfgruppes," were billeted north and northeast of Arnhem.[32] General der Waffen SS Wilhelm "Willi" Bittrich commanded the II SS Panzer Corps, which included SS Brigadeführer (Colonel) Heinz Harmel's 10th SS Frundsberg and SS Obersturmbannführer (Lt.-Colonel) Walter Harzer's 9th SS Hohenstaufen.[33] Field Marshal Model had previously issued orders that the Fifth German Panzer Army release the II SS Panzer Corps during the first week of September for rest and refitting deep behind the front lines in Holland.[34]

Remotely akin in regimental tradition to their British counter-parts, both panzer divisions retained names evoking centuries old military history. The Hohenstaufers were formed in western France in the late fall of 1942 as the 9th SS Panzergrenadierdivision and commanded by then SS Brigadeführer Willi Bittrich. The name "Staufers" originated in the Duchy of Swabia, where several members of this royal family were German Imperial kings throughout the 12th and 13th century. The Staufers' reign ended after the defeat of Freidrich II, but the spirit of knightly culture was revived through the name of the Hohenstaufens.[35] The 10th SS Division was also organized in France in 1942, and later named Frundsberg after the 15th century Imperial Captain Georg von Frundsberg. The family name was associated with "Landsknechts," or mercenaries renowned for their hard fighting under numerous German kings, including the German Emperors Maximilian I and Karl V.[36]

Both elite divisions included a large contingent of officers and volunteers from the Erganzungsamt (Replacement Bureau) Waffen SS. The 9th and 10th SS Divisions were quickly transformed into highly mechanized armor formations, then transferred to the Eastern Front until the summer of 1944. Bittrich's II SS Panzer Corps returned to France during the closing weeks of the Allied breakout only to suffer nearly seventy percent losses in combat strength.[37]

By late August, Field Marshal Model decided to withdraw Bittrich's II SS Panzer Corps through France and Belgium and establish a mobile reserve in the west. Despite suffering numerous casualties attributed to Allied *Jabos* (fighter-bombers) and the French Maquis (Underground), both formations managed to escape into Holland. Model intended to replenish these forces, but the severity of troop and armor losses on both fronts limited rebuilding to the 10th SS Frundsberg. By September 9, the Hohenstaufen was ordered to transfer all its heavy equipment to Frundsberg and entrain for Siegen, Germany. However, many veteran officers and NCOs were reluctant to surrender any of their carefully husbanded equipment, rendering them "out of order" when attempts were made to transfer scarce armored fighting vehicles to Frundsberg.[38]

By September 12, only the combat formations of the 9th SS Hohenstaufen remained within a ten-mile radius of Arnhem. The 2,500 troops were organized into nineteen company strength *Alarmeinheiten* (quick reaction) groups spread over twelve locations within the Apeldoorn-Arnhem-Zutphen triangle.[39] These *Alarmeinheiten* could reach any attempted British airborne landings within several hours by foot or 30 minutes by vehicle.[40]

The 10th SS Frundsberg was positioned further east of Arnhem, with three Panzer-grenadier battalions at Deventer, Diepensen, and Rheden, a tank headquarters with Mark IVs at Vorden (Panzerjaeger 39), and artillery in Dieren. The total force numbered nearly 3,000 troops and awaited re-equipment with new Panther Mark V tanks. The Panthers, however, would not arrive until several days following the British First Airborne Division's landings west of Arnhem.[41] Somewhat paradoxically on September 14, the British First Airborne Division announced that the "enemy would not be able to muster any mobile force exceeding a brigade."[42]

A number of Bittrich's II SS Panzer Corps units were trained by General der Panzertruppen Baron Geyr von Schweppenburg in 1943 to "aggressively repel airborne landings."[43] In addition to anti-airborne training, many of the corps' logistical units had survived the costly withdraw from France, and provided much needed assistance during formation rebuilding.

Rear Echelon North - Armed Forces Command Netherlands
The northern German rear lay safely ensconced behind the defensive shield of von Zangen's 15th and Student's First Fallschirmjäger Armies. Commanded by General der Flieger Friedrich Christiansen, Regional Commander in Chief of the Wermacht in Holland, its area spanned the entire Dutch coast and ran along the Waal and Maas rivers to Nijmegen. Christiansen's duties were essentially administrating civil government, protecting military installations, and coordinating various German support units. Christiansen remained under direct command of Oberkommando Wermacht (OKW) in Berlin, and exerted no tactical authority over either Bittrich's II SS

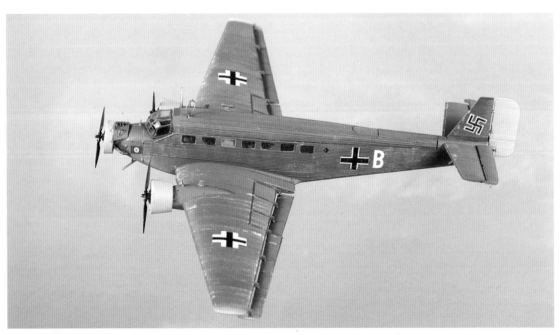

The build up in the Arnhem area continued unopposed.

Panzer Corps or the infamous Hoherer SS und Polizeiführer und General der Waffen SS Hans Albin Rauter, Commander-in-Chief of the German SS police in Holland.[44]

General Christiansen reorganized his "mixed bag" of military personnel into light infantry battalions, many lacking front line experience. Generalleutnant Hans von Tettau, Christiansen's inspector of military training, was assigned the tactical role of establishing reception centers at bridges and ferries along the Maas and Waal in order to reorganize the demoralized remnants into a number of battalions under "Division von Tettau." Former Luftwaffe support personnel were transformed into Fliegerhorst battalions, coastal and garrison artillery battalions into Schiffstammabteilungen (naval training divisions), and Dutch sympathizers and draftees into SS Dutch surveillance battalions.[45] These inadequately trained support troops would be the first German ground forces to encounter the British First Airborne Division west of Arnhem, suffering heavy casualties in the process. But Chistiansen's command was not entirely predestined to misfortune. SS Colonel Hans M. Lippert's SS NCO School and SS Sturmbannführer Sepp Krafft's SS Panzergrenadier Depot and 16th Reserve Battalions would play a key role in successfully harassing and delaying the advances of British First Airborne west of Arnhem.[46]

Lippert's SS NCO School, composed mostly of NCO veterans from the Russian Front, included two infantry companies and a heavy weapons platoon. Lippert's forces, positioned west of the British airborne landing sites, would eventually penetrate and overrun landing zones defended by the British First Airlanding Brigade. Krafft's troops, which included one heavy weapons and two infantry companies, would play a pivotal role in halting the British First Parachute Brigade during the first crucial hours following the airborne landings.[47]

Rear Echelon East -Wehrkreis VI
The second support echelon, similar to General Christiansen's command, was located east of the Allied landing zones near the Reichswald Forest and Groesbeek Heights. Military District Wehrkreis VI—located near the Allied invasion corridor—was responsible for training replacements, organizing new units, and directing supply units. This military district was reduced though battle attrition to merely one full division, the 406th "Landesschützen" Division, numerous Alarmeinheiten, various "eyes and ears battalions," and several Luftwaffe NCO training battalions. After reaching the front of the First Parachute Army, Wehrkreis VI came under the command of General der Kavallerie Kurt Feldt, or "Corps Feldt."[48] Feldt's mixed units would be the first German formations to contest the American 82nd Airborne division landings at Nijmegen until the arrival of Bittrich's 10th SS Kampfgruppe from Arnhem and General Meindl's II Parachute Corps from Cologne several days later.[49]

Army Group B: Final Disposition
Several days before Operation Market Garden, Model's reconstituted forces had reached nearly 130,000 troops, including von Zangen's 15th Army, Student's First Parachute Army, Christiansen's Armed Forces Command, and Corps Feldt. General Student's First Fallschirmjäger Army alone held a 75-mile front stretching from the North Sea to Maastricht, supported by an effective network of several hundred medium to heavy batteries, anti-tank weapons, tanks, and self-propelled guns. Behind Student's defensive network and across the Lower Rhine lay Bittrich's formidable II SS Panzer Corps. Following the arrival of the First British Airborne near Arnhem an additional 50,000 to 75,000 German troops, hundreds of tanks, artillery, self-propelled guns, and light armor would converge on the Market Garden Corridor. A final Allied intelligence summary stated:

"The enemy is fighting determinedly along the general lines of Albert and Escaut canals from inclusive Antwerp to inclusive Maastricht. His line is held by the remnants of some good divisions, including Parachute divisions and by the new arrivals from Holland. They are fighting well but have very few reserves. The total armored strength is probably not more than 50-100 tanks, mostly Mark IV. There is every sign of the enemy strengthening the defenses of the river and the canal lines through Arnhem and Nijmegen, especially with Flak, but the troops manning them are not numerous and many are of low categories…"[50]

The Allies had concluded that the proposed air landings would be initially hazardous but ultimately successful. The advance of Lt.-General Horrocks' XXX Corps through the "crust of resistance" would be swift, and Market Garden a success within a few days. The German defenses were considered weak, but the relatively flat, sandy heathlands and peat bogs, cross-stitched with numerous water courses, would confine heavy vehicles to raised highways, making them easy prey for flat trajectory 88mm guns and pockets of anti-tank troops.

The Allies would also fail to appreciate a number of the intangibles within the core of the Army Group B: a significant number of seasoned campaigners, most likely non-commissioned officers trained to perform duties with the highest degree of efficiency; young recruits compensating lack of experience with fanaticism; and old soldiers driven by fear of dire consequences for not carrying out orders by Goebbel's propaganda.

Just ten days earlier the British 21st Army Group could have reached the Zuider Zee along an almost totally defenseless highway.[51]

Notes

[1] Correlli Barnett, ed., *Hitler's Generals: Authoritative Portraits of the Men Who Waged Hitler's War* (New York: Quill/William Morrow, 1989), p.201. Based upon the Office of the US Chief Counsel for Prosecution of Axis Criminality interviews with Fieldmarshall Keitel. Cornelius Ryan contends that von Rundstedt's chief of staff Major General Blumeritt recalls the Fieldmarshall's comments: "I said nothing…. if I opened my mouth, Hitler would have talked 'at me' for three hours."

[2] Winston G. Ramsey, *"Prelude to Market Garden", The Battle of Arnhem, After the Battle Magazine: Special Issue* (London: Battle of Britain Prints International Ltd., 1986), pp.1-3.

[3] Robert Jackson, *Arnhem: The Battle Remembered* (Shrewsbury: Airlife Publishing, 1994), p.39.

[4] B.H. Liddell Hart, *The Other Side of the Hill* (London: Cassell, 1951), pp.442-443.

[5] F.H.Hinsley, ed., *British Intelligence in the Second World War, III Volumes* (London: HMSO, 1988), Vol. III, Part 2, p.380.

[6] Reporting to Field-Marshal von Rundstedt effective September 4, 1944, Commander-in-Chief , West (OKW).

[7] OKW was similar to SHAEF and all field commanders reported to a centralized command.

[8] Cornelius Ryan, *A Bridge Too Far* (New York: Simon and Shuster, 1974), pp.53-55.

[9] Ibid., p.58

[10] Charles B. MacDonald, *The Siegfreid Line Campaign* (Washington DC: U.S. Military Institute, 1993), p.19.

[11] Barnett, op.cit., p.319.

[12] Robert J. Kershaw, *It Never Snows in September* (Ramsbury: Crowood Press, 1990), p.35.

[13] Cornelius Bauer, *The Battle of Arnhem: The Betrayal Myth Refuted* (London: Hodder and Stoughton, 1963), pp.48-49.

[14] Ibid., pp.47-53. Required reading for a comprehensive review of the alleged conspiracy plot contradicting Cornelius Ryan's "A Bridge Too Far."

[15] MacDonald, op.cit., p.123.

[16] Russell F.Weigley, *Eisenhower's Lieutenants* (Bloomington: Indiana University Press, 1990), p.293.

[17] MacDonald, op.cit., p.125.

[18] Lt.- General Sir Brian Horrocks, *"A Full Life"* (London: Collins, 1960), p.204.

[19] Jackson, op.cit., p. 37.

[20] MacDonald, op.cit., p.123.

[21] Hinsley, op. cit. p.378.

[22] Jackson, op.cit., p.38.

[23] Kershaw, op.cit., p.22.

[24] MacDonald, op.cit. pp.123-125. The kampfgruppe or "battle group" became the basic German fighting unit throughout Operation Market Garden. These groupings were essentially improvised formations equal to an Allied Brigade or Regiment in terms of combat power. The battle group was inherently a fluid organization whereby it incorporated numerous combinations of Wermacht, Kreigsmarine, Luftwaffe, and Waffen SS. The overall performance of these formations varied throughout the Market Garden campaign.

[25] Jackson, op.cit., p.38.

[26] Ibid., p.124.

[27] Kershaw, op.cit. p.23.

[28] Jackson, op.cit., p.38.

[29] Ibid., pp.28.

[30] Ibid., pp.28-29.

[31] MacDonald, op.cit., p.125.

[32] Wilhelm Tieke, In the Firestorm of the Last Years of the War: II SS-Panzerkorps with the 9. and 10. SS-Divisions "Hohenstaufen" and "Frundsberg" (Winnipeg: J.J. Fedorowicz Publishing, 1999), p.222.

[33] Kershaw, op.cit., p.16. An SS panzer division was traditionally 18,000 strong, including 170 tanks, 21 self propelled guns, 287 armored half-tracks, 16 armored cars, 18 self propelled artillery pieces, and 3,670 support vehicles.

[34] MacDonald, op.cit., p.127.

[35] Tieke, op.cit., p.3.

[36] Tieke, ibid., p.10.

[37] Kershaw, op.cit., p.38.

[38] Ryan, op.cit.,pp.150-151. Harzer issued orders for his troops to render their armor and vehicles unserviceable by "removing caterpillar tracks, wheels, or guns."

[39] Jackson, op.cit., p.43.

[40] Kershaw, op.cit., p.41.

[41] Jackson, op.cit., p.43.

[42] Ibid., p.40.

[43] Tieke, op.cit., p. 4.

[44] Bauer, op.cit., pp.48-51.

[45] Ibid., pp.54-55.

[46] Bauer, op.cit., p.56.

[47] Jackson, op.cit., p.41.

[48] Macdonald, op.cit., p.126.

[49] Ibid., p.142.

[50] Hinsley, op.cit., pp.385-386.

[51] Ibid., p.22

3

"The Light Brigade and All That"[1]

*"We must be very careful what we do with British infantry. Their
fighting spirit is based largely on morale and regimental espirit de corps.
On no account must anyone tamper with this...."*

- Lord Montgomery of Alamein [2]

The British Regiment

Before proceeding into the battle, one must renew an appreciation of the centuries-old legacies that preceded many British fighting formations. The tradition and historic achievements of British airborne and ground forces provide a case study of twentieth century warfare infused with Victorian regimental tradition.

By September 1944, many of the British ground and airborne forces remained an amalgam of regimental organizations. Numerous critics have assailed the regimental system as a key reason for XXX Corps' lethargic and sometimes nearly non-responsive performance during several key engagements. In one instance, the Irish Guards failed to mix armored forces with Grenadier Guards infantry during an engagement near Nijmegen. On the other hand, the valiant stand of British First Airborne troops at Arnhem Bridge and inside the Oostebeek Pocket could be best ascribed to the inherent strength of the regimental system.

The Regimental System

The British Army's regimental system had existed since St. Valentine's Day in 1661, and its essence remained prevalent among Field Marshal Montgomery's 21st Army Group. By the outbreak of the war, the British Army was organized into five Foot Guard Regiments, or Brigades of Guards, and sixty-four regiments of the line. Each regiment represented a parent organization and generally retained two to five regular infantry battalions. The infantry battalion was considered the basic British combat unit. The battalions associated with each regiment rarely served together but shared the same regimental training depot. Many of the new battalions that eventually served in Market Garden retained unique geographic distinctions, such as the South Staffordshires, Borders, and Household Calvary.[3]

Both officers and lower ranks considered the regimental organization a private club with a well-understood hierarchy. The regiment was also considered an extended family whose individuals could earn and learn self-respect, take pride in regimental tradition, and add to its glory. Each regiment of the British Army had its own customs and traditions based upon some historical accomplishment. A British volunteer joined the regiment more so than the army it-self, and in many cases both officers and enlisted soldiers rarely left the regiment. An officer might assume other duties outside the regiment but remain on its roles, wearing a symbol of his affiliation until promoted to general or death.[4]

British Military historian Byron Farwell best described the general attitude prevalent among many British officers and soldiers "of the line." While walking with a retired Guards regimental colonel, the topic of a distinguished military writer arose. The colonel simply responded "He was not a real soldier, you know; he was only in the war."[5]

The Kern of the British Parachute Regiment ….
"Whoa Mohammed!"[6]

The Parachute Regiment

In the spirit of regimental tradition, the British Parachute Regiment arrived. During June 1941, the British Joint Chiefs of Staff approved the formation of two parachute brigades, one based in the United Kingdom and the other in North Africa. The parent Parachute Regiment was not officially established until 1942.[7]

A glider force eventually supplemented the parachutists, along with medium bombers that were converted for parachuting and glider towing. By September 1941, the First Parachute Battalion was formed at Hardwick near Chesterfield, commanded by Lt.-Colonel Eric Down. No. 11 Special Air Service (SAS) Commando Battalion provided the nucleus of the unit. Brigadier Richard N. Gale would eventually command the 1st Parachute Brigade, which expanded to three infantry battalions, including the 2nd, 3rd, and 4th Parachute Battalions. Later in October, Brigadier F.A.M. "Boy" Browning, a former commander of the elite 24th Independent Guards Brigade, was elevated to Major General in command of all airborne troops. The three brigades and support units were later renamed the British First Airborne Division.[8]

Airlanding Units and the Glider Pilot Regiment

The 1st Airlanding Brigade Group, commanded by Brigadier G.F. Hopkinson, was established in late 1941. It consisted of the 1st Battalion, the Border Regiment; 2nd Battalion, the South Staffordshire Regiment; the 2nd Battalion, the Oxforshire and Buckinghamshire

Light Infantry; 1ˢᵗ Battalion, the Royal Ulster Rifles; and various support elements. Unlike the paratroopers, the glider troops were Regular Army infantry converted to airborne duty. The Glider Pilot Regiment was also formed from soldiers of the line willing to fly gliders under the tutelage of the Royal Air Force, and would differ significantly from their American counterparts, fighting alongside the ground troops they delivered.[9]

Organic Composition of Parachute and Airlanding Battalions
Each parachute battalion was lightly armed, with three rifle companies and three platoons instead of the traditional four. A rifle company included 120 troops divided into Company HQ and three thirty-six man platoons. The best troopers were traditionally assigned to infantry companies, and a disproportionate number of sections (three to a platoon) were commanded by sergeants instead of corporals.

There were numerous weapons found in each battalion, including 2-inch and 3-inch mortars, Vickers heavy and Bren light machine guns, PIATS, and Gammon bombs.[a] Few of these parachute battalions reached an established fighting strength of 36 officers and 696 men, and those arriving near Arnhem would average less than 550 troops, seven jeeps, and two Bren carriers.

The airlanding battalions possessed a similar high caliber of troops, including four rifle companies, each with four platoons. The airlanding battalions arriving at Arnhem would average nearly 770 troops, with a greater number of heavy weapons and support vehicles.[10]

Filling the Ranks
The exemplary yet somewhat ruthless airborne training programs directed by former SAS commandos and elite Guards officers yielded a number of crack battalions ready for combat. The ranks were filled with exiled soldiers from Czechoslovakia, Norway, France, Belgium, Holland, and Poland. The Poles provided the largest contingent of foreign troops forming the Independent Polish Brigade Group commanded by Major General Stanislaw Sosabowski.

In March 1942, the 1st Parachute Brigade relocated from the Hardwick training facilities to Bulford Camp on Salisbury Plain. Brigadier Gale was replaced by Brigadier E.W.C. Flavell, former commander of the 2ⁿᵈ Parachute Battalion. A new air transport arm, Number 38 Wing of the Royal Air Force, established the foundation for delivering parachute and glider troops. The British War Office later implemented a critical decision to draft entire infantry battalions because of the low rate of volunteers and high rate of training attrition. Additional battalions were drawn from county regiments, retaining their unique traditions, comradeship, and pride of locality. The Queen's Own Cameron (Scottish) Highlanders provided its 7ᵗʰ Battalion, and the Royal Welch Fusiliers its 10ᵗʰ Battalion. Both became the 5ᵗʰ and 6ᵗʰ Parachute Battalion, respectively.[11]

Lt.-General F.A.M. "Boy" Browning
Major General Frederick Arthur Montague Browning GCVO, KBE, CB, DSO appreciated the mixed nature of the First Parachute Division. In 1942 Browning established the maroon beret, with the emblem of Bellerophon mounted on the winged horse Pegasus, as the distinctive headgear of the airborne divisions. A maroon arm patch with a blue symbol of Pegasus was worn on airborne battle dress.[12]

Browning's career resembled so many of his officered counterparts: he was educated at Eton and Sandhurst Academies; commissioned in the Grenadier Guards; and served with distinction in World War I. While serving at the front he once shared a dugout with Winston Churchill. Browning later received the prestigious Distinguished Service Order and Croix de Guerre in World War I. After serving in various administrative capacities during the interwar years, Browning was appointed commander of the British First Airborne. The first commander of the British First Airborne Division was also best remembered as "Boy" Browning, because of his movie star looks, splendiferous uniform, and marriage to the famous novelist Daphne du Maurier.[13]

Browning was adroit in molding both parachute and airlanding battalions into effective fighting formations. Browning applied the well honed "Brigade of Guards" discipline to both the 1ˢᵗ and 6ᵗʰ British Airborne formations. The British 6ᵗʰ Airborne Division served with distinction during D-Day, while the British First Airborne Division remained in England. From its inception, Browning envisioned self-supporting airborne divisions replete with light artillery and organic support. Browning emerged in August 1944 as Deputy Commander of the First Allied Airborne Army and Commander of the First British Airborne Corps, which included the British First Airborne Division, 52ⁿᵈ Lowland Division, and the 1ˢᵗ Polish Independent Parachute Brigade Group.

The Concept of Airborne Corps Command
The First Allied Airborne Army (FAAA) included two airborne corps: the First British Airborne Corps and American XVIII Airborne Corps. These organizations served primarily as administrative and training formations until the airborne divisions were delivered and subsequently linked with British ground forces in Operation Market Garden.[14] This concept of corps headquarters was previously employed in June 1944, but the headquarters remained behind in England during the invasion. However, Browning obtained permission from his commander, Lt.-General Lewis H. Brereton, to airland his corps headquarters along with the first wave of Brigadier General Gavin's 82ⁿᵈ Airborne Division at Nijmegen. A number of historians, most notably Martin Middlebrook, contend that the thirty-eight gliders employed by Browning's tactical headquarters, which also included a portion of his wine collection, should have been allocated to several combat-ready companies of the 2nd South Staffordshires west of Arnhem.[15] Within hours after airlanding, Browning's administrative and communications staffs were rendered powerless spectators to the fighting in nearby Nijmegen until XXX Corps arrived. In Browning's defense, the delayed landing of sev-

---

[a] **PIAT**, or the Projector Infantry Anti-tank Mk I, was introduced in 1940. It was similar to the American bazooka and designed to fire a spring loaded 3-lb. hollow-charge grenade. The **Gammon Bomb** or No. 82 grenade was a plastic explosive placed in a stockinet bag containing a screw cap detonator at the neck. This particular weapon was effectively used against enemy armor in Arnhem.

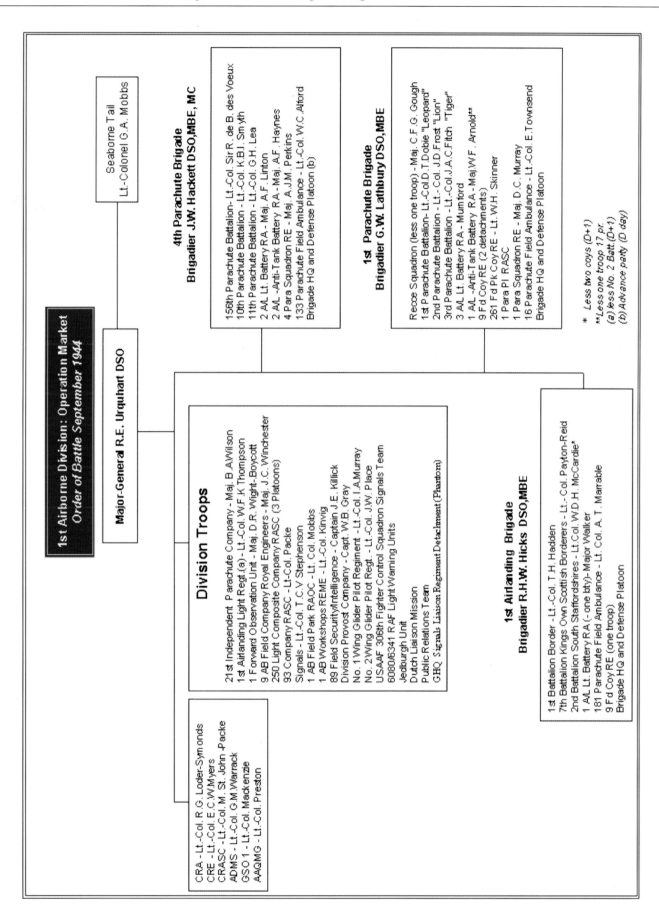

1st Airborne Division: Operation Market
Order of Battle September 1944

Major-General R.E. Urquhart DSO

CRA - Lt.-Col. R.G. Loder-Symonds
CRE - Lt.-Col. E.C.W.Myers
CRASC - Lt.-Col. M. St. John -Packe
ADMS - Lt.-Col. G.M.Warrack
GSO 1 - Lt.-Col. Mackenzie
AAQMG - Lt.-Col. Preston

Seaborne Tail
Lt.-Colonel G.A. Mobbs

4th Parachute Brigade
Brigadier J.W. Hackett DSO,MBE, MC

156th Parachute Battalion- Lt.-Col. Sir R. de B. des Voeux
10th Parachute Battalion - Lt.-Col. K.B.I. Smyth
11th Parachute Battalion - Lt.-Col. G.H. Lea
2 Alt. Lt. Battery RA - Maj. A.F. Linton
2 Alt. -Anti-Tank Battery RA - Maj. A.F. Haynes
4 Para Squadron RE - Maj. A.J.M. Perkins
133 Parachute Field Ambulance - Lt.-Col. W.C.Alford
Brigade HQ and Defense Platoon (b)

1st Parachute Brigade
Brigadier G.W. Lathbury DSO,MBE

Recce Squadron (less one troop) - Maj. C.F.G. Gough
1st Parachute Battalion- Lt.-Col D.T.Dobie '"Leopard"
2nd Parachute Battalion - Lt.- Col. J.D.Frost "Lion"
3rd Parachute Battalion - Lt.-Col.J.A.C.Fitch "Tiger"
3 Alt. Lt. Battery RA - Mumford
1 Alt. -Anti-Tank Battery RA - Maj.W.F. Arnold**
9 Fd Coy RE (2 detachments)
261 Fd Pk Coy RE - Lt. W.H. Skinner
1 Para Pl RASC
1 Para Squadron RE - Maj. D.C. Murray
16 Parachute Field Ambulance - Lt.-Col. E.Townsend
Brigade HQ and Defense Platoon

*   Less two coys (D+1)
**Less one troop 17 pr.
(a) less No. 2 Batt.(D+1)
(b) Advance party (D day)

Division Troops

21st Independent Parachute Company - Maj. B.A.Wilson
1st Airlanding Light Regt.(a) - Lt.-Col. W.F.K.Thompson
1 Forward Observation Unit - Maj. D.R. Wight.-Boycott
9 AB Field Company Royal Engineers - Maj. J.C. Winchester
250 Light Composite Company RASC (3 Platoons)
93 Company RASC - Lt.-Col. Packe
Signals - Lt.-Col. T.C.V Stephenson
1 AB Field Park RAOC - Lt. Col. Mobbs
1 AB Workshops REME - Lt.-Col. Kinvig
89 Field SecurityIntelligence - Captain J.E. Killick
Division Provost Company - Capt. W.B. Gray
No. 1 Wing Glider Pilot Regiment - Lt.-Col. I.A.Murray
No. 2 Wing Glider Pilot Regt. - Lt.-Col. J.W. Place
USAAF 306th Fighter Control Squadron Signals Team
6080/6341 RAF Light Warning Units
Jedburgh Unit
Dutch Liaison Mission
Public Relations Team
GHQ Signals Liaison Regiment Detachment (Phantom)

1st Airlanding Brigade
Brigadier R.H.W. Hicks DSO,MBE

1st Battalion Border - Lt.-Col. T.H. Hadden
7th Battalion Kings Own Scottish Borderers - Lt.-Col. Payton-Reid
2nd Battalion South Staffordshires - Lt.Col. W.D.H. McCardie*
1 Alt. Lt. Battery RA (-one bty)- Major Walker
181 Parachute Field Ambulance - Lt. Col. A. T. Marrable
9 Fd Coy RE (one troop)
Brigade HQ and Defense Platoon

eral hundred troops in Arnhem would have had little impact against the overwhelming German armor and troops rushing to counter-attack the British First Airborne Division.

"He Must Be Hot From Battle"...Major General Roy E. Urquhart CB DSO[16]

Commanding an airborne formation was quite new to Major General Robert Elliot Urquhart, CB DSO, the recently appointed commander of the British First Airborne Division. On January 1, 1944, he reported to Lt.-General Browning's headquarters near St. James Court attired in regimental tartan trews and white spats of the Highland Light Infantry Regiment. Upon seeing his new division commander for the first time, Browning dryly remarked "You had better go and get yourself properly dressed."[17]

An accomplished athlete, Major General Urquhart was educated at St. Paul's School, West Kensington, and also attended the same school as Field Marshal Montgomery. A career soldier, he was commissioned to the Highland Light Infantry, served in Ireland, Malta, India, and had recently fought with distinction in North Africa, Sicily, and Italy as Commander of the 231st Independent Brigade. In similar fashion to his airborne corps commander, Urquhart's career path was accelerated indirectly by his uncle, to whom Prime Minister Churchill was greatly indebted during his escape from the Boers.[18]

Following several months of intense preparations, Urquhart faced the unenviable task of planning and canceling sixteen airborne operations. Frustration among the ranks intensified as Urquhart's troops sat idly in England while Allied forces rapidly advanced across Western Europe.

On September 15, Urquhart received confirmation from Browning of a seventeenth plan, code-named Operation Market Garden. After reviewing the operational plans, Urquhart expressed concerns that spreading several airborne lifts over three days could preclude British First Airborne from attaining its key objectives. Urquhart then requested that Major General Paul Williams, commander of the American USAAF IX Troop Carrier Command, reconsider two lifts on D-Day in lieu of one, but was ultimately refused. Urquhart finally requested that at least several British Horsa gliders be dispatched from the main armada and land only two miles distant. By this suggestion he intended to employ somewhat similar tactics as Major General Gale's 6th Airborne Division at Pegasus Bridge. The request was also denied, this time by Air Vice-Marshal Leslie Hollinghurst, commander of the British Number 38 and 46 (Air Transport and Tug) Group.

The troop carrier plan would only allow the British 1st Airlanding Brigade, 1st Parachute Brigade, and support units to arrive west of Arnhem, near the town of Wolfheze, on D-Day. A portion of the Glider Regiment and 1st Airlanding Brigade was to

"Brian Horrocks was the best wartime commander I ever came across."

defend, while the 1st Parachute Brigade, composed mostly of three light assault battalions, armored jeeps, and several support companies, was to capture the Arnhem Bridge nearly six miles to the east. On D-Day +1, the 4th Parachute Brigade would arrive even further west of Wolfheze and capture the high ground north of Arnhem. On D-Day +2, the Independent Polish Parachute Brigade Group was to land several miles south of the Arnhem Bridge to reinforce the British First Airborne Division, by now comfortably occupying a relatively weakly defended city.

Urquhart would later contend that he was unaware of the presence of German armor near Arnhem, leading to his agreement with the airlift commanders' decision to land his troops more than six miles away from key Arnhem objectives over three days.

Brigadier Gerald Lathbury and the 1st Parachute Brigade

The core of the British First Airborne Division was the venerable 1st Parachute Brigade, commanded by Brigadier Gerald Lathbury of the Bucks Light Infantry. Made up of Dunkirk survivors and Guardsmen, the 1st Parachute Brigade had suffered heavy casualties the prior year in the Tunisian and Sicily campaigns. Despite this, the brigade had refilled half its ranks with returning campaign veterans, and the balance with 2nd Parachute Brigade transfers and recently trained parachutist volunteers.

The brigade included the original 1st Parachute Battalion, commanded by Lt.-Colonel David Dobie, a Tunisia veteran. The 1st Parachute Battalion included a large contingent of Dunkirk and Tunisia survivors, former Commandos, SAS members, Grenadier Guards, and 10th Royal Welch Fusiliers from the 6th Parachute Division.[19]

The 2nd Parachute Battalion, commanded by ex-Cameronian Highlander Lt.-Colonel John Frost, was formed in 1941. In 1942, Frost led C Company during the successful Bruneval Raid, and in 1943 assumed command of the 2nd Battalion in Tunisia. Frost was considered the most experienced officer within the brigade, and his cool temperament throughout the defense of the northern ramp at Arnhem would prove key to its surprising success. The 2nd Parachute Battalion also included a number of recruits from the Royal Ulster Rifles and 7th Cameron Highlanders, giving it a strong Scot and Irish character.

The 3rd Parachute Battalion, formed in 1941, was the last addition to the brigade, and it possessed neither the regional nor historical ancestry. Many veterans were survivors of the Algerian and Tunisian campaigns, including the commander, Lt.-Colonel John Fitch, and were formally of the Manchester Regiment.[20]

Brigadier John "Shan" Hackett and the 4th Parachute Brigade

The 4th Parachute Brigade was formed in the Middle East in late 1942 as an independent formation, but was transferred to the British First Airborne Division in 1943. Brigadier John "Shan" Hackett, its original commander, was an Oxford-educated and battle-seasoned officer commissioned into the 8th Royal Irish Hussars. Hackett served with distinction in North Africa,: he was wounded in Syria in 1940 and again in North Africa while leading his armored unit against Rommel in 1942.[21]

The 156th Parachute Battalion, raised in India in 1941, was the senior unit in the brigade and included troops from more than twenty British regiments of the line. The 156th Parachute Battalion was commanded by Lt.-Colonel Sir Richard des Voix of the Grenadier Guards, a former member of Browning's airborne staff. Prior to the unit's arrival in England in 1943, the 156th Battalion served in India and later moved to Egypt under the command of the 4th Parachute Brigade.

The 10th Parachute Battalion was formed in 1942 and included a large number of British Eighth Army veterans. Following the battle of El Alamein, hundreds of surviving troops from the 2nd Royal Sussex Brigade volunteered for parachute training. The battalion commander was Lt.-Colonel Kenneth Smyth of the South Wales Borderers.

The 11th Parachute Battalion, commanded by Lt.-Colonel George Lea of the Lancaster Fusiliers, was formed in North Africa in 1943 under the command of the 4th Parachute Brigade. Hackett considered the battalion to be somewhat of a disciplinary problem, and it contained a number of less suitable volunteers. The battalion fought its first and last battle at Arnhem.[22]

Brigadier P.H.W. "Pip" Hicks DSO MC and the 1st Airlanding Brigade

The 1st Airlanding Brigade, formally the 31st Independent Infantry Brigade from India, was the largest formation in the British First Airborne Division. The brigade included three battalions infused with centuries-old regimental heritage: the 1st Battalion, the Border Regiment; 2nd Battalion, South Staffords; and the 7th Battalion Kings Own Scottish Borderers (KOSB). The 7th KOSB was a recently reconstituted battalion from the Territorial Army, while the 2nd South Staffords and 1st Borders were Regular British Army battalions previously posted to the original brigade. The commander, Brigadier P.H.W. "Pip" Hicks of the Royal Warwicks, was one of few World War I veterans found in the division. At forty-nine, Brigadier Hicks was the oldest of the commanders at Arnhem.

The 1st Battalion Borders, commanded by Lt.-Colonel Tommy Haddon, was one of only two Regular British Army units to fight at Arnhem. The Borders had served in France early in the war under the command of the British Expeditionary Forces (BEF), and later in Sicily under Allied command. The Borders suffered nearly three hundred casualties during a hard-fought withdrawal from France in 1940, and later sustained catastrophic losses after nearly two-thirds of the battalion glider force had crash landed in the Mediterranean during Operation Husky.[23] By 1944, many veterans were replaced by young and untested reinforcements from the heavy industrial regions of Lancashire and the North-East.[24]

The 2nd Battalion South Staffordshires, commanded by Lt-Colonel Derek McCardie, had served in India under the command of the 31st Independent Infantry Brigade and later suffered heavy casualties during the glider-borne assault of Sicily. The battalion was rebuilt with a number of surviving troops and recruits from the Staffordshire region.

The 7th Battalion Kings Own Scottish Borderers served as an apotheosis of the tradition prevalent among the British First

Airborne's nine battalions. The regimental colors were raised, but this time by the sounds of pipers playing "Blue Bonnets O'er the Border." The KOSB's heritage dated to 1689, when the 3rd Earl of Leven authorized the formation of the 800-strong Edinburgh Regiment to defend the Lowlands of Scotland. Since then, the regiment had served in many parts of the world and had expanded to twelve battalions by the conclusion of World War I. Following the end of the Great War, the battalions were disbanded except for several assigned to the Territorial Army. In 1938, the 7th KOSB (Galloway) split from the 5th Battalion (Dumfries and Galloway) of the Territorial Army.[25] The 7th Battalion remained part of the Orkney and Shetland Defense Force until conversion to gliders in 1944. The Borderers retained a significant number of its Scottish and Territorial troops, and Arnhem would be the 7th KOSB's first and last battle of the war.[26]

The role of the 1st Airlanding Brigade was to quickly dispatch concentrations of troops and heavy weapons onto landing areas west of Arnhem. The troops were expected to secure five landing and drop zones until all six parachute battalions and divisional support had arrived. Each battalion averaged nearly seven hundred seventy men divided into four rifle companies, for a total of sixteen platoons compared to the smaller nine-platoon parachute battalions. The rifle platoons were reduced to twenty-six troops in order to fit inside a standard British Horsa glider. A full-sized battalion required sixty-two Horsa gliders and one Hamilcar. Heavy weapons allocations were doubled, especially with additional 3-inch mortar, Vickers machine guns, and six pounder anti-tank guns.[27]

Despite the formidable size and firepower, the 1st Airlanding Brigade suffered a significant loss of experienced glider veteran parachute units, which offered better compensation and safer landing techniques. A large number of these losses were replaced with young and inexperienced infantry recruits. The battalions were well-suited for defense, but following the battle for Arnhem the troops incurred criticism for lacking the panache so prevalent among the attack oriented parachute battalions:

> "Their Character was probably halfway between the doggedness of Ordinary British infantry and the dash of parachute troops"[28]

Many officers filling the battalion ranks of the 1st Airlanding Brigade arrived from British infantry regiments, but a large number of Canadian officers—called CANLOANS—mitigated the shortage of platoon commanders. More than twenty fought at Arnhem, and five would perish in battle.[29]

Divisional Units

The remaining forces under Major General Urquhart's command included: Division Headquarters; a defense platoon of the 2nd Oxford and Bucks Light Infantry; the "pathfinder" 21st Independent Parachute Company; the Reconnaissance Squadron; the 1st Airlanding Light Regiment; 1st and 2nd Airlanding Anti-Tank Batteries; and various supply, support, and medical units. The division also included some rather atypical units, including a Dutch Liaison Mission; a Public Relations Team; and the GHQ Signal Liaison Regiment Detachment, or "Phantom" Unit, responsible for having direct radio contact with London.

The "Coup de Main"

One of the critical units assigned to the British First Parachute Division, the Reconnaissance Squadron commanded by Major C.F.G. "Freddie" Gough, was an oversized motorized company divided into four troops. The jeep borne unit was expected to play a pivotal role by rushing the defenders of the Arnhem highway bridge in jeeps specially fitted with single .303 inch Vickers machine guns. Major Gough's motorized troops were to lead the foot-borne 1st Parachute Brigade, which required several hours to assemble and march to the bridge. The Reconnaissance Squadron had substituted the light "Tetrarch" tanks traditionally assigned to British airborne divisions with jeeps. Much to Urquhart's misfortune, the anticipated dash and surprise of Gough's small 275-man unit would crumble against the formidable 9th SS Hohenstaufen laying in wait.[30]

The "Horse Gunners"

The British Royal Artillery, renowned for its mastery of heavy weaponry, retained a large presence within the British First Airborne Division. The airborne artillery regiment, commanded by Lt.-Colonel Robert Loder-Symonds, included twenty-four American PAK 75 mm guns, two anti-tank batteries of thirteen troops (units) armed with fifty-two six-pounders, and four troops of sixteen 17-pounder guns. The regiment also fielded a small group of artillery observers disseminated amongst the battalions, brigades, headquarters, and XXX Corps. Nearly 800 artillerymen arrived at Arnhem in 170 Horsa and Hamilcars on the first day—nearly 40% of the D-Day glider allocation, or the equivalent of one additional airlanding infantry regiment. The artillery and anti-tank batteries were distributed among the three brigades with the exception of the 1st Airlanding Light Regiment, commanded by Lt.-Colonel W.F.K. Thompson. Major General Urquhart had previously decided to "front load" the first day's lift with artillery in place of assault infantry. The Royal Artillery would provide critical support throughout the battle until their guns were destroyed and troops withdrawn from the Oosterbeek pocket.[31]

The Gap between the "Goose-Eggs"[32]

Another key organization in the British First Airborne Division was the Divisional Signals Unit, commanded by Lt.-Colonel T.C.V Stephenson. This unit was distributed among infantry and artillery units and arrived in Arnhem with inadequate equipment, as well as an ill-prepared contingency plan. The communications equipment had a history of performing marginally under perfect conditions—so long as infantry battalions stayed within a "net" radius of three miles and brigades within six miles. The signals commander was quite aware that the heavy woods and buildings prevalent in the Arnhem area would seriously impair inter-unit communications.[33]

The table below summarizes the limitations of the communications units, and helps explain the difficulties they faced following their arrival in battle:

Type	User	Range/Conditions	Requirements
"19" Set	Artillery	12 miles/Good	Jeep with battery charger
"22" Set	Brigade	6 miles/Good	Jeep with battery charger
"68" Set	Battalion	3 miles/Good	Small man-pack/batteries

Urquhart's decision to retain Division Headquarters near the landing sites while his battalions proceeded beyond the radio net rendered the battalion and regimental sets inoperable within hours. The limited first-day airlift capacity and ten day "sorting out" period prevented re-supply of the more powerful "19" sets. The signalmen were aware that the battalions would be out of touch throughout the first twenty-four hours, and that a communications gap would exist between the communication nets, or battalion "goose eggs" (so-named for their shape when plotted on maps). Even with this knowledge, the communications units did not make a concerted effort to utilize the available and intact Dutch underground phone lines. [34]

The Glider Pilot Regiment

The estimated 1,300 British glider pilots required for Market Garden were well-versed in both flight and infantry tactics, and expected to serve as reserve ground troops after landing. Colonel G.S. Chatterton commanded the regiment, which was split into two wings of three squadrons apiece: No.1 Wing commanded by Lt.-Colonel I.A. Murray; and No. 2 Wing commanded by Lt.-Colonel J.W. Place. [35] This strictly voluntary assemblage of highly trained troops retained close links with the RAF, and was available whenever airborne operations were needed. The glider pilots were initially trained by the RAF to fly powered aircraft up to solo flight standards, then moved on to Horsa and Hamilcar gliders. This elite unit included a significant number of Guards NCOs. [36] The glider pilots provided a needed divisional reserve equivalent to two additional battalions of fighting infantry, and would perform well during the closing days of the battle. The glider pilot's dual role would result in the highest level of unit fatalities among British First Airborne troops, exceeding seventeen percent. [37] Unlike many British regiments of the line, the Glider Pilot Regiment would quickly disappear following the end of the war because of more efficient and safer means of delivering troops. [38]

RAF Transport No 38 and 46 Groups

Similar to the Americans in many respects, the Air Ministry initially lacked sufficient resources and interest in developing a full-scale air transport formation for airborne troops. Throughout 1940 and 1941, the Royal Air Force desperately hoarded resources to support strategic bombing and mainland defense. Only a limited quantity of outdated aircraft were available, such as the Armstrong Whitworth Whitley, to support airborne troop training and conduct small-scale operations. The first integrated operation by British paratroops and aircraft occurred in February 1941, when thirty-eight volunteers were dropped in southern Italy to attack the Tragino Aqueduct. [39]

No. 38 Wing RAF initially served as a training and support formation until Bomber Command expanded operations to group level, boosting its strength to six Sterling, two Albermarle, and two Halifax front line squadrons. [40] Unlike American transport crews, many RAF pilots were former medium bomber pilots and were allowed to participate in bombing or resupply missions across the English Channel to retain a keen sense of *espirit de corps*. A significant number of RAF transport pilots excelled in night navigation and were "flak inoculated," resulting in steady aircraft handling during heavily resisted operations. [41]

While the RAF transport wing slowly expanded, the 1st Parachute Brigade was rushed to the Mediterranean Theater to participate in the Algerian and Tunisian landings. The first brigade-scale operation took place in November 1943, when the American 60th Group of the 51st Troop Carrier Wing dropped the British 3rd Parachute Battalion on an Algerian airfield with good results. On the night of July 9, 1943, the 1st Airlanding Brigade set out to capture the Ponte Grande Bridge near Syracuse. The gliders were towed by the American 51st Troop Carrier Wing and a handful of Albermarle aircraft from the recently arrived RAF No.38 Wing. Unfortunately, nearly fifty percent of the British gliders crashed into the Mediterranean, and only seventy-three troops of the entire brigade reached the objective. Troops casualties were heavy, and over three hundred deaths were attributed to drowning. The last major airborne operation in the Mediterranean occurred over Sicily on the night of July 13, 1943, when the 2,000 troop 1st Airborne Brigade, carried by the American 51st and British No. 38 Wing, set out to capture the Primosole bridge. Despite an accurate landing with a new "pathfinder" unit, only four of seventeen gliders landed safely, and nearly thirty percent of the 135 transport aircraft suffered flak damaged from uncoordinated Allied anti aircraft guns. [42]

By the fall of 1944, RAF Transport Command expanded No.38 Group to ten squadrons of obsolete Halifaxes, Albermarles, and Stirlings. British air transport capacity was further augmented by the formation of No. 46 Group, which included six squadrons of recently arrived American C-47 Dakotas. Air Vice-Marshal L. N. Hollinghurst, CB OBE DFC, commanded No. 38 RAF Group, and No. 46 RAF Group was commanded by Air Commodore L. Darvall. The experienced air wing members included a number of Commonwealth air crews from Canada, New Zealand, and Australia. [43]

By the time Operation Market Garden took place, a formidable force of nearly one thousand transport aircraft and gliders had replaced the handful of obsolete Whitley bombers.

The 1st Polish Independent Parachute Brigade Group

Nearly 1,700 Polish volunteers of the 1st Polish Independent Parachute Brigade joined the British First Airborne Division. Colonel Stanislaw Sosabowski formed the 1st Polish Independent Parachute Brigade in 1941 with the intent of dropping his troops onto occupied Poland soil to assist the Polish Home Army. The oft-obstreperous Colonel Sosabowski was a veteran of the First World War, and had served as an infantry commander until the fall of Warsaw in 1940.

When it became apparent in March 1944 that safe passage to Poland was highly unlikely, the British Imperial General Staff informed General Kazimierz Sosnkowski, the exiled Polish Army Commander in Chief, that the parachute brigade would be transferred to SHAEF airborne reserves. The request triggered a series of diplomatic proposals and counter-proposals between the Polish government-in-exile and British Imperial General Staff concerning the Poles' primary mission. The Poles requested a number of conditions, especially retention of national unit identity, brigade-level access to training facilities at Ringway, and transfer of much needed airborne equipment. The Polish government eventually agreed on June 15 to the status of SHAEF airborne reserves, along with the relocation of recently-promoted Major General Sosabowski's command to Scotland for full unit operational exercises. The Poles eventually joined the British First Airborne Division following transfer to Britain in June 1944.[44]

The 1st Polish Parachute Brigade Group was eventually transformed into a self-contained formation with three infantry battalions, light artillery and anti-tank batteries, and requisite support companies. By late August, the brigade was fully equipped with standard British airborne issue, with the exception of steel gray berets and a Polish eagle cap badge. The Poles were to suffer numerous misfortunes throughout Market Garden, and their contributions would be unduly criticized.[45]

"All Battle Dressed Up With No Place to Land"
Speculation remains among many historians concerning what might have happened if the air-transportable 52nd Lowland Division had landed west of Arnhem to assist Urquhart's forces. The 52nd Lowlands, commanded by Major General Hakewill Smith, was a standard British Army Infantry formation attached to Lt-General Browning's First Allied Airborne Army as an air-transportable reserve. Hakewill-Smith's troops were scheduled to land on D+4 at Deelen airport, located four miles north of Arnhem, following its capture and occupation by the British First Airborne Division. By Thursday, September 21, Urquhart's troops were isolated at Oosterbeek, and Frost's command driven from the northern ramp at Arnhem. Sensing a desperate situation at Arnhem and the impossibility of landing at Deelen, Major General Hakewill-Smith offered to land a brigade of Lowlanders on D+3 close to Urquhart's besieged forces.

Lt.-General Browning's response to Hakewill-Smith was "Thanks for your message, but the offer not – repeat not – required as situation better than you think…"[46] This response clearly indicated a lack of battle condition awareness on Browning's part.

The Market Relief Forces – XXX Corps
Lieutenant General Brian Gwynne Horrocks
At Dunkirk, "Jorrocks" led a battalion, then the II Brigade of the 4th British Infantry Division commanded by Lt.-General Montgomery.[47] Later in 1942, Horrocks assumed command of XIII Corps prior to the battle of El Alamein and turned the Mareth Line with IX Corps. At Salerno, Lt.-General Horrocks was severely wounded, which apparently ended his distinguished career. However, during the summer of 1944 Field Marshal Montgomery judged Horrocks

fit again to command XXX Corps, valuing his sparkling presence and ability to command front line troops. Unfortunately, Horrocks was plagued with recurring bouts of pain from his past wounds. This condition may have weakened his decision-making abilities as XXX Corps Commander during the first critical forty-eight hours of Market Garden.[48]

By the time Market Garden began on September 17, 1944, Lt.-General Horrocks commanded the powerful Guards Armored Division, 43rd Wessex Infantry Division, 50th Northrumbian Infantry Division, 2nd Household Cavalry Regiment, several large formations of the Royal Artillery and Royal Engineers, 8th Armored Brigade, and Princess Irene Brigade of the Free Dutch. Supporting the XXX Corps' flanks were XII Corps, commanded by Major General L. G. Whistler, and VIII Corps, commanded by Lt.-General N.M. Ritchie. The British XII Corps' objectives included protecting the left flank of XXX Corps and proceeding to the Maas River, while the VIII Corps was to protect the right flank of XXX Corps and advance north to the town of Helmond. British XXX Corps would deliver a "mailed fist" of six hundred tanks and 20,000 vehicles to pierce the outer crust of enemy resistance and relieve the surrounded pockets of airborne forces along the "Club Route," which was Horrocks' axis of advance.[49]

"This is a tale you will tell your grandchildren"[50]
On September 16, 1944, Horrocks assembled his senior officers, down to the rank of lieutenant colonel and brigade majors, in a cinema located in the Belgium town of Bourg Leopold. The atmosphere was full of optimism and regal gaiety:

> "….No one deigned to wear a steel helmet. The Royal Armoured Corps affected brightly coloured slacks or corduroys. The Gunners still clung for the most part to riding breeches or even jodhpurs. Few had retained their ties, but wore in their place scarves of various colours, dotted with white spots. Sniper's smocks, parachutists' jackets, jeep coats all contributed to the amazing variety of costume…."[51]

The meeting ascended to high excitement in the late afternoon as the tall commander with flowing silver hair, good looks, and great personal charm made his entrance into the hall. British troops fought well for Horrocks because of his trustworthiness under severe battle conditions. Horrocks greeted many of his senior commanders as he stepped onto the stage, where a large map stood with colored tape piercing through Dutch cities, towns, and rivers to the Zuider Zee. Horrocks spoke for an hour and explained the complexities of Market Garden, reinforcing his points with inspiring comments such as "keep going like hell" and "pass 20,000 vehicles over the highway to Arnhem in sixty hours."[52] As soon as the first airborne troops landed in Holland, Lt-General Horrocks would personally give the order for XXX Corps to attack along the "Club Route" and reach Arnhem in three to four days.

"It Was Novel in the Extreme"[53]
Horrocks had instructed his commanders that if any major crossings were destroyed, the Guards were to allow the 43rd Wessex Division to pass through with 9,000 sappers and 2,300 vehicles to rebuild any key bridges.[54] Once the Arnhem Bridge was seized, the

43rd Infantry Division was to proceed further north over the Ijssel River near the city of Deventer, Holland. The 50th Northrumbian Infantry Division was to follow as a mobile reserve. Horrocks' experienced commanders were keenly aware that the sixty-four mile trip to Arnhem was a gamble, and enemy resistance had increased significantly over recent weeks. The British were no longer facing weary German soldiers such as the 719th Coastal Division, but fanatical and battle hardened paratroopers and SS troops from all points in Germany.

The road to Arnhem was a narrow two-lane highway, easily defensible, and quite difficult to traverse because of the surrounding soft polderland. The leading Guards Armor required heavy artillery and Tactical Air Support to complete an audacious schedule:

Eindhoven	1715 hours	September 17
Veghel	2400 hours	September 17
Grave	1200 hours	September 18
Nijmegen	1800 hours	September 18
Arnhem	1500 hours	September 19

The Guards Armored Division – "The All Seeing Eye"[55]
The Guards Armored Division, commanded by Major General Allan Adair, would break out west of the Neerpelt bridgehead, crossing at "Joe's Bridge" (named after the commander of one of the leading 5th Brigade formations, Lt.-Colonel J.O.E. Vandeleur). The Guards Armored Division was echeloned into two brigades. The 5th Guards Brigade, commanded by Brigadier N.W. Gwatkin, which included an infantry and armored battalion from the Irish and the Grenadier Guards Battlegroups, along with supporting anti-tank units. The second echelon, the 32nd Guards Brigade commanded by Brigadier G.F. Johnson, also included armor and infantry battalion parings of the Coldstream and Welsh Guards Battlegroups, supported by anti-tank units.

The Guards Armored Division included a large contingent of Royal Engineers, commanded by Lt.-Colonel C.P. Jones; heavy artillery of the 153rd and 55th Field Regiment Artillery; the 64th Medium Regiment Royal Artillery; and 94th Light Anti-Aircraft Regiment. The 43rd Wessex Infantry Division, commanded by Major General Ivor Thomas, would immediately follow the Guards. The 50th Northrumbian Division, commanded by Major General D.A.H. Granham and part of VIII Corps, would support the breakout at the Neerpelt Bridgehead on September 17, 1944, and eventually the right flank of the Guards Division. The Royal Netherlands Princess Irene Brigade Group, commanded by Colonel Ruyter van Stevenwick, would follow the 43rd Wessex infantry Division.

Major General Allan Adair of the British Guards Armored Division
The Regiment of the Guards originated over three centuries earlier as the personal protectors of the Royal Palace and members of the royal family. Throughout the centuries, the Guards continued a tradition of exemplifying the highest military standards of the British Army. The Guards, like the Household Cavalry, remained an exclusive organization, selecting officers with social connections and enlisted ranks according to regional areas and height.[56]

Many Foot Guards Battalions displayed strict discipline and ferocity in World War I, leading Lord Kitchener to create a Guards Division as a permanent and exemplary component of the British Army. A number of Guards Battalions participated in the 1940 Battle for France, and surviving numbers were assigned to building a mobilized division in 1942. The Guards Armored Division would spend the following two and a half years training and strengthening its brigades in Great Britain for the return to France in June 1944.

Major General Allan Adair had assumed command of the Guards in the fall of 1942. The new commander was appropriately a descendent of a military family since the reign of James I, and had served with the Guards since 1916. Adair commanded the Guards through Operation Goodwood, the Liberation of Brussels, and the two hundred mile drive to the Meus-Escaut Canal, building two strong regiments with a history of excellent infantry and armor cooperation.

Following the Normandy breakout, Major General Adair regrouped both the 5th and 32nd Guards Brigades into four Regimental Battle Groups (a "battle group" pairs like armor and infantry units to form a more cohesive fighting force). The resulting Guards Battle Groups were as follows:

Armor	**Infantry**
2nd Armored Irish Guards	3rd Irish Guards
2nd Armored Guards	1st Motor Grenadier Guards
1st Armored Coldstream Guards	5th Coldstream Guards
2nd Armored Reconnaissance	1st Welsh Guards
Welsh Guards	

Major General Adair believed that "like" battalion formations would engender better performance under battle conditions. However, in his memoirs Lt.-General Horrocks commented that Adair's approach may have hampered the flexibility required for successful mobile warfare.[57]

Nevertheless, at the start of Operation Market Garden the Guards Armor Division was positioned to cross into Holland with over 3,000 vehicles, 300 tanks, and nearly 14,700 well-trained troops. The division would advance across a six hundred yard front at maximum speed and secure the corridor for the subsequent arrival of the 43rd Wessex Infantry Division.

Major General G.I. Thomas and the 43rd Wessex Division
Major General Thomas and his commanders prepared the 5,000-vehicle division for its key role in Market Garden with less theatrical effect. The 43rd "Wessex" Division wore the sign of the wyvern, a blend of cunning snake and winged dragon, which symbolized the fifth century arrival of the West Saxons and was the emblem worn by Wessex kings.[58] The division was formed in England and arrived in late June 1944 with Montgomery's 21st Group in Normandy. The division suffered heavy casualties during the opening weeks, especially among battalion commanders.

The Garden aspect of the plan required the Wessex Division to follow the Guards Armor Division along the main "Club Route," and once the Lower Rhine was crossed, secure the high ground running south from Apeldorn to the northern outskirts of Arnhem.

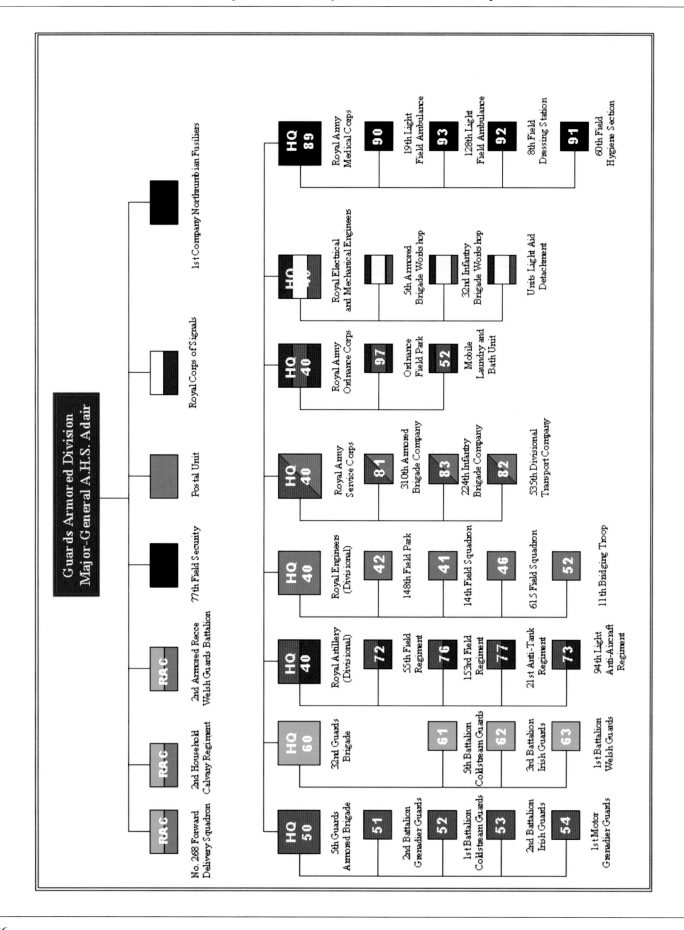

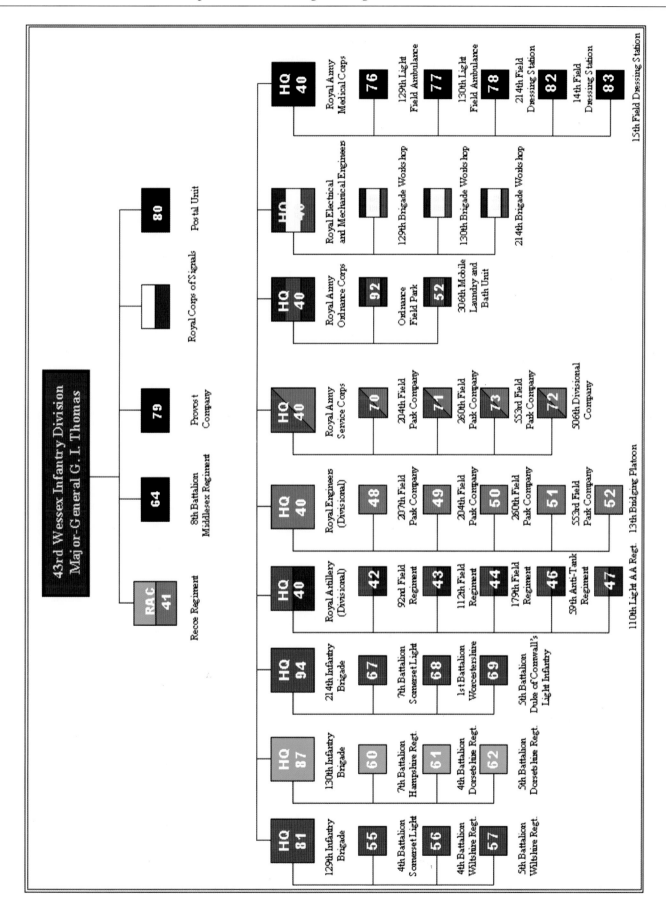

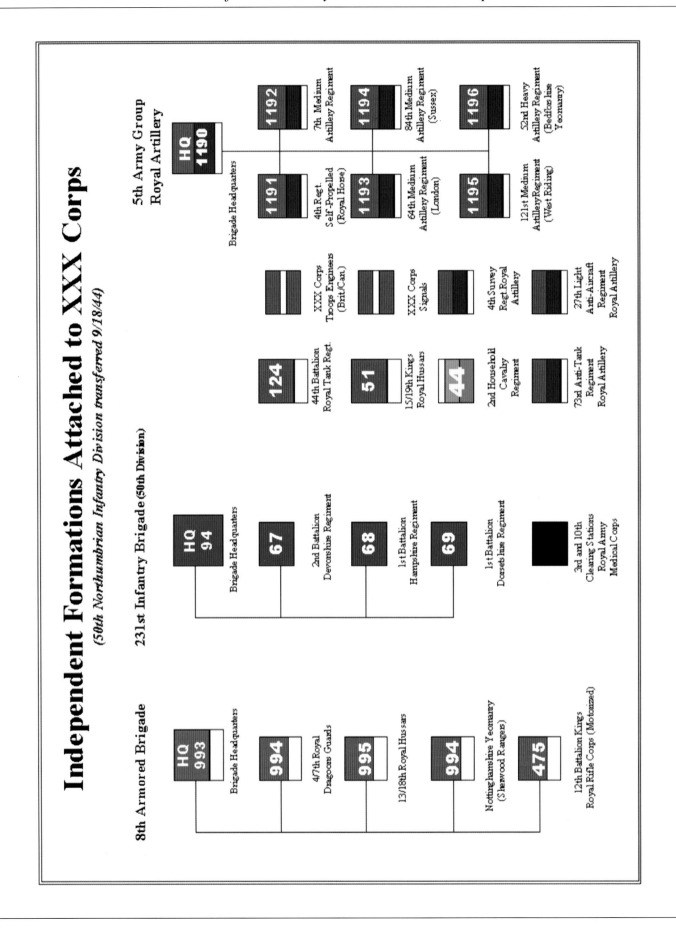

Independent Formations Attached to XXX Corps

(50th Northumbrian Infantry Division transferred 9/18/44)

5th Army Group Royal Artillery

HQ 1190 — Brigade Headquarters

- **1191** — 4th Regt. Self-Propelled (Royal Horse)
- **1192** — 7th Medium Artillery Regiment
- **1193** — 64th Medium Artillery Regiment (London)
- **1194** — 84th Medium Artillery Regiment (Sussex)
- **1195** — 121st Medium Artillery Regiment (West Riding)
- **1196** — 52nd Heavy Artillery Regiment (Bedfordshire Yeomanry)

- XXX Corps Troops Engineers (Brit/Can)
- XXX Corps Signals
- 4th Survey Regt Royal Artillery
- 27th Light Anti-Aircraft Regiment Royal Artillery

- **124** — 44th Battalion Royal Tank Regt.
- **51** — 15/19th King's Royal Hussars
- **44** — 2nd Household Cavalry Regiment
- **73rd Anti-Tank Regiment Royal Artillery**

231st Infantry Brigade (50th Division)

HQ 94 — Brigade Headquarters

- **67** — 2nd Battalion Devonshire Regiment
- **68** — 1st Battalion Hampshire Regiment
- **69** — 1st Battalion Dorsetshire Regiment

- 3rd and 10th Clearing Stations Royal Army Medical Corps

8th Armored Brigade

HQ 993 — Brigade Headquarters

- **994** — 4/7th Royal Dragoons Guards
- **995** — 13/18th Royal Hussars
- **994** — Nottinghamshire Yeomanry (Sherwood Rangers)
- **475** — 12th Battalion King's Royal Rifle Corps (Motorized)

If any major crossings were destroyed, the 43rd Wessex Division was to "fan out to the flanks," carry out river assault crossings, and construct temporary bridges using the three Army Groups of Royal Engineers.[59]

The 43rd Gloucestershire Reconnaissance Regiment would lead the formation in Humber armored and light reconnaissance cars, followed by the 12th Motor Battalion, King's Royal Rifle Corps; 130th Infantry Brigade; 214th infantry Brigade; the Royal Netherlands Princess Irene Brigade Group; and 129th Infantry Brigade. The 43rd Wessex Division was also supported by the 8th Armored Brigade, 147th Essex Yeomanry Field Regiment, 64th Medium Regimental Royal Artillery, and a battery of heavy artillery.

Four days rations and fuel were allotted, with considerable contingency plans if any of the major bridges were destroyed.[60] Upon arriving at Arnhem, the 43rd Reconnaissance, 12th Motor Battalion, and a squadron of the Royal Hussars Armor were to seize the crossings over the Ijssel River. The 130th and 214th Infantry Brigades were to hold an area near Apeldorn while the 129th Infantry Brigade linked up with the British First Airborne Division. The Royal Neth-erlands Brigade was to seize Apeldorn and raise the Dutch citizenry against the German occupation troops.[61]

Major General D.A.H. Graham and the 50th Northumbrian Infantry Division
A veteran of Dunkirk and the desert campaigns in North Africa, the British 50th Infantry Division provided valuable support to the XXX Corps' right flank along the Meuse-Escaut Canal. The division would serve as Corps reserve and was limited in mobility, since most of its supply lorries were surrendered to the Second British Army. Two infantry battalions from the 69th Infantry regiment were to provide assistance in counterattacking German attempts to sever the corridor during the closing days of Market Garden.

44th Royal Tank Regiment
The 44th "Home Counties" Armor Regiment fought in the Middle East under the command of Horrock's XIII Corps. This "ubiquitous" Royal Tank Regiment would provide critical assistance to the American 506th Infantry Parachute Regiment along "Hells Highway" near Veghel on D+ 4.[62]

Notes
1. Byron Farwell, *Queen Victoria's Little Wars* (New York: W.W. Norton & Company, 1972), p.69.
2. Byron Farwell, *Mr. Kipling's Army* (New York: W.W. Norton & Company, 1981), p.23.
3. Brian Davis, *The British Army in World War II: A Handbook on the Organization, Armament, Equipment, Ranks, Uniforms, etc., 1942* (London: Lionel Leventhal Limited, 1990), p.22.
4. Farwell, op. cit., p.25
5. Ibid., p.11.
6. *By Air to Battle: The Official Account of the British Airborne Divisions* (London: HMSO, 1945), p.46.
7. Martin Middlebrook, *Arnhem 1944* (Boulder: Westview Press, 1994), p.23.
8. Barry Gregory, *British Airborne Troops 1940-45* (Garden City: Doubleday and Company, 1974), p. 25.
9. Ibid., p.25.
10. Middlebrook, op.cit., pp.456-457.
11. Gregory, op.cit., p.38.
12. Ibid., p.39.
13. *Legend has it that du Maurier the novelist influenced Browning's decision to select Bellerophon as the symbol of the British Airborne Forces.*
14. *Lt.- General Matthew B. Ridgway commanded XVIII American Airborne.*
15. Middlebrook, op.cit., pp.11-13.
16. Major General R.E. Urquhart CB DSO (Wilfred Greatorex), *Arnhem, The Epic Story of the Greatest Airborne Assault of World War II* (Derby: Monarch Books, 1960), p.17. *Urquhart describes words used by Browning to describe the type of commander needed to command the British First Airborne Division.*
17. Ibid., p.17.
18. Major Victor Dover, *The Sky Generals* (London: Cassell, 1981), pp.120-124.
19. Middlebrook, op.cit., p.24.
20. Ibid., p.25-26.
21. Ibid., p.26.
22. Ibid. pp. 27-28.
23. Stuart Eastwood, Charles Gray, and Alan Green, *When Dragons Flew: An Illustrated History of the 1st Battalion The Border Regiment 1939-45* (Peterborough: Silver Link Publishing Ltd., 1994), p.217.
24. Ibid., p.31.
25. Robert Sigmond, *Off At Last, An Illustrated History of the 7th (Galloway) Battalion The King's Own Scottish Borderers 1939-1945* (Ede: Veenman Drukkers, 1997), pp. 9-11.
26. Ibid., pp.28-31.
27. Middlebrook, op.cit., pp.28-29. *The standard load also included a handcart containing the platoon ammunition reserve and a small motorcycle.*
28. Ibid., p.30.
29. Ibid., p.31.
30. Cornelius Ryan, *A Bridge Too Far* (New York :Simon and Shuster, 1974), pp.140-141.
31. Middlebrook, op.cit. pp.34-36.
32. Middlebrook, op.cit., p.37. *"Goose Egg" is the oval circle drawn on planning maps to denote unit location.*
33. Ryan, op.cit., p.179.
34. Middlebrook, op. cit., pp.37-38.
35. Ibid., pp. 459-460. *The Glider Pilot Regiment also included HQ Squadron serving as a seventh unit.*
36. Ibid., pp. 39-40.
37. Ibid..p.439.
38. Ibid..p.447.
39. Robert Jackson, *Arnhem: The Battle Remembered* (Shrewsbury: Airlife, 1994), p.9.
40. Gregory, op.cit., pp.41-42.
41. From Air to Battle, op.cit., pp.23-24.
42. Jackson, op.cit., pp.10-14. *Ten C-47s were shot down*
43. Ibid., p.15.

[44] George Cholewcynski, *Poles Apart: The Polish Airborne at the Battle of Arnhem* (New York: Sarpedon Publishers, 1993), pp. 66-71.

[45] Ibid., p.311.

[46] Middlebrook, op.cit., p.413.

[47] John Keegan, *Churchill's Generals:" The First Authoritative Look at the Men Who helped Churchill Win the War"* by Alan Shepperd, (Quill William Morrow, New York, 1991), p. 231.

[48] Oliver Lindsay, ed., *A Guards' General: The Memoirs of Major General Sir Allan Adair* (London: Hamish Hamilton, 1986), p. 150.

[49] Ibid., p.153.

[50] Geoffrey Powell, *The Devil's Birthday* (London: Leo Cooper, 1984), p.84.

[51] Ibid., pp.83-84.

[52] Ryan, op.cit., p.166.

[53] op.cit., p.163. *Quote from Major General Sir Allan Adair in describing the riskiness of the plan.*

[54] Ryan, op.cit., p.166.

[55] Mike Chappell, *The Guards Division 1914-1915* (London, Osprey, 1995), p.6.*The All Seeing Eye was the division sign designed in 1916 by Major Sir Eric Avery. The sign was a white eye with a black pupil on a blue background appearing on most Guards vehicles and as Guardsmen shoulder patches.*

[56] The author encountered a number Second World War Guards at the Commemorative 50th Anniversary of Operation Market Garden and was quite taken by the preponderance of six foot plus veterans. A veteran Grenadier Guardsmen stated that a selective regimental traditional encouraged above average height among recruits, despite an acute manpower shortage in late 1944.

[57] Lindsay, op.cit., p. 152.

[58] Major General H.Essame, *The 43rd Wessex at War 1944-1945* (London: William Clowes and Sons Limited, 1952), p.1.

[59] Ibid. p.9.

[60] Ibid., pp.116-117. *Over 2,200 vehicles and nearly twenty Royal Engineering troops were assigned to Market Garden.*

[61] Ibid., p.118.

[62] Powell, op.cit., p.154.

4

The Americans
"Gory, Gory, What a Helluva Way to Die!"[1]

"I saw one or two boats hit the beach, followed immediately by three or four others. Nobody paused. Men got out and began running toward the embankment. My God, what a courageous sight it was!"

- Lt.-Colonel Giles Vandeleur[2]

During the closing months of World War I, Brigadier General William "Billy" Mitchell proposed airdropping American infantry behind the German fortress of Metz. This idea represented the first full-scale plan to vertically envelop an opposing force in combat. Mitchell later delegated detailed planning to a young Air Service staff officer named Lewis H. Brereton, future commander of the First Allied Airborne Army.[3] This first attempted airborne assault was nullified by the November 1918 Armistice, and the plans were buried within the War Department's bureaucracy. However, the spectacular yet costly Fallshirmjäger success on the island of Crete in 1940 rekindled both American and British interest in developing a standing airborne formation. The founders of the nascent American airborne forces would encounter challenges very similar to those faced by their British counterparts during the early war years.

The Birth of American Airborne Forces

On May 6, 1939, the Office of the Chief of Infantry authorized the formation of a small detachment of "air" infantry. From its outset, differences of opinion clashed over operational control of the "airborne project." Following nearly a year of debate, the project was placed directly under the command of then Brigadier General Leslie J. McNair, Chief of Army General Headquarters.[4] Shortly thereafter, a test parachute platoon at the Fort Benning Infantry School became the 501st Parachute Battalion. Development progressed quickly: the Provisional Parachute Group Headquarters received regimental authority, and in 1941 the Parachute School at Fort Benning was established. The first airlanding unit, the 550th Infantry Airborne Battalion, was also activated in July 1941 at Fort Kobbe in the Panama Canal Zone. Three parachute infantry brigades (the 501st, 502nd, and 503rd) were authorized in July 1942, culminating with the activation of the "All American" 82nd Division and "Screaming Eagles" 101st Airborne Division by late summer of the same year.[5] The Provisional Parachute Group Headquarters, commanded by Lt.-Colonel William Lee, became the headquarters of Airborne Command, and retained sole responsibility for centralized control of any ground elements. Although Lt.-Colonel (Later Major General) Lee was quite instrumental in overseeing the development of airborne forces, he would not lead airborne troops into combat be-

cause of a heart condition.

In late 1942, the Army Air Force established the First Troop Carrier Command as a training agency for all airborne related operations, including the movement of glider borne troops and paratroopers. Qualified troop carrier crews were provided by the Army Air Force, but the selection process became a weak link throughout the development of integrated Allied Airborne operations. Insufficient numbers of qualified airborne and troop carrier staff advisers also hampered development of a truly unified airborne-transport command, and would plague airborne operations until the end of the war.

The lack of unified command for both airborne and transport operations compounded these difficulties. Inter-service rivalries and scarce allotments of aircraft, gliders, aircrews, and equipment hampered the development of a unified command structure until the First Allied Airborne Army was formed in 1944. The complex tasks of communicating and coordinating with higher headquarters, troop carrier command, tactical air support, civilian control, traffic control, and operational ground forces required additional divisional general staff, but General McNair failed to support the much needed expansion.[6]

General Formation of American Airborne Divisions

General Leslie McNair, Chief of the Army General Headquarters and the top ranking officer in the U.S. Army, did not view the concept of employing large-scale airborne divisions as a serious possibility until the end of the North Africa and Sicily operations in 1943. McNair grudgingly approved the expansion of both parachute and glider battalions to regimental formations of three battalions apiece. Divisional formations, previously proposed by Major General Matthew Ridgway, included three regiments: two gliders and one parachute. The new formations were equivalent to a downsized American infantry division of 504 officers and 8,321 troops. The proposed table of organization included glider and parachute borne division artillery, an engineer battalion, medical company, and signals and quartermaster companies.

By the fall of 1944 the 82nd Airborne Division and the 101st Airborne Division were expanded to four regiments each: three parachute and one glider. To support each parachute regiment, the 82nd Airborne Division incorporated a provisional fourth company into the engineer battalion, added a provisional parachute maintenance company, and converted an anti-aircraft battalion into a fourth anti-tank battery.

**Brigadier General James Maurice Gavin
and the 82nd Airborne Division**

Thirty-six year old Brigadier General James M. Gavin commanded the volunteer "All American" 82nd Airborne Division. Brigadier General Gavin, a West Point graduate, was already a seasoned veteran of Sicily, Italy, and Normandy. Gavin's tenacity and skillful command under heavy enemy pressure drew the admiration and respect of his airborne troops: "in battle (he) would could cut your (the enemy's) throat and then laugh...."[7]

Despite its brief history as an airborne unit, the troops of the 82nd Airborne Division were battle hardened following campaigns in Sicily, Salerno, and Normandy. The 82nd was also known as the "All American" division because it included troops from all 48 states. The division served with distinction in World War I, and its battle streamers included Lorraine, Saint Mihiel, and Meuse-Argonne. The 82nd Airborne Division's most distinguished veteran was Sergeant Alvin C. York.[8] Following the widespread dispersal of American airborne troops throughout the Cotentin Peninsula in Normandy, Gavin's troops displayed individual toughness, bravery, and initiative by reforming into small units and successfully disrupting German defenses. The 82nd Airborne Division gained world renown for capturing the key town of Saint Mere-Eglise, but suffered heavy losses during the operation.

Following the conclusion of D-Day operations, the 82nd Airborne Division returned to England in late summer for recuperation and refitting. However, Gavin was informed at Lt.-General Brereton's FAAA Headquarters at Sunninghill Park that the division would return to Europe and participate in a daring daylight operation code named Operation Market Garden. It would require at least two days to deliver Gavin's troops along a ten-mile stretch of highway close to the Dutch-German border. The 82nd Airborne Division was expected to capture a major road bridge over the Maas River at Grave and at least one of four canal bridges over the Maas-Waal Canal, and finally the 1,800 foot long Nijmegen span over the Waal. Gavin's division was also expected to capture a high hill mass known as the Groesbeek Heights southeast of the city of Nijmegen. The triangular shaped heights consisted of a series of 300 foot-wooded ridges facing the German Reichswald.[9]

Lt.-General Browning also informed Gavin that enemy armor had massed near the proposed landing sites. A swift counterattack by these concealed forces could result in the seizure of Gavin's landing sites, as well as direct artillery interdiction of XXX Corp traffic moving north towards the Nijmegen. Gavin's unfortunate fate—having to attempt so many objectives spread over a twenty-five square mile area with three regiments—would delay the capture of the pivotal Nijmegen span and the subsequent relief of the British First Airborne Division in Arnhem.[10]

"All American" Airborne Regiments

Brigadier General Gavin would command four regiments throughout Operation Market Garden: the 504th, 505th, and 508th Parachute Infantry Regiments (PIR) and the 325th Glider Infantry Regiment (GIR). In addition, the 82nd Airborne Division included several artillery batteries: the 456th and 376th Parachute Field Artillery Battalions (PFAB); the 319th and 320th Glider Field Artillery (GFA); and the 80th Anti-Tank Battalion (ATB).

The 82nd "All American" Airborne Division dropping into Holland.

Colonel Rueben Henry Tucker III and the 504th Parachute Infantry Regiment

Colonel Rueben Henry Tucker III, commander of the 504th PIR, was nearly as legendary as Gavin himself. Tucker was a rough-and-tumble Connecticut Yankee, a West Point graduate, and a fearless infantry leader, gaining a "tough-as-nails" reputation throughout the Italian campaigns in Sicily and Salerno in 1943 and Anzio in early 1944.[11] At Salerno, Tucker's regiment successfully completed a night drop and captured Hill 424. Later, Tucker's command was nearly victimized by an ill-conceived plan to airdrop the 504th PIR onto a strongly defended Rome. Major General Mark Clark would retain Tucker's forces in the Mediterranean to fight as sea-borne infantry at Anzio, leading to heavy casualties and a Presidential Unit Citation.[12] Colonel Tucker's actions were best described as being "up to his ears in battle…. having a hell of a good time."[13]

Tucker's 504th PIR would miss the Normandy invasion in June 1944 because of heavy casualties sustained in Italy, but its depleted ranks were quickly refilled with green replacements from the United States and recent graduates of the Ashwell Jump School in England.[14] The 504th PIR's primary mission in Market Garden was to capture the nine-span, 1,800 foot iron highway bridge over the Maas River north of Grave. Tucker's regiment was also assigned the tasks of capturing the following: at least one bridge over the Maas-Waal Canal; the combination highway-railroad bridge at Honinghutje; and the canal bridges at Malden and Heumen.

Colonel William E. Ekman and the 505th Parachute Infantry Regiment

The commander of the 505th Parachute Infantry Regiment, Colonel William E. Ekman, was another West Point graduate and replacement of the recently promoted Brigadier General Gavin. During the Normandy airborne landings, Colonel Ekman's "lost" battalions would capture the famous French town of Saint Mere-Eglise and the La Fiere bridge along the Merderet.[15] During Market Garden, Colonel Ekman would be responsible for securing the town of Groesbeek and the adjacent heights until the airhead build-up was complete.

Colonel Roy Lindquist and the 508th Parachute Infantry Regiment

Colonel Roy Lindquist, a 1930 graduate of West Point, was the original commander of the 508th Parachute Infantry Regiment. The 508th PIR also experienced wide dispersion in Normandy, but regrouped to secure key invasion routes adjacent to the Merderet River bridgehead. During Market Garden, Colonel Lindquist's regiment was responsible for securing the Groesbeek Heights with the 505th PIR until the 325th Glider Infantry arrived on D+1, then assist Tucker's 504th PIR in capturing two bridges over the Maas-Waal Canal and the five-span highway bridge across the Waal River at Nijmegen.

Colonel Charles Billingslea and the 325th Glider Infantry Regiment

Colonel Charles Billingslea assumed command in August 1944 after Colonel Harry Lewis fell victim to combat fatigue in Normandy.

During the early hours of the Normandy landings, the 325th GIR had assumed a critical role in capturing the key La Fiere Bridge at the Merderet River. The less-than-popular "Light Horse Harry Leigh" Lewis had commanded the regiment throughout the North Africa, Sicily, and Salerno campaigns until he collapsed under fire at Normandy. Colonel Lewis would die of cancer the following year.[16]

A 1936 graduate of West Point, Billingslea was best remembered for his "six foot three inch tall and taciturn frame." He served with distinction as executive officer of Colonel Tucker's 504th Parachute Infantry Regiment in the Salerno, Volturno River, Anzio, and Normandy operations.[17] The 325th GIR was assigned the role of divisional reserve, and would relieve Colonel Tucker's 504th Parachute Regiment on D+1.

"All American" Divisional Units

The 376th Parachute Field Artillery Battalion, commanded by Lt.-Colonel Wilbur Griffith, fought in Sicily, Salerno, Naples, and Anzio with each battery attached to a parachute regiment. The battalion included four batteries: Headquarters/Service battery, and three batteries equipped with four disassembled 75-mm pack howitzers, for a total of twelve guns.[18] Although Griffith's parachute battalion was never dropped in combat, it would arrive on Market D-Day along with the glider-borne infantry. Throughout the battle, the 376th would provide fire support for the 505th PIR with its ten surviving howitzers and tenaciously defend the Groesbeek Heights.[19]

The 80th Anti-Tank Battalion, commanded by Lt.-Colonel Raymond E. "Tex" Singleton, fought in Sicily, Salerno, and Normandy. It included four batteries of 57mm anti-tank guns, each battery with four guns. Half of the 80th ATB, with eight guns, would arrive on Market D-Day. Two guns each were assigned to the 504th, 505th, and 508th PIRs and the balance held in reserve. The remaining divisional artillery, the 319th and 320th Glider Field Artillery and the 456th Parachute Field Artillery, would arrive on D+1.

Three companies of the 307th Airborne Engineers, commanded by Lt.-Colonel Edwin A. Bedell, would arrive with the paratroopers on D-Day. Many of the remaining administrative and support troops would arrive on D+1 and +2.

Major General Maxwell Taylor and the 101st Airborne Division

Major General Maxwell Taylor's 101st "Screaming Eagles" Airborne Division fought a series of vicious battles in Normandy until relieved by the American 4th Infantry Division arriving at Utah Beach. The 101st Airborne Division was the first Allied formation to land in France, but also experienced wide dispersion and failed to capture several key objectives on schedule.

The 101st Airborne Division would land at the southernmost end of the Market Garden corridor, ten miles ahead of the British XXX Corps positioned near the Neerpelt Bridgehead. The three parachute regiments (the 501st, 502nd, and 506th), plus attached engineering and reconnaissance units, were to seize three canal crossings along the Wilhelmina Canal near Son. The division was also expected to secure a fifteen-mile stretch of highway between Veghel and Eindhoven, later known as "Hell's Highway." The lead 506th PIR was to capture Eindhoven, located five miles south of the town of Son, block the Son/St.-Oedenrode Highway, and send detachments to road and railway bridges over the Wilhelmina Canal south and southeast of Best. The rest of the division would secure the remaining crossings of the Willems Vaart Canal and the Aa River in the Veghel area.[20] Other divisional assets included the 327th Glider Infantry Regiment, three artillery batteries—the 377th and 907th Parachute Field Artillery Battalions and the 321st Glider Field Artillery—and the 81st Anti-Tank Battalion.

Colonel Howard Johnson and the 501st Parachute Infantry Regiment

One of the legendary 101st Airborne Division officers was Colonel Howard "Skeets" Johnson, commander of the 501st Parachute Infantry Regiment. Colonel Johnson was an All-American boxer and former Annapolis midshipman who had transferred to the Army. Before Market Garden he had amassed over one hundred parachute jumps, and developed a reputation for his ruthless agenda in training and fearlessness under fire. During the Normandy invasion, the 501st PIR captured key positions near the Douve River.

The 501st PIR, along with two platoons of the 326th Airborne Battalion, was ordered to secure crossings over the Willems Vaart Canal and Aa River near the town of Veghel.

Colonel Johnson would die several months after the conclusion of Market Garden in the Betuwe.

Colonel John H. Michaelis and the 502nd Parachute Infantry Regiment

Colonel John H. Michaelis, West Point class of 1936, assumed command of the 502nd Parachute Infantry Regiment during the Normandy operation. Michaelis replaced Colonel George Moseley, Jr., who was wounded in action. The 502nd PIR assisted in opening key invasion causeways for the 4th Infantry Division at Utah Beach. Colonel Michaelis' regiment would serve as the 101st Airborne Division reserve, block the Son-St. Oedenrode Highway, send detachments to the nearby railroad and highway bridges over the Wilhelmina Canal, and support the 506th PIR advance towards Eindhoven. Colonel Michaelis was known to remain cool and capable under battle conditions. He was seriously wounded during Market Garden and replaced by Lt.-Colonel Steve Chappius.

Colonel Robert F. Sink and the 506th Parachute Infantry Regiment

Colonel Robert F. Sink, West Point 1927, was the original commander of the 506th Parachute Infantry Regiment and a survivor of the Normandy campaign. The 506th PIR had opened key causeways for the 4th Infantry Division on the Cotentin Peninsula. Colonel Sink was known as "One of the Bravest, most able men …never to be promoted."[21] During Market Garden the 506th PIR, along with one platoon of the 326th Airborne Engineers Battalion and division reconnaissance, was to seize the crossings over the Wilhelmina Canal near Son and the canal crossings at Eindhoven.

Colonel Joseph Harper and the 327th Glider Infantry Regiment

Colonel Joseph Harper was the original commander of the 401st Parachute Infantry Regiment (PIR), but his command was split in order to provide a temporary third battalion to the 325th and 327th Glider Infantry Regiments for the Normandy operations. Colonel Harper later relieved the commander of the 327th GIR, George S. Wear, during a series of critical engagements near the Douve River crossings. Harper's crucially needed troops would not arrive in Holland until the third day of operations

"Screaming Eagles" Divisional Units

Lt.-Colonel Benjamin Weisberg commanded the 377th Parachute Field Artillery Battalion (FAB) during the Normandy operation, where the unit was scattered and rendered ineffective. Weisberg was relieved and replaced by Lt.-Colonel Harry W. Elkins. The 377th FAB included four batteries: Headquarters/Service plus three firing batteries, each equipped with four disassembled 75-mm pack howitzers.[22] Only Company D of the 377th FAB would arrive on Market Garden D-Day along with the parachute infantry regiments. The remainder of the battalion would arrive on D+1 and support the 505th Parachute Infantry Regiment.

The 81st Anti-Tank Battalion, commanded by Lt.-Colonel X. B. Cox, Jr., fought in Normandy. The battalion included three anti-aircraft batteries and one battery of 57mm anti-tank guns. The 81st ATB would arrive in Holland on D+2 with only fourteen guns available. The remaining artillery units, the 321st Glider Field Artillery (GFA) and the 907th Parachute Field Artillery (PFA), would arrive on the second day of the Holland operations with their snub-nosed 105mm guns. Three platoons of the 326th Airborne Engineers would arrive with the paratroopers. The remaining administrative and support troops would arrive throughout the first several days of the operation.

The Pathfinders

The independent Pathfinder units would precede both American airborne divisions. The pathfinders were to mark the drop and landing zones with "Eureka" compass beacons, colored panels, and colored smoke.[a] The Pathfinder aircraft would carry special radar equipment by which crews would find the targeted landing areas.[23]

Condition of Readiness

During the early weeks of September 1944, both the 82nd and 101st Airborne Divisions were recovering from costly casualties suffered in Normandy. The 82nd Airborne Division, originally 12,000 strong, was reduced by nearly 5,300 troops, of which 1,300 were killed. The cost to the 101st Airborne Division was also severe: nearly 5,000 casualties, including two regimental and five battalion commanders lost. The 17th Airborne Division would not participate in Market Garden because it had recently arrived from the United States.

Airborne Transportation: Major General Paul L. Williams

On September 10 a meeting was held with commanders and staff officers from airborne and troops carrier units at Sunninghill Park. Lt.-General Browning named Major General Paul L. Williams operational air commander of all transport forces for Operation Mar-

---

[a] "Eureka" devices were radio beacons used to assist incoming transports in locating drop zones with relative precision.

ket. Williams' command included the USAAF IX Troop Carrier Command, British No. 38 Group commanded by A.V.M. Leslie Hollinghurst, and British No. 46 Group commanded by Air Commander L. Darvall, as well as Allied bomber aircraft allocated for resupply missions.[24] Major General Williams would oversee sixty-four troop carrier squadrons totaling 2,000 transports and gliders. Williams faced the unenviable task of deploying nearly forty-five thousand men—twenty thousand parachutists, fifteen thousand glidermen, and ten thousand regular infantry—over a three- to five-day timeframe. Williams had recently commanded operations in Sicily, Normandy, and Southern France, but his accuracy in troop delivery was poor.[25]

"Second-Class" Transport Pilots

Before proceeding to the execution of the Market Garden airborne phase, a review of fundamental issues regarding air transport support is in order. The air transport wings had suffered from a series of poorly executed operations in Sicily and Anzio. Prior to Market Garden, Allied troops maintained the general perception that many American airborne transport crews were essentially "washouts" and second-class compared to the more illustrious daytime bomber crews. Airborne transport pilots were not considered combatants, despite the fact they flew less than 120 miles per hour at three hundred feet without armor or self-sealing tanks in the wings of their Douglas Dakota C-47s. The airlife of a Dakota C-47 following a flak induced wing fire was less than five minutes, yet scores of British and American airmen would bravely sacrifice themselves while delivering vitally needed supplies. Unlike their British counterparts, American glider pilots did not receive flight or combat pay, and more importantly, basic infantry training to allow them to fight effectively after a successful landing. It was not until the conclusion of Operation Market Garden that transport pilots finally received long-deserved recognition.

The Challenges of Market

Major General Williams faced several challenges throughout the planning process: night versus day drop; distance of troop carrier routes; flak suppression; safe drop zones; ground support capacity; and effective resupply flights. The first major decision was to conduct a major daylight operation in place of the traditional night drops. Both the Sicily and Normandy night operations resulted in wide dispersion of troops and a significant number of landing casualties. Delivery of heavy equipment such as artillery was considered a total failure in Normandy. Another concern was the deadly effectiveness of German night fighters and the inadequate Allied defensive measures used against them.[26] Unlike the British 38 and 46 Groups, the American IX Troop Carrier Command had not practiced night operations since Normandy. The month of September was also a "no moon" period, making night navigation nearly impossible. In light of these facts, Lt.-General Brereton decided to conduct a daylight invasion of Holland.

A second issue concerned the selection of troop carrier routes. Since airfields on the European continent were exclusively used by

TAC fighter support, the entire air operation would originate from twenty-two airfields located throughout southern and eastern England. The routes needed to be direct, since the armada would extend over fifty miles in length.

The third issue was flak suppression, but Lt.-General Brereton remained confident that the Eighth Air Force, Air Defense of Great Britain, the British 2nd TAC, and No. 2 Group RAF would provide ample coverage for the lumbering transports and gliders. Based on recent intelligence, flak defenses were increasing around Arnhem, and the RAF feared that air transport casualties could reach forty percent losses.[27] Heavy flak and soft polderland led to a crucial decision by the British 38 and 46 Groups to deliver the British First Airborne Division on high ground between five and eight miles west-northwest of the Arnhem objectives. Despite historical proof that landing a handful of forces directly on an objective (the British 6th Airborne's capture of the Orne River Bridge) might be the best means of attaining success, Air Vice-Marshall Hollinghurst of 38 Group insisted that the surrounding polderland was too soft to support a glider borne *coup de main*. Both Williams and Taylor also determined that the 101st Airborne Division should drop eight miles north of Eindhoven. Finally, Gavin elected not to land any forces near the Nijmegen Bridge, which would contribute to the three-day delay in capturing the major objective.[28]

The fourth issue was Major General Williams's concern that there were insufficient gliders and transport to deliver three airborne divisions and a brigade to Holland on D-Day. Using every available aircraft, only two-thirds of the fighting infantry could be delivered. Heavy equipment gliders could only be parceled to key units expecting counterattacks immediately after airlanding. Williams remained adamant that ground support units and pilots were physically incapable of conducting two missions in a single day, despite the fact that two flights were successfully conducted during the daylight *Operation Dragoon* in southern France in July 1944.

Major General Williams concluded that the entire First Allied Airborne Force could only be delivered over a three-day timeframe. Lt.-General Brereton supported Williams, realizing that a three-day drop would essentially eliminate the key factor inherent in airborne operations—*surprise and efficient use of firepower*. After the first lift the enemy would be alerted, resulting in counterattacks and increased anti-aircraft fire.

Finally, there remained the danger of unpredictable weather conditions throughout September on the European continent and England. The night operations oriented RAF had previously suggested initiating the first lift before dawn, but the overwhelming number of untrained night flying U.S. aircrews precluded such an option.

Resupply of airborne troops would continue for no longer than ten days, and Williams would not approve gliders in double tow. The First Allied Airborne made arrangements with the Eighth Air Force to use B-24 Liberator bombers for dropping supplies on D+2.[29] This attempt would prove to be quite unsuccessful. The shortage of aircraft also made it unlikely that the air transportable British 52nd Lowland Division would arrive any sooner than D+5.

Notes

1 Gerard M. Devlin, *Paratrooper!* (New York: St.Martins, 1979), p.660. *Sung by American troops to the tune of "Battle of the Republic."*

2 Vandeleur describing Major Julian Cook's amphibious crossing of the Waal. James M. Gavin, *On To Berlin: Battles of an Airborne Commander, 1943-1946* (New York: The Viking Press, 1978), p.179.

3 Lt.-General Lewis Hyde Brereton, *The Brereton Diaries: The War in the Pacific, Middle East, and Europe 3 Ocober 1941-8 May 1945* (New York: DaCapo Press, 1976), p.309. *First published by William Morrow and Sons in 1946.*

4 James A. Huston, *Out of the Blue: U.S. Army Airborne Operations in World War II* (Nashville: The Battery Press, 1972), p.65.

5 Ibid., p.66.

6 Ibid., pp.68-69.

7 Ibid., p.53.

8 *Including the author's father, Technical Sergeant Paul E. DeLillio, Combat Infantryman, Bronze Star.*

9 Charles MacDonald, *The Siegfried Line Campaign* (Washington DC: Center of Military History, 1963), pp.155-156.

10 James M. Gavin, op.cit., p.147.

11 Clay Blair, *Ridgway's Paratroopers: The American Airborne in World War II* (New York: William Morrow, 1985), pp.302-303.

12 Ibid., pp.350-351.

13 Ibid., p.159.

14 Ibid., p.476.

15 Gerard M. Devlin, op.cit., pp. 384-385.

16 Ibid., p.43.

17 Ibid., pp.65-67, and p.510.

18 Ibid., pp.521-525.

19 Huston, op.cit., p.8

20 Ibid., p.21.

21 Devlin, op.cit., p.223. *Quote from Lt.-General Maxwell Taylor.*

22 Blair, op.cit., pp.521-525.

23 Huston, op.cit., p.23.

24 Robert Jackson, *Arnhem, The Battle Remembered* (Shresbury: Airlife Publishing, 1994), p.26.

25 Blair, op.cit., p.88 and p.315. Williams claimed that his troop carriers dropped 80% of the paratroopers on designated drop zones in Sicily and 85 to 90% in Operation Dragoon but unfortunately these estimates were not challenged by Senior FAAA Command until 1955. Actual figures were closer to 15-20%. Bair concluded that William's overestimates may have unduly encouraged further airborne operations in the European Theater of Operations.

26 Cajus Bekker, *The Luftwaffe War Diaries* (London: MacDonald and Company, 1966), p.356. By Autumn 1944 the Allies implemented new tactics of jamming the night –fighters "Liechtenstein" SN 2 radar sets out of action.

27 Jackson, op.cit., p.29.

28 Ibid., p.30.

29 Huston, op.cit., pp.16-17

5

Operation Market:
"Warriors from the Sky"

"Red Devils," "Screaming Eagles," and "All Americans"….

"I look back at the door and the pilot gives me the clenched-hand salute, like a boxer about to jump… The ships ahead of us are still going on. There's a burst of flak.

You can see it right from the side. It's coming from the port side just across our nose, but a little bit low. Tracers going across us, in front of our nose. I think it's coming from that little village just beside the canal. More tracer coming up now, cutting across in front of our nose. A lovely orange color it is… In just about 40 seconds now our ship will drop the men; they will walk out onto Dutch soil. You can probably hear the snap as they check the lashing on the static line. There they go!

Do you hear them count? Three… four… five… six… seven… eight… nine… ten… eleven… twelve… thirteen… fourteen… fifteen… sixteen… Now every man is out…!

Every man is clear…they're dropping…like nothing so much as khaki dolls hanging beneath green lampshades…the whole sky is filled with parachutes…."[1]

The Opening Attack: September 16-17, 1944[a]

The much anticipated weather report arrived at the office of the First Allied Airborne Army commander, Lt.-General Lewis H. Brereton, late Saturday afternoon on September 16, 1944. Meteorologists predicted favorable weather conditions over Holland throughout the next four days, with intermittent haze and morning fog. After sixteen cancellations the "party was on," with Brereton issuing the final airborne orders setting H-Hour as 1300 hrs on Sunday, September 17, 1944.

The First Allied Airborne Army, organized only 40 days earlier, would spearhead Field Marshal Montgomery's attack towards the heart of industrial Germany.[2] Allied airborne forces were expected to take control of five major crossings over a series of canals and bridges located along the sixty-four mile British XXX Corps axis of attack. The British First Airborne Division and First Polish Airborne Brigade Group were to capture and hold the Arnhem bridges for three days, while the American's 82nd and 101st Airborne Divisions occupied principal crossings at Eindhoven, Grave, and Nijmegen. Within a few hours of the initial airborne assault, Lt.-General Brian Horrock's XXX Corps would lead the Second British Army towards the Zuider Zee from their starting point near the Albert and Escaut canals in northern Belgium, while the British XII and VIII Corps provided flanking support. Advancing along a single Dutch road in three days seemed quite plausible, given the recent 280-mile advance of Lt.-General Sir Miles Dempsey's Sec-

ond British Army and the successful American First and Third Army drives toward the Moselle River. Speed was essential in order to relieve airborne troops before they ran out of supplies or were overwhelmed by German counterattacks.

Daily airlift limitations imposed by Major General Paul L. Williams, overall chief of air transport operations, compelled both the British and American airborne generals to reconsider the offensive capabilities of their respective landing forces. However, the commander of the First British Airborne Division, Major General Robert E. Urquhart, elected to transport only two infantry brigades, the 1st Parachute and 1st Airlanding Brigade, plus a significant number of divisional support and artillery to a point nearly seven miles west of Arnhem on D-Day. The remaining British First Airborne Division troops, which included the 4th Parachute Brigade and 1st Polish Parachute Brigade, would arrive in the second and third lift. The air transportable British 52nd Lowland Infantry Division would not arrive until the fourth lift, following the capture of airfields north of Arnhem.

The American 82nd and 101st Airborne Divisions would land the equivalent of six infantry brigades, placing a total of eighteen

---

[a] Because of the complexity of the operation the forces in this chapter are directed towards the airborne elements during the first forty-eight hours. The detailed actions of the British Second Army are described in Chapter Six.

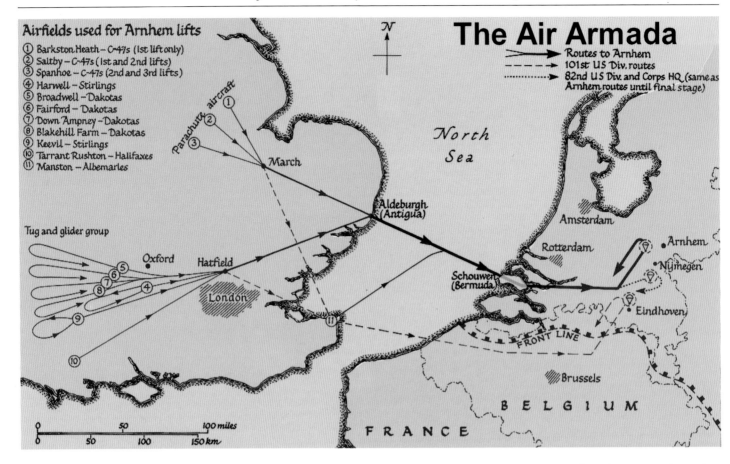

Airfields used for Arnhem lifts
1. Barkston Heath – C-47s (1st lift only)
2. Saltby – C-47s (1st and 2nd lifts)
3. Spanhoe – C-47s (2nd and 3rd lifts)
4. Harwell – Stirlings
5. Broadwell – Dakotas
6. Fairford – Dakotas
7. Down Ampney – Dakotas
8. Blakehill Farm – Dakotas
9. Keevil – Stirlings
10. Tarrant Rushton – Halifaxes
11. Manston – Albemarles

The Air Armada

Routes to Arnhem
101st US Div. routes
82nd US Div. and Corps HQ (same as Arnhem routes until final stage)

American combat battalions on the ground in comparison with only six British battalions. Significantly fewer American support troops arrived on D+1, reinforced by two additional glider infantry regiments and supporting artillery battalions on D+2/3. Unlike Urquhart's forces, both Gavin's and Taylor's troops were permitted by Troop Carrier Command to land within three miles of town and crossing objectives, with the unfortunate exception of the main road bridge at Nijmegen.

Softening the Enemy Air Defenses
The battle for the Market Garden corridor began on a nearly cloudless September 16th evening as RAF Bomber Command's Avro Lancasters and de Havilland Mosquitos dropped nearly 900 tons of high explosive bombs on suspected fighter fields at Leeuwuwarden, Steenwijk-Havelte, Hopsten, and Rheine.[3] The next morning, two flak-suppressing waves of Lancasters and Mosquitos targeted anti-aircraft defenses lining the airborne corridor and landing zones. Several thousand tons of 260-lb fragmentation bombs were dropped from 10,000 to 20,000 feet, but less than half hit their mark. The Allies were fortunate in that a significant number of the superior Messerschmitt 262 fighter-bombers of Kampfgeschwader 51 were temporarily put out of action by British bombs.[4]

The bombing missions continued throughout the early morning of D-Day, September 17th, as a large force of 1,100 Eighth USAAF B-17 Flying Fortresses, escorted by P-51 Mustangs and P-47 Thunderbolts, attacked nearly 100 coastal flak and inland anti-aircraft batteries. Later that morning, additional waves of RAF

Lancasters and Mosquitos conducted diversionary attacks against suspected anti-aircraft positions on Walcheren Island. Mosquito Squadrons Nos. 107 and 613, from Lasham and Thorney Island, also attacked targets in Nijmegen and Arnhem. Second TAC B-25 Mitchell and Boston bombers attacked Ede, several miles west of the designated drop zones. Despite this massive effort, few bombers achieved material success.

Several minutes after the last bombing run, over eight hundred Eighth and Ninth Air Force P-51 Mustangs, P-38 Lightnings, and P-47 Thunderbolts flew fighter escort or engaged enemy anti-aircraft batteries along the corridor. Eighteen British Spitfire squadrons flew escort protection for the lumbering armada from England to a designated hand-off area where their American counterparts would take over. The Mustangs flew over the Belgium and Dutch countryside in layers of 2,500 and 5,000 feet, shooting down several Fw-190s and Messerschmitts with minimal loss. The closing attacks included four Ninth Air Force fighter-bomber groups, as well as rocket and strafing attacks along the corridor by RAF Tempests and Typhoons. Visibility remained poor, resulting in a significant number of aborted attacks. Even so, the initial air suppression phase appeared successful.[5]

This particular Sunday also marked the fourth anniversary of the Battle of Britain. At approximately 9:30 a.m., transport squadron formations at RAF and American bases initiated preparations for what many considered a momentous flight to the Dutch Gelderlands. As the largest air armada ever assembled prepared to follow the bombers mid-morning, not one Englishman, Pole, Canadian, or American expected that losses over the next nine days would exceed those suffered by the RAF during Britains' "Finest Hour" in 1940.[6]

The Airborne Troop Armada
Early Sunday morning on September 17, 1944, Allied transport and First British Airborne troops at eight RAF and three American airfields rested on grassy fields adjacent to hundreds of tugs, gliders, and transports. One last cup of tea or sandwich was consumed; one last newspaper acquired from WAAF staffed "Sally Anne" wagons.[7] The dissipating Sunday morning haze revealed scores of RAF Horsa and Hamilcar gliders; their camouflage punctuated with thick black and white invasion stripes on wings and fuselages. Closer inspection of the midnight black glider underbellies revealed many a chalk-written graffiti scrawled by confident troops. A memorable inscription on one Horsa read "no barrel rolls, please!" The RAF squadrons would primarily fly tow-and-glider combinations, with the exception of twelve Stirlings assigned to deliver 186 pathfinders of the Independent 21st Parachute Company.[8]

At the bases of Broadwell, Down Ampney, and Blakwell Farms the high-pitched whines of American Pratt and Whitney "Twin Wasp" engines abruptly filled an already excited atmosphere, while huge 1,600 hp Bristol Hercules XVI radial engines perched on ancient wings of Stirlings laboriously reached deafening crescendos at Harwell, Keevil, and Fairford. Fifteen minutes later, the tugs and gliders carrying the 1st Airlanding Brigade and various support units commenced their ascent to formation height.

Approximately half an hour later the British 1st, 2nd, and 3rd Parachute Battalions of the 1st Parachute Brigade departed from American troop carrier bases at Barkston Heath, Saltby, Spalding, and Fairford.[9] This difference in departure times was due to the slower 120-mph speed of the Albemarles and Stirlings, as well as the lengthy

assembly time inherent in pre-invasion tug-glider formations. Commencing at 10:30 a.m., the British Airborne 21st Independent Parachute Company departed in converted Stirling troop carriers from Fairford, while the American pathfinder teams took off in C-47 Dakotas minutes later from Chalgrove airfield.

Eventually the five hundred ship British and American air transport armada carrying the British First Airborne (not including over a thousand fighter-escorts from the US VIII Airforce) would rendezvous with two massive waves of three paralleled streams of aircraft heading east over London and then towards the English Channel. The first wave, totaling 3,500 Allied aircraft, would reach its final destination in less than five hours. From port to starboard one witnessed an incredible 100-mile stream of planes, tugs, and escorts floating effortlessly through clear weather and over calm seas. A few gliders would plummet into the North Sea by accident, but many aboard were saved by air-sea rescue.[10] Later that evening British transports dropped "Rupert" dummy parachutists west of Utrecht to confuse and mislead enemy ground troops.

The RAF transport and tug squadrons included Douglas Dakotas, Albermarles, Stirlings, Halifaxes, and Horsa gliders of the 38th and 46th Group. The British squadrons towing glider-borne vehicles, heavy weapons, line infantry, and divisional support would rendezvous with transport serials of American IX Troop Carrier C-47s (and a few C-53s) transporting the British 1st Parachute Brigade and lead elements of the 4th Parachute Brigade near Aldeburgh, England. This joint force then proceeded southeast along the designated "Northern Route" until arriving at the coast of Holland, near Schouwen Island. Only thirty-five gliders would fail to reach the landing zones. The average flight time was two hours from England to the European continent and thirty to fifty minutes over enemy held Holland. After reaching the Dutch coast, air transit casualties remained light due to the effectiveness of the anti-air sup-

British 2nd TAC attacking flak positions along the Market Garden corridor.

pression campaign. Simultaneously, the British 2nd Tactical Air Force attacked German barracks at Nijmegen and Arnhem. Not one British transport or glider was lost to enemy ground fire during the opening air phase of Market Garden, and many of the aborted thirty-five Horsa gliders returned in the second airlift.[11]

Despite the enormity of the air phase, a key issue remained: there simply were not enough transports and tow-tug combinations to deliver the entire First British Airborne Division in the first lift. Major General Paul Williams of the American IX Troop Carrier Command considered it impossible to launch two airborne waves in a single day. The key factors contributing to Williams' decisions were insufficient American training and experience in night navigation, understaffed ground maintenance crews, lack of continental airbases for rapid turnaround, potential pilot fatigue, and the danger posed by enemy anti-aircraft defenses put on full alert after the first wave. This decision led to plans to transport Urquhart's forces over a three-day period, assuming that the unpredictable September weather would remain favorable and enemy build-up at the landing sites minimal.

First British Airborne Troops Land on Dutch Soil

At precisely 12:40 p.m., pathfinders of the 21st Independent Parachute Company dropped from twelve lumbering British Stirlings onto freshly harvested fields near the towns of Wolfheze, Heelsum,

and Renkum. In a matter of thirty minutes, squads from each pathfinder platoon completed the task of laying out large air recognition panels to assist Allied tug and transport pilots in identifying airdrop area "X" and glider landing areas "Z" and "S." The remaining pathfinders set up a "Eureka" transmitting beacon, a large "T" in the designated airdrop area, or prepared smoke canisters to indicate wind direction.[12] The panels were made from nylon and colored crimson, white, or orange.[13]

In less than ninety minutes nearly three hundred gliders and one hundred and fifty Douglas Dakota C-47s would deliver over 5,000 British troops six and a half miles west of the Arnhem Bridge.

Arrival of British 1st Airlanding Brigade and Division Support

At 1:00 p.m. the commander of the 21st Independent Parachute Company, Major B.A. "Boy" Wilson, peered southwest to observe scores of Horsas, Hamilcars, and a smattering of American Wacos approaching Landing Zone S near Reijers-Camp Farm and the southern Landing Zone Z located west of Wolfheze.[14] The British Horsas were released nearly two and a half miles from the landing sites, and the gliders descended at speeds of less than 90 miles per hour, arriving every nine seconds with full flaps onto the recently harvested Dutch fields.[15] The glider pilots were instructed to commence their landings at the northern end of the two large fields to leave enough room for following gliders to land behind them; this unfor-

The high pitched whine of American Pratt and Whitney Twin Wasp engines abruptly filled an already excited atmosphere.

tunately led to a number of casualties among the Horsa gliders. Several of the Horsas overshot, landing in the surrounding undergrowth or atop trees along the northeastern corner of Landing Zone Z and resulting in several fatalities. The soft ground also contributed to the destruction of four heavy Hamilcars carrying the much-needed 17-pound anti-tank guns and Bren carriers. Other pieces of equipment believed to be well fastened to the floors of the gliders broke loose on landing, resulting in a number of sprains and broken bones.

The Horsa-borne infantry of the 1st Borders, 7th Kings Own Scottish Borderers (KOSB), and 2nd South Staffordshires were the first to arrive onto Landing Zone S. After jumping through the large aft loading doors, the platoons of the 7th KOSB, 2nd South Staffordshires, and 1st Borders immediately assumed defensive positions around Drop Zones X/Y and Landing Zones Z/L. Fortunately, the airlanding troops encountered little enemy opposition until General von Tettau's probing companies arrived in the late afternoon.

Additional glider troops arrived between 1:19 p.m. and 1:40 p.m. onto Landing Zone Z, including the 1st Airlanding Anti-tank Battery, as well as vehicles and support equipment belonging to the 1st Parachute Brigade, Airlanding Light Regiment, Reconnaissance,

and RASC and RAMC units. Almost ninety percent of the gliders arriving from England experienced an average unloading time of thirty minutes.[16]

Nearly two-thirds of the Division, including Headquarters, the Airlanding Light Regiment, and the 1st Airlanding Brigade, remained within a ten-mile triangular shaped perimeter nearly eight miles west of Arnhem. These troops were to remain until second lift forces arrived on D+1, including Brigadier Hackett's 4th Parachute Brigade at Drop Zone Y near Grote Heide, the 1st Polish Parachute Brigade Group gliders carrying anti-tank guns and support troops at Zone L near Johannahoeve, and a resupply drop (Point V) near Warnsborn. The 1st Borders, commanded by Lt.-Colonel T.H. Haddon, were assigned to defend the airlanding zones near Wolfheze, then proceed several kilometers south to occupy the town of Renkum near the Lower Rhine. The 7th KOSB, commanded by Lt.-Colonel R. Payton-Reid, proceeded three miles northwest to defend Drop Zone Y near the Ede-Arnhem road or Amsterdamseweg, then awaited the arrival of Brigadier Hackett's 4th Parachute Brigade. The 2nd South Staffordshires, commanded by Lt.-Colonel W.D.H. McCardie—missing an entire company and delayed until the second lift—would remain in Wolfheze as brigade reserve.[17]

Huge 1,600 hp Bristol Hercules XVI radial engines reached deafening crescendos at Harwell, Keevil, and Fairford.

American C-47s from IX Troop Carrier Command transporting British First Parachute Brigade to drop zones near Wolfheze.

RAF 38 Group Horsas transporting the British First Airlanding Brigade to Wolfheze.

Above: American C-47s from IX Troop Carrier Command dropping Frost's 2nd Parachute Battalion over Drop Zone X north of Heelsum.

RAF 43 Group transporting PAK 75mm guns of the 1st Airlanding Light Regiment to Landing Zone Z southwest of Wolfheze.

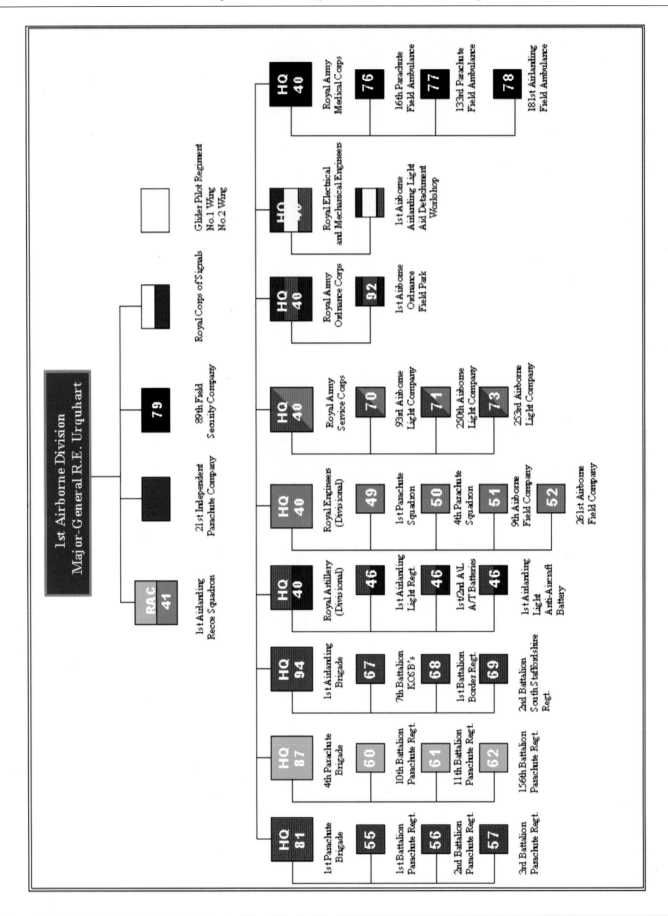

Arrival of the 1st British Parachute Brigade

At 1:50 p.m. over 2,200 red, white, khaki, and yellow parachutes debauched from hundreds of "vic" arrayed Douglas C-47 Dakotas converging on Drop Zone X. The entire drop lasted only eighteen minutes, and all but four troops failed to jump successfully.[18] The drop sequence included a mixture of brigade and division support troops:

1st Parachute Brigade (1st, 2nd, 3rd Battalions)
Brigade HQ and Defense Platoon
1st Airlanding Anti-Tank Battery
16th Field Ambulance (RAMC)
1st Parachute Squadron
Reconnaissance Squadron
RASC (Royal Army Service Corps) platoon
Brigade and Division Headquarters
Advanced landing parties of the 4th Parachute Brigade

While Brigadier Hick's 1st Airlanding Brigade protected the landing sites, the three assault battalions of Brigadier Gerald Lathbury's 1st Parachute Brigade assembled within ninety minutes and prepared to set out along three converging routes leading to Arnhem. The 1st Parachute Brigade was augmented with the 1st Parachute Squadron, troops of the 9th Field Company of the Royal Engineers, most of the 1st Airlanding Anti-tank Battery, a platoon of RASC, glider pilots, artillery observers, and brigade headquarters. Several troops of the Armored Reconnaissance Squadron, commanded by Major Freddie Gough, were assigned to the brigade and proceeded ahead of Lathbury's troops in an attempt to seize the Arnhem Bridge.

Lathbury's Decision to divide the 1st Parachute Brigade

Even though Brigadier Lathbury's command was larger than traditional parachute brigades, he divided the formation into three over-sized assault battalions. Lathbury's critical decision to divide his forces was based on estimates that the Second British Army had provided to the First Allied Army Headquarters in England. Based on this information, First Allied Airborne Corps concluded that enemy opposition would be "light." This conclusion, combined with the six and a half mile distance from landing sites to the brigade objectives, influenced Lathbury's decision to rely on speed of movement in lieu of depth and concentrated firepower. Thus, the brigade would proceed along a thin three-battalion front without sufficient reserves.

At precisely 3:00 p.m., both the 2nd and 3rd Parachute Battalions set off for Arnhem from Landing Zone Z near Heelsum. Half

Rescue craft immediately arrived to recover survivors of ditched gliders.

An ancient but noble Sterling tug from 299 Group.

an hour later the 1st Battalion, commanded by Lt.-Colonel D.T. Dobie, followed Major Freddie Gough's Reconnaissance jeeps along the main Ede-Arnhem roadway (code-named "Leopard") towards the high ground north of Arnhem. Within forty-five minutes the 1st Parachute Battalion was moving along the Ede-Arnhem Railway. The 2nd Parachute Battalion, commanded by Lt.-Colonel John D. Frost, advanced along a secondary road (code-named "Lion") north of the Lower Rhine. They were accompanied by a troop of 1st Airlanding A/T six-pounders and Royal Engineers. Frost's multiple tasks were to capture a pontoon, ferry, and railway bridge in Oosterbeek and the main roadway bridge in Arnhem.[19] The 3rd Battalion, commanded by Lt.-Colonel J.A.H. Fitch, set out along the upper Heelsum-Arnhem road (code-named "Tiger") accompanied by engineers and Anti-tank (A/T) troops. The battalion was assigned the single task of reinforcing Frost, eventually entering parkland near a hotel called the Hartenstein.

The balance of Lathbury's troops closely followed Frost's 2nd Battalion into Arnhem, including brigade headquarters, the 1st Parachute Squadron, the RASC Platoon, headquarters of the 1st Airlanding Anti-Tank Battery, Military Police troops, and the 16th Parachute Field Ambulance. The medical unit would locate at St. Elizabeths Hospital.

In less than two hours Lathbury's battalions would lose radio contact with one another, and his attacking force of nearly 2,200 lightly armed troops would encounter serious difficulty along a bisecting road called the Dreyenseweg. Only a mixed force of about seven hundred troops, mostly from Frost's 2nd Battalion, would arrive safely in Arnhem late on Sunday evening.

Right: A Horsa arriving "flaps down" with First British Airborne heavy weapons.

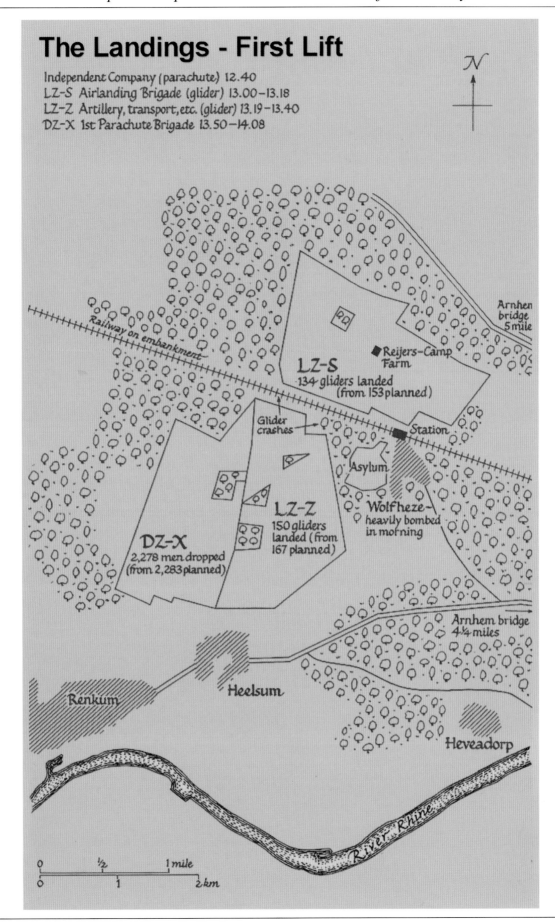

The Landings - First Lift

Independent Company (parachute) 12.40
LZ-S Airlanding Brigade (glider) 13.00–13.18
LZ-Z Artillery, transport, etc. (glider) 13.19–13.40
DZ-X 1st Parachute Brigade 13.50–14.08

Railway on embankment

Arnhem bridge 5 mile

Reijers-Camp Farm

LZ-S
134 gliders landed
(from 153 planned)

Glider crashes

Station

Asylum

LZ-Z
150 gliders
landed (from
167 planned)

Wolfheze –
heavily bombed
in morning

DZ-X
2,278 men dropped
(from 2,283 planned)

Arnhem bridge
4¼ miles

Renkum

Heelsum

Heveadorp

River Rhine

½   1 mile
1   2 km

The First Airlanding Brigade were the first troops to arrive on Landing Zone Z south of Wolfheze.

British troops quickly assembled, and within several hours began the epic march eastwards to Arnhem.

The Divisional Sea-Borne Tail

Some 2,300 troops of the First British Airborne "sea tail" had arrived in Belgium in late August composed of Royal Army Service Corps (RASC), Royal Engineer Mechanical Engineers (REME), and over 1,000 support vehicles. The convoy carried ammunition, rations, and the personal kits. Other second echelon troops of the First Polish Airborne Brigade Group and 52nd (Lowland) Division were moving behind the XXX Corps spearhead along the "Garden" or "Club Route," with the expectation of linking up with the assault troops at Arnhem by D+2.[20] They would never reach the division in time.

The American Airborne Forces Arrive in Holland

As British ground operations began to unhinge west of Arnhem, both American airborne divisions were experiencing greater success in capturing and holding nearly every D-day objective. Almost the entire first lift of 15,000 American troops landed within a mile of planned airheads, seizing scores of under-defended objectives, many less than three miles away. Only a handful of disorganized enemy troops were encountered, and TAC support was readily available to deal with any armor or heavy infantry counterattacks. Despite the initial success, three key objectives would not be captured on schedule: the major city of Eindhoven; the Wilhelmina Canal Bridge at Son; and the main roadway bridge at Nijmegen. Within the next seventy-two hours, the American buildup would experience troop transport delays attributed to increasingly bad weather, confusion concerning tactical assignments near Nijmegan and Groesbeek, a slow-moving XXX Corps relief force, and a resilient enemy capable of imposing critical delays on the entire Market Garden operation.

The Arrival of the American 101st "Screaming Eagles"

As a pair of American Douglas C-47s from Chalgrove carried two serials of 101st Airborne Division pathfinders across the starting point of XXX Corps, German light arms and anti-aircraft fire erupted immediately. One of the planes caught fire and plummeted in flames, while the second transport lumbered forward to Drop Zone A, west of the Dutch town of Veghel. A second serial of transports continued towards a large grassy field located three miles west of Son and St. Oedenrode to mark adjacent Drop Zones B/C and Landing Zone W.[21] The 101st Airborne Division pathfinders arrived at 12:47 p.m. and within minutes set up special radar and "GEE" homing beacons. They also deployed large yellow "A" and "T" identification panels for the incoming air armada. The pathfinders began to set off red smoke as the 53rd Troop Carrier Wing (TCW) appeared over the horizon carrying nearly seven thousand troops of Major General Maxwell Taylor's 101st Division.

Despite heavy ground fire, the American transport formation arrived relatively intact, dropping all three airborne regiments and support battalions with nearly pinpoint accuracy in the following order:

12.47 p.m.	Pathfinders	DZ-A/A1, B, C, LZ-W
1: 01 p.m.	501st Parachute Infantry	DZ-A, A1
1: 12 p.m.	502nd Parachute Infantry	DZ-C
1: 24 p.m.	506th Parachute Infantry	DZ-B
1: 48 p.m.	377th Parachute Artillery	LZ-W
1: 48 p.m.	Division Support	LZ-W

The 501st Parachute Infantry Regiment: Drop Zones A and A-1

It was nearly a perfectly executed arrival. The lead serials of the 434th and 442nd Troop Carrier Groups carried 2,505 troops of Colonel Howard Johnson's 501st Parachute Infantry Regiment (PIR) plus two platoons of the 325th Airborne Engineer Battalion over the wide expanse of Drop Zones A and A1, both situated between the Dutch towns of Veghel and Eerde.

Only the lead serial transporting Lt.-Colonel Harry W.O. Kinnard's 1st Parachute Battalion appeared to miss the drop zone, but the American pilots delivered nearly 90 percent of the paratroopers sufficiently close to capture both the Willems Vaart Canal and the Aa River bridge east of Veghel by 4:00 p.m. The second serial arrived at 1:06 p.m., dropping Major Pelham's 2nd Parachute Battalion onto Drop Zone A east of the town of Eerde. By 3:15 p.m. the 2nd Parachute Battalion had seized the road and railway bridges over the Willems-Vaart Canal. The third transport serial dropped Lt.-Colonel Julian Ewell's 3rd Parachute Battalion onto Drop Zone A at 1:11p.m, and Ewell's unit captured the village of Eerde within two hours.

By nightfall several westerly attacks by lead elements of Kampfgruppe Chill were repulsed, and all three battalions remained closely linked. Lt.-Colonel Howard Johnson's 501st Parachute Infantry Regiment had achieved all its objectives in less than four hours with only ten casualties.[22]

The 506th Parachute Infantry Regiment: Drop Zone B

The three transport serials carrying 2,200 troops of Colonel Robert F. Sink's 506th Parachute Infantry Regiment, along with a platoon of Company C of the 325th Airborne Engineer Battalion and a detachment from the division reconnaissance platoon, arrived at Drop Zone C along the northern edge of the Sonsche Forest. The transports encountered heavy flak and light arms fire, but only one Douglas C-47 was lost. The regiment arrived at 1:12 p.m. without additional casualties, and Sink's battalions quickly assembled at planned rendezvous points.

The 1st Parachute Battalion, commanded by Lt.-Colonel James LaPrade, assembled within 45 minutes. LaPrade's troops then proceeded towards Son along the Willems Canal to seize the main Highway Bridge and two smaller bridges. Lt.-Colonel Robert Strayer's 2nd Parachute Battalion was delayed thirty minutes because of ground assembly confusion and troops running off to assist division headquarters untangle and unload fifty Waco gliders, many of which were damaged, on nearby Landing Zone W. Once order was restored, Strayer's troops set out for Son through the Sonsche Woods

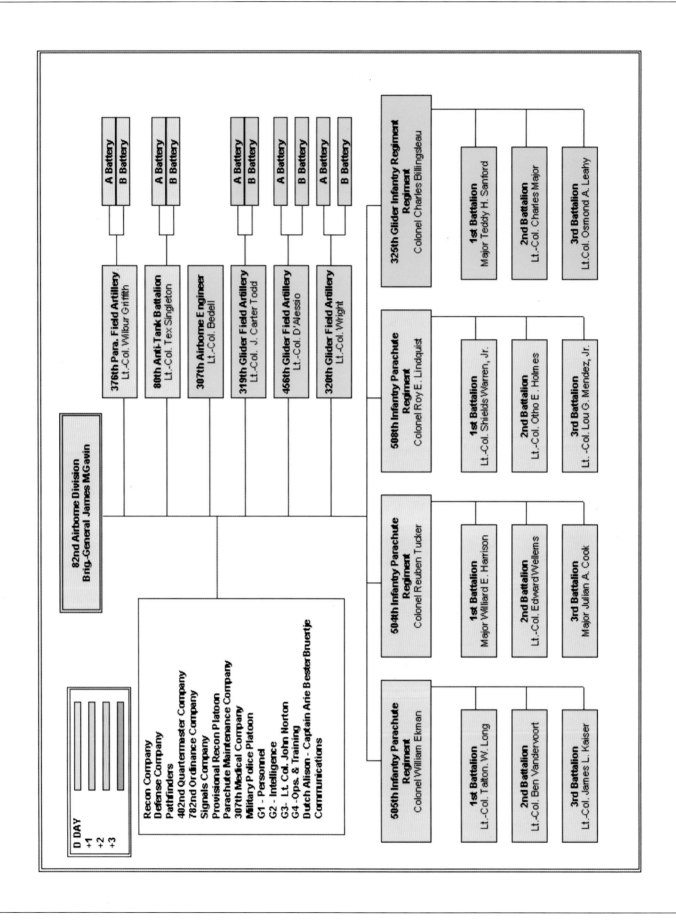

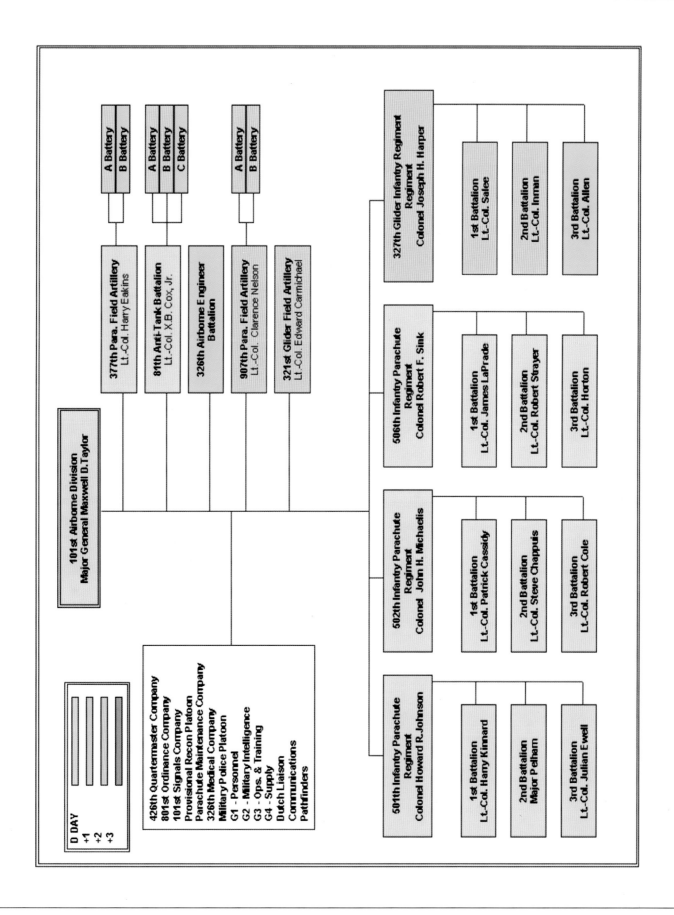

to eventually link up with LaPrade's 1st Battalion. Incoming 88mm artillery bursts and a series of firefights with enemy roadblocks hampered the advance of both battalions. Just as LaPrade's troops reached the main road bridge at Son, enemy troops from Major Jungwirth's Fallschirmjäger Training Battalions destroyed it. A handful of American paratroopers, including LaPrade, jumped into the canal and reached the south side.[23] Airborne engineers accompanying the 1st Parachute Battalion worked frantically to complete a footbridge by 5:30 p.m., and by late evening the entire regiment had crossed the Wilhelmina Canal and established a defensive perimeter one-half mile south of the canal. Lt.-Colonel Strayer, however, decided to halt the advance of his troops and regroup to attack Eindhoven the following morning. According to the original plan, Sink should have entered Eindhoven by 8:00 p.m. on D-Day.[24]

The 502nd Parachute Infantry Regiment: Drop Zone C
At 1:24 p.m. the 435th and 438th TCG began dropping 2,400 troops of Colonel John H. Michaelis' 502nd Parachute Infantry Regiment, the advance headquarters of Major General Maxwell Taylor's 101st Airborne Division, and engineers onto Drop Zone C, located north of the Sonsche Forest. The 502nd PIR was tasked with a number of key objectives: blocking the Son-St. Oedenrode Highway; establishing a vital four-mile link between the 501st and 506th Parachute Infantry Regiments; sending a small detachment to capture the Wilhelmina Canal bridges east of Best; serve as division reserves; and assume control of the Son perimeter after 506th PIR departed for Eindhoven.[25]

The 1st Parachute Battalion, commanded by Lt.-Colonel Patrick Kennedy, advanced north along the main roadway towards St. Oedenrode but did not reach the town until nightfall, when it finally seized the Dommel River Bridge. The 3rd Battalion, commanded by Lt.-Colonel Robert Cole, was less fortunate, and failed to capture a secondary bridge west of the main highway along the Wilhelmina Canal Bridge near Best. The remaining regimental forces, including Lt.-Colonel Steve Chappuis's 2nd Parachute Battalion and regimental headquarters, remained close to the drop zone to await the second lift on D+1.[26]

Cole originally sent a single company from 3rd Battalion to seize the secondary road bridge, but the fighting intensified and drew the entire battalion into the fray. Eventually the entire regiment would fight nearly one thousand enemy troops belonging to Generalleutnant Walter Poppe's 59th Infantry Division over the next two days.[27]

Divisional Support
Unlike the British First Airborne and American 82nd Airborne Divisions, Major General Maxwell Taylor's forces were mostly composed of infantry battalions. Since Horrocks' forces were expected to relieve the 101st Airborne Division within twenty-four hours, the need for organic medium artillery support was minimized.

The Arrival of the "All American" 82nd Airborne Division
American C-47s from Chalgrove carried two serials of pathfinders towards Drop Zones N/T/O and Landing Zone N/T northeast of

Grave. Enemy flak intensified, but escorting waves of P-47 Thunderbolts from the 78th Fighter Group swooped down and silenced the batteries within minutes.[28] The first serial of pathfinders landed within 500 yards of Drop Zone O at 12:30 p.m., setting up radar and Eureka homing beacons and deploying a large yellow "O" identification panel within twenty minutes.[29] Drop Zone N remained unmarked, since navigational references were considered excellent and marker smoke was deemed sufficient. Minutes later nearly five hundred planes of the 50th and 52nd Troop Carrier Wing began dropping 7,300 troops of the 82nd Airborne Division onto a series of drop and landing zones within a twenty five-mile division perimeter.[30] The 82nd Airborne Division arrived in the following order:

12.50 p.m.	Pathfinders	
1.08 p.m.	505th Parachute Infantry	DZ-N
1.15 p.m.	504th Parachute Infantry	DZ-O
1:21 p.m.	307th Engineer Battalion	DZ-N
1:26 p.m.	508th Parachute Infantry	DZ-T
1:41 p.m.	376th Parachute Artillery	DZ-N
1:41 p.m.	80th Antiaircraft Battalion	DZ-N
1:47 p.m.	Division/Support	DZ-N
2.00 p.m.	British I Airborne Corps	DZ-N

Brigadier General Gavin was expected to capture over a dozen objectives spread over a division perimeter of twenty-five square miles.

The 505th Parachute Infantry Regiment: Drop Zone N
The first drops were completed by the 313th and 316th Tactical Carrier Groups, carrying 2,300 troops of Colonel William Ekman's 505th Parachute Infantry Regiment and 376th Parachute Artillery Battalion to Drop Zone N, one mile southeast of the town of Groesbeek. In addition to securing, clearing, and marking the drop zone for subsequent glider and supply lifts, Brigadier General Gavin assigned Ekman the mission of securing the town of Groesbeek and the base of the Groesbeek heights southwards near the town of Mook. Unfortunately, marshalling errors and confusion near the unmarked Drop Zone N resulted in misplacing troops of the 2nd Parachute Infantry Battalion and regimental headquarters over a three-mile area. The remaining troops of the 3rd and 1st Parachute Battalions and General Gavin's Division Headquarters landed relatively intact and within proximity to their objectives. The misplaced 2nd Battalion, commanded by Lt.-Colonel Ben Vandervoort, quickly reassembled and occupied the western perimeter of the regiment located on the high ground near Groesbeek. Two companies of the 3rd Battalion, commanded by Lt-Colonel James Kaiser, captured the town of Groesbeek, while a third company dug in near the Reichswald. The 1st Parachute Battalion, commanded by Lt.-Colonel Talton Long, occupied the southern end of the Groesbeek ridge near the towns of Mook and Riethorst.

Within six hours the 505th Parachute Infantry Regiment had captured all objectives, forming a scythe-like perimeter spanning the town of Riethorst in the south to Heikant in the east. Surprise was achieved, and casualties among Colonel Ekman's 505th Parachute Infantry were minimal.[31]

The 504th Parachute Infantry Regiment: Drop Zone O

The 315th and 316th Tactical Carrier Group carried 2,000 troops of Colonel Reuben Tucker's 504th Parachute Infantry Regiment and Company C of the 307th Airborne Engineers Battalion over the triangularly shaped Drop Zone O at 1:15 p.m.[32] The 1st Parachute Battalion, commanded by Major Willard Harrison, assembled within fifty minutes and set out for the three canal bridges over the Mass-Waal Canal. Company E of Lt.-Colonel Edward Wellems' 2nd Battalion landed on the south side of the 640-foot Maas River bridge, while Company D/2nd Battalion attacked from the north side. After a brief but violent exchange with enemy infantry and several flak towers, Tucker's troops captured the key span and eventually the town of Grave. The town was considered a critical link, where the spearheading British Guards Armor was expected to cross within the next twenty-four hours.

The balance of Tucker's troops attacked northeastward towards three crossings over the Mass-Waal Canal. The south crossing at Molenhoek was number 7, the next bridge near Malden was number 8, and the largest was the Hatert bridge, number 9. Both the Hatert and Malden crossings were immediately destroyed, but the assault companies captured the third bridge (number 7) near the town of Molenhoek. The bridge would serve as the only crossing capable of supporting XXX Corps armor and heavy equipment in the ensuing days.[33]

The 3rd Parachute Infantry Battalion, commanded by Major Julian Cook, set up a defensive perimeter north of Grave and would remain in regimental reserve near the landing perimeter. Colonel Ruben Tucker's 504th Infantry Regiment had succeeded in capturing all objectives and linking up with the 505th Parachute Infantry Regiment, located east of the Maas Waal Canal, within eight hours.[34]

The 508th Parachute Infantry Regiment: Drop Zone T

The 1,900 troops of Colonel Roy Lindquist's 508th Parachute Infantry Regiment were expected to secure Drop Zone T for the D +1 arrival of the 325th Glider Infantry Regiment, secure three and half miles of the Groesbeek Ridge, assist the 504th Parachute Infantry Regiment in capturing two bridges across the Maas-Waal Canal, and finally capture the Nijmegen Bridge.[35] The 440th and 441st Tactical Carrier Group encountered heavy anti-aircraft fire near Nijmegen, eventually losing eight C-47s, but nearly 1,900 troops and pathfinders of the 325th Glider Infantry Regiment arrived at Drop Zone T at 1:26 p.m. The troops immediately overwhelmed several German 88mm anti-aircraft gun batteries near the town of Wyler, captured the northern ridge of the Groesbeek between the hamlets of De Ploeg and Bergen Dal, and prepared the landing zone for the next day's arrivals.

Lindquist's troops made an attempt to capture the rail bridge and largest of the road bridges at Honinghutie (number 10), but the

British officers paused near a white hotel called the Hartenstein.

enemy eventually organized an effective defense and destroyed both bridges. This represented a serious setback, since the road span served as a direct route between Grave and Nijmegen. Lindquist's 508[36] PIR had the most difficult assignment, which included securing DZT until the arrival of the 325th Glider Infantry, occupying part of the Groesbeek Heights, and assisting Tucker's 504th PIR east of the Waal Canal in capturing the main 1,960 foot highway bridge over the Waal.[36] The 1st Parachute Battalion finally set off from the hamlet of De Ploeg late in the evening with three companies to seize the Nijmegen bridge, but one of the companies became lost. The remaining two companies continued along the wide boulevards of Nijmegen until reaching a circular park called the Keizer Karel Plein. The Americans suddenly encountered withering heavy fire from the leading battle group of the 10th SS Panzer Division and were stopped within 400 yards of the bridge. Despite this initial setback the 1st Parachute Battalion, with the help of several brave Dutch citizens, managed to seize and destroy the building containing the demolition controls for the bridge.[37]

Divisional Support

On D-Day seventy American Waco gliders towed by the 437th Group suffered nearly 25% losses in gliders and troops. Only fifty-three Wacos reached their objectives due to various mechanical failures and German flak. The Wacos began arriving at 1:48 p.m., carrying the Divisional Signals Company, Reconnaissance Platoon, Medical Company, headquarters personnel, British liaison personnel, and a "Phantom Radio" Detachment. Many gliders crashed-landed, requiring assistance that delayed the departure of one of the 501st Parachute Infantry Regiment's key assault battalions. Another group of 80 C-47s finally arrived carrying headquarters artillery staff, the 307th Engineer Battalion, the 376th Parachute Field Artillery Battalion (with twelve PAK 75mm guns), the 80th Airborne Anti-tank Battalion (with eight 57mm guns), additional staff personnel, and an air support party.[38]

First Allied Airborne Corps Headquarters Arrives in Nijmegen

The final serial of twenty-nine Horsa gliders, towed by British 38 Group aircraft, arrived with Lt.-General Browning and a substantial First Airborne Corps Headquarters staff. Despite his presence Browning would exert little influence over the battle, since the 101st Airborne Division immediately came under the command of XXX Corps and the British First Airborne Division was virtually isolated in Arnhem. Browning's extensive signals staff would prove of little value, and considerable criticism surfaced after the battle for committing such a large number of gliders to transport staff and even part of a wine collection while the 2nd South Staffordshire Battalion arrived at half-strength near Arnhem on D-Day due to lack of available transport.

Opposite: Initiative was lost as the British stopped to regroup after arriving only six hours earlier.

Fog of War, Malfunctioning Wireless, and Missing Division Commander

The British First Parachute Division Loses Momentum

Later in the afternoon of September 17, a major mix-up occurred among Major General Urquhart's troops when only a handful of the specially equipped jeeps with twin Vicker's machine guns from Major Freddie Gough's C Troop were available for the planned Arnhem *coup de main*. Many of the jeeps had either failed to arrive, were shot up, or were simply mixed up with other British units. The 1st Parachute Battalion had set off earlier than expected after Brigadier Lathbury was informed that Gough's vehicles had not departed for the bridge. The 1st Parachute Battalion was the intended brigade reserve, but Lathbury elected to commit all three battalions with the hope that one battalion, at minimum, could reach the Arnhem road span before nightfall. The road span was less than a half-hour drive away, and enemy resistance was not anticipated alongside the railway running parallel to Dobie's 1st Parachute Battalion axis of advance. Minutes later, several of the leading reconnaissance vehicles attempting to make a dash for the bridge were met by a hail of sniper, flame-thrower, heavy machine gun, and mortar fire from ad hoc formations of German troops and armored vehicles. While Gough's reconnaissance vehicles and Dobie's battalion encountered severe difficulties, both the 2nd and 3rd Parachute Battalions continued almost unobtrusively along the tree-lined center and lower roads towards their respective objectives.[39]

As Lathbury's troops moved eastwards through the streets of Arnhem, Major General Urquhart also received word of the reconnaissance squadron setback. Urquhart immediately became frustrated with his inability to reach Gough to reorganize another attempt at a *coup-de-main*. Being a relatively inexperienced division-level commander in battle, Urquhart decided to take his jeep to the sharp end of the action.[40]

Urquhart would become lost and isolated somewhere within the labyrinth of the Arnhem city streets only several hours following his arrival in Holland. Urquhart's absence would contribute to the fatal confusion among his brigade and battalion commanders throughout the first crucial forty-eight hours.

3rd Parachute Battalion is Halted

Following their arrival near Heelsum, Lt.-Colonel John Fitch's 3rd Parachute Battalion marched almost unopposed along the "main" road, or Utrechtsestraatweg, for nearly two hours. The troops advanced in parallel sections along the road, observing how peaceful and architecturally attractive the Dutch residences and streets appeared; even the road signs clearly pointed to the bridge. The Dutch suburbs reminded many of them of England. Many Dutch citizens waved small tricolor flags of the Netherlands and shared there limited inventories of dairy products and wartime preserves with their liberators. As the lead sections moved forward, sporadic sniper fire increased and infantry casualties began to mount. Suddenly, a camouflaged Citroen appeared between the lead scouts and the main assault company. Bren and Lee Enfield fire erupted immediately, bringing the careening vehicle to a bullet-riddled halt. Moments later several troops opened both bullet riddled doors to discover the

Lt.-Colonel John Frost's 2nd Parachute Battalion immediately set out along the lower road code named "Lion" and reached Arnhem by early evening.

now ex-commandant of Arnhem, Major General Fredric Kussin. Minutes earlier, subordinates had warned Kussin to avoid travel along the main road to Arnhem.[41]

Fitch's battalion advanced another several hundred yards, only to be halted by a mixed battalion of self-propelled guns and infantry. The fighting intensified near the Doorwertsche Woods, and the companies became separated after a series of brief but violent engagements. The advance of Fitch's battalion eventually slowed to a snail's pace, possibly compounded by the presence of both Major General Urquhart and Brigadier Lathbury among its ranks. Finally by 8:30 p.m., darkness had reduced visibility along the tree-lined streets and Lt-Colonel Fitch decided to establish a defensive perimeter near a white stucco building called the Hartenstein. Lathbury ended the attack for the evening with the knowledge that Frost's reinforced 2nd Battalion had reached the Arnhem Bridge. Lathbury was also aware that the lower road taken by the 2nd Battalion lay virtually unopposed a half-mile south of the newly formed Hartenstein perimeter.[42]

1st Parachute Battalion is Halted

Lt.-Colonel Dobie planned to follow the "Leopard" route taken by Gough's reconnaissance vehicles, which ran from a railroad path near Wolfheze Station past Johannahoeve Farm and onto the main Ede-Arnhem Road, or Amsterdamseweg. The battalion quickly fell behind schedule awaiting the status of Gough's jeeps, then lost critical time following flanking attacks by hastily formed German defenses, including armored elements of the 9th SS Panzer Division.

The 1st Battalion, which began with three full Companies R, S, and T, plus Headquarters, consumed considerable time while attempting to bypass increasing enemy opposition along the Amsterdamseweg. Dobie's companies later became separated and sustained heavy losses in the surrounding dense woods. By late evening, the exhausted ranks moved southeastwards in the direction of the 3rd Battalion, now resting near the Hartenstein. The 1st Battalion had advanced only three miles, suffered nearly 100 casualties, and had countless troops missing in the surrounding woods. Even though Dobie received a clear transmission from Frost requesting reinforcements, his troops were unable to move eastwards until next light.[43]

2nd Parachute Battalion Reaches the Arnhem Bridge

Lt.-Colonel Frost's 2nd Battalion proceeded along the most southern of the three easterly routes, through the town of Heelsum along a narrow brick road shrouded by thick trees and overgrowth. The 2nd Battalion numbered less than 500 troops but was further augmented by half of B Troop of the 1st Parachute Squadron, part of the 9th Field Company (Royal Engineers), five six-pounders, headquarters of the 1st Parachute Brigade, the 1st Parachute Squadron and battery, and battalion support staff. Frost's battalion passed the Heveadorp ferry and continued east, leaving it undefended. By 6:00 p.m., the 2nd Battalion reached the built-up area of Oosterbeek, where they were joyously greeted by throngs of Dutch citizens. After wading through the crowds, Frost instructed C Company to split from the battalion and seize the railway span.

Company C, commanded by Major Dover, split off from the battalion and attempted to capture the railway bridge, while Company A, commanded by Major Tatham-Water, assumed the lead for the battalion. As Company C approached the rail bridge, enemy machine fire erupted from the southern end. Within minutes a huge explosion lifted the main span, which then settled into the bottom of the Neder Rhine. The troops were halted by elements of Battalion Krafft, and any attempt to surprise enemy defenders near the southern ramp of the Arnhem Bridge abruptly ended.

Company A continued eastward along Koninginne Laan until heavy German fire erupted near a small rise called Den Brink, located to the left of a railroad underpass. Company B, commanded by Major Doug Crawley, remained near Den Brink to deal with the German defenders, while the rest of the column continued east with Company A in the lead. Further ahead Dutch civilians continued greeting the column, saying that the Germans had fled, but sniping continued until nightfall.

As dusk settled, Tathan-Warter's troops cautiously walked along the Weerdjestraat through the wide Eusebiusplein, sighting the huge silhouette of the Arnhem Bridge. It appeared intact, but German vehicles were moving south across the span.

Lt.-Colonel Frost immediately instructed his commanders to capture a number of buildings located on both sides of the northern ramp. Frost established a command post on the corner of Oranjewachstraat, then ordered a patrol onto the bridge to seize the southern approaches. The small force was immediately halted by a hail of machine gun fire from a pillbox situated on the span. Heavy enemy fire emanating from the southern approaches contributed to the confusion. Frost reacted quickly, ordering Company B downstream to search for a barge or pontoon bridge in order to outflank German defenses at the southern approaches. Nothing was found, and the troops returned to the battalion defensive perimeter.[44] However, it was 8:00 p.m. and the 2nd Battalion now controlled the northern ramp of the Arnhem Bridge.

Throughout the first night Frost's force of over six hundred fifty British paratroopers would prepare themselves for the defense of the Arnhem Bridge until the expected arrival of XXX Corps in forty-eight hours.[45] Little did anyone realize that the small force would bear the brunt of the 9th SS Panzer Division now slowly amassing in the east.

First Airlanding and Division Troops Dig In

Only five hours had passed since landing in Holland, but by 8:00 p.m. both the 1st and 3rd Parachute Battalions were stopped halfway short of their objectives, while the 2nd Parachute Battalion had reached the northern Arnhem ramp. Less than one-third of the 2,200 troops of the 1st Parachute Brigade reached preplanned objectives. The remaining 3,000 troops in the west would eventually withdraw into the Hartenstein pocket.

The 1st Borders deployed headquarters plus A, C, and D Companies around Landing Zone X and Drop Zone Z, with B Company a mile and a half south near a brick factory in the town of Renkum.

German armored vehicles could be heard approaching the perimeter.

British troops dug in near the tennis courts behind the Hartenstein where captured German troops were held prisoner.

The 7th KOSBs positioned headquarters and B, C, and D Companies around the perimeter of Drop Zone Y near Ginke-Heide to await the second lift of the 4th Parachute Brigade. The final unit, A Company, was positioned further east along the Ede-Arnhem road near the Planken Wambuis.[46] The two companies of 2nd Battalion South Staffords remained in brigade reserve near Wolfheze. Enemy action against the landing sites was minimal throughout the first night, except for the KOSBs mauling a company of Dutch Volunteers from the 9SS Wach Battalion.[47]

**German Forces: Model, II Panzer SS Corps,
and Division von Tettau**

On Monday morning, 18 September, both the 1st and 3rd British Parachute Battalions would attempt a second attack by shifting southeastwards towards the lower road previously taken by the 2nd Battalion. As the two battalions made surprisingly good progress, no one realized that Army Group B Commander Walther Model and II SS Panzer Corp Commander Willi Bittrich were preparing a large-scale counterattack.[48] The cohesive effect of having an Army Group General and Corps Commander so close to the landing areas would facilitate quick reaction and the subsequent repulse of two British brigades.

Quick Reaction of II SS Panzer Corps

The II SS Panzer Corps was commanded by Obergruppenführer und General der Waffen SS Willi Bittrich. The formation had two major units: Kampfgruppe 9th SS Hohenstaufen commanded by Obersturmbannführer Walther Harzer and Kampfgruppe 10th Frundsberg commanded by Standartenführer Heinz Harmel. Both Harzer and Harmel had unknowingly positioned their forces close to Arnhem, while General Bittrich's headquarters was located just fifteen miles to the east in Doetinchem.

Hohenstaufen had been reduced to a weak brigade of 2,500 troops and segmented into nineteen assault companies, but was within thirty minutes of the city by motor vehicle.[49] The brigade-size formation possessed a paltry mix of Captain Viktor Graebner's 9th SS Reconnaissance force of thirty armored vehicles, some self-propelled 20mm half-tracks, and quantities of artillery, but lacked tanks or heavy weapons.[50] Frundsberg was also reduced to brigade size but produced a number of Mark IV, Panther, and Tiger tanks throughout the battle.[51] Model ordered Harzer's 9th SS Hohenstaufen to eliminate the British Airborne at the Arnhem Bridge, then isolate and destroy the remaining pockets of British airborne troops in Oosterbeek.

Elements of the 9th SS Hohenstaufen had previously halted the 1st and 3rd British Parachute Battalions and established strong blocking positions west and east of Arnhem Bridge.[52] The 10th SS Frundsberg was ordered to cross the Lower Rhine and prevent the American 82nd Airborne Division from seizing the key crossings at Nijmegen. Another division was formed from ad-hoc battalions, including a mixture of Naval, Dutch SS, NCO School, and rear echelon troops. The force was commanded by Wermacht General Hans von Tettau and ordered to attack British landings from the east and northeast. Compounding the impending difficulties of the British assault, the Germans facilitated inter-battalion communications through extensive use of the Dutch telephone network.

Dark Foreboding

Within forty-eight hours of arrival, the First Airborne Division would stretch ten miles across the Lower Rhine in three precariously linked forces: the northern ramp of the Arnhem Bridge; the Hartenstein perimeter in the center; and a cluster of thinly defended airdrop and airlanding fields located near Wolfheze and Ginkel-Heide. Casualties remained acceptably low, but the Division Commander Urquhart was missing somewhere forward, inter-battalion communications were almost non-existent, and the element of surprise was certainly lost.

The Americans at Eindhoven and Grave had successfully landed near their objectives in great numbers, and encountered only mod-

Everyone suddenly looked in the direction of the distant sounds of the heavy 15cm Nebelwerfer launchers. Even a well-protected slit trench could not withstand a near miss.

erate opposition throughout the first forty-eight hours. However, the American 506th PIR delayed capturing Eindhoven, while the key Wilhelmina Canal Bridge lay destroyed at Son. Both Lt.-General Browning and Brigadier General Gavin withheld major attacks against the Waal River Bridge at Nijmegen until the arrival of the delayed second lift, and XXX Corps struggled to reach Grave. Enemy flanking pressure along the corridor increased as nearly 4,000 troops from the German 59th Infantry Division and several Fallschirmjäger battalions attacked the western perimeter of the 101st Airborne Division between Eindhoven and Grave. The powerful 107th Panzer Brigade, commanded by Major Freiherr von Maltzahn, was fast approaching Son from the east and included a formidable battalion of Panther Mark V tanks. Nearly 6,000 enemy troops, albeit of marginal fighting quality, and scores of armored vehicles under the command of Corps Feldt and 406th Landesschützen Division, amassed along the eastern Groesbeek perimeter of Gavin's 82nd Airborne Division. The enemy bridgehead at Nijmegen expanded as elements of the 10th SS Panzer Division arrived, including heavy guns and Panzerjäger Mark IV assault tanks.

Time appeared to favor the defenders, whose reserves were now arriving at a faster rate than the Allies.

Notes
[1] Edwin R. Murrow, Columbia Broadcasting System, 1944. (tape and transcript)
[2] Lt.-General Lewis Hyde Brereton, *The Brereton Diaries: The War in the Pacific, Middle East, and Europe 3 October 1941-8 May 1945* (New York: DaCapo Press, 1976), pp.342-345. First published by William Morrow and Sons in 1946.
[3] Robert Jackson, *Arnhem: The Battle Remembered* (Shrewsbury: Airlife Publishing, 1994), p.46.
[4] Ibid., p.47.
[5] Brereton, op.cit., p.345.
[6] Martin Middlebrook, *Arnhem 1944* (San Francisco: Westview Press, 1994), p.75.
[7] Barry Gregory, *British Airborne Troops* (London: MacDonald and Jane's, 1974), p.116.
[8] Middlebrook, op.cit., pp.458-459.
[9] Ibid., p.456.
[10] Brereton, op.cit., p.345.
[11] Many authors have incorrectly indicated that the Arnhem bridge *coup de main* was delayed by the failed arrival of a large number of Major C.F.H. Freddie Gough's special Recce jeeps with twin Vickers. Most Recce jeeps did in fact arrive but for some reason failed to assemble in time resulting in the decision to send 2nd Battalion and 1st Parachute Brigade Headquarters ahead to seize the Arnhem Bridge.
[12] Gliders had "Rebecca" receivers to home in on the "Eureka transmissions."
[13] Barry Gregory, op.cit., p.118.
[14] Middlebrook, op.cit., p.460. Four American Wacos were assigned to the First Airborne drop carrying two five man teams of American from the 306th Fighter control Squadron ground to air communications equipment. All of the equipment was destroyed shortly.
[15] Middlebrook, op.cit., p.99. *Unlike their American counterparts, the glider pilots were fighting infantrymen attached to the Glider Pilot Regiment.*
[16] Middlebrook, op.cit., p.105.
[17] *The South Staffs were undermanned since thirty-two of their Horsa infantry gliders were assigned the task of transporting Lt.-General Browning's Airborne Corp staff, including a selection of his wine collection to Nijmegen.*
[18] Ibid., p.111.
[19] *By Air to Battle: The Official Account of the British Airborne Divisions* (London: HMSO, 1945), p.102.
[20] Martin Middlebrook, op.cit., pp.60-61.
[21] James A. Huston, *Out of the Blue: U.S. Army Airborne Operations in World War II* (Nashville: The Battery Press, 1972), p.28.
[22] Robert Jackson, op.cit., pp. 50-51.
[23] Mark Bando, *The 101st Airborne,: From Holland to Hitler's Eagles Nest* (Osceola: Motorbook, 1995), p.24.
[24] Ibid., p.53.
[25] Huston, op.cit., p.21.
[26] Ibid., p.53.
[27] Cornelius Ryan, *A Bridge Too Far* (New York :Simon and Shuster, 1974), p.252.
[28] Ibid., pp.50-51
[29] Ibid., pp.50-51
[30] Ibid., p.53.
[31] Ibid., pp.54.
[32] Huston, op.cit., p.21.
[33] Gavin, op.cit., p.157.
[34] Jackson, op.cit., p.55.
[35] Huston, op.cit., p.21.
[36] Ryan, op.cit., p.474.
[37] Devlin, op.cit., p.476.
[38] Huston, op.cit., p.22.
[39] Middlebrook, op.cit. p. 127. *Landed 2:10 p.m. departed from Drop Zone –X at 3:00 p.m.*
[40] *Gough's squadron was attached to the First Parachute Brigade communications net, therefore he could not be reached over the Division wireless.*
[41] Cornelius Bauer, *The Battle of Arnhem* (New York: Hodder and Stoughton, 1966), p.106.
[42] Middlebrook, op.cit., p.137.
[43] Ibid., p.142.
[44] By Air to Battle, op.cit., p.102.
[45] *C Company 3rd Battalion would arrive late Sunday night.*
[46] Middlebrook, op.cit. p.163. *Lt.- Colonel Haddon would never reach his battalion following two failed attempts to reach his troops at Arnhem.*
[47] Bauer, op.cit., p.112.
[48] *Model had unknowingly located his headquarters near the landings at the Tafelberg Hotel in Oosterbeek.*
[49] Robert J. Kershaw, *It Never Snows in September* (Ramsbury: Crowood Press, 1990), p.41
[50] Ibid., p.327.
[51] Ibid.,p.332.
[52] Middlebrook, op.cit., pp.118-119. *Division Artillery Commander (Obersturmbannführer) Spindler and SS Panzer Grenadier Depot and Reserve Battalion Commander (Sturmbannfuhrer) Josef Kraft.*

6

Garden:
"Hell's Highway"

"Brian Horrocks was the best war time commander I ever came across. He was a great leader and I found him much more impressive than Monty. When giving orders, he was very clear, and he was always right up with one and helping one along. He was full of grip and insisted on pushing us along as much as possible.

He had been shot in the stomach by a low flying German fighter near Bizerat and on occasions was clearly still in pain for periods which lasted for anything up to a week. On several occasions when he was under great strain his mind seemed to be wandering, due to the drugs he was receiving."

-Major General Sir Allan Adair, Commander Guards Armored Division[1]

XXX Corps Spearhead and Airborne Link-Up[a]

Garden D-Day

On September 17 at 1:00 p.m., Lt.-General Brian Horrocks received confirmation that the airborne landings were successfully taking place in Holland. Shortly thereafter, Horrocks ordered nearly four hundred medium and heavy guns of the British Royal Artillery to commence firing a series of rolling barrages onto suspected enemy defenses alongside the narrow roadway leading to Eindhoven:

"There was a sudden deafening roar and a noise as though an express train was passing overhead. Our guns had opened their counter-artillery programme and the battle of Arnhem was on..."[2]

After nearly a half-hour of devastating bombardment extending five miles deep and one mile wide, the Guards Armor Division, which included the 5th Guards Brigade and the 32nd Guards Brigade, began pushing at maximum speed towards Valkenswaard and Eindhoven. The breakout from the Neerpelt Bridgehead was again spearheaded by the Irish Guards Group, which included the 2nd Armored Battalion Irish Guards, commanded by Lt.-Colonel G.A.M. Vandeleur, and the 3rd Battalion Irish Guards Infantry, commanded by his cousin, Lt.-Colonel J.O.E. Vandeleur.[3]

Several hundred Typhoon fighter-bombers of the RAF 83rd TAC Group flew in "cab ranks" above the slow procession of 20,000 vehicles, awaiting radio instructions or purple marking smoke fired by Guards tanks onto suspected enemy positions that survived the initial artillery bombardment. As the Guards advanced in single file, the 231st Infantry Brigade of the 50th Northrumbian Division spread out for several hundred yards to either side to protect its flanks.[4]

Falling Immediately Behind Schedule

Tank squadrons of the Irish Guards Group slowly trundled along the two-lane road leading to Valkenswaard at eight miles an hour, many laden with Irish Guards infantry. A number of armored vehicles also appeared to have their rear hulls marked with yellow air recognition streamers. The lead Shermans and Fireflies[b] proceeded for several hundred yards as the high explosive shells of the 64th Medium Artillery barrage crept a mere hundred yards ahead of the column.

As the first troop of armor disappeared into the smoke and haze, a sudden series of loud bangs rang out, and three tanks of the lead squadron burst into flames. Six more in the second squadron were hit and began burning within minutes. High velocity armor-piercing shells screamed from the nearby pine forests, punching holes in the hulls and turrets of the thin-skinned British "Tommy Cookers."[c] Thick oily smoke poured from commander copulas and forward hatches of the now immobilized armor.[5] Other vehicles and infantry caught along the road and between the stricken armor immediately fell prey to the staccato bursts of heavy machine gun fire. The half-mile phalanx of burning armor indicated that a significant number of enemy anti-tank gunners and infantry with panzerfausts under the command of Kampfgruppe Walther survived

---

[a] Because of the complexity of the operation, the focus of this chapter is directed towards the efforts of XXX Corps and the ensuing link up with the American 82nd and 101st Airborne Divisions. The Battle for Arnhem by the British First Airborne will be treated separately in Chapters VII – IX.
[b] Sherman tanks fitted with long barreled high velocity 17-pound guns equal to the American 76mm.
[c] German term describing the inherent flammability of the gasoline powered Sherman tanks.

"Hell's Highway."

XXX Corps "Garden" Order of Battle

21st ARMY GROUP

Commander: Field Marshal Sir Bernard L. Montgomery
Chief of Staff: Major General Freddy de Guingand

Second British Army : Lt.-General Sir Miles Dempsey

XXX Corps: Lt.-General Brian G. Horrocks

Guards Armor Division - Major General A.H.S. Adair

2nd Household Cavalry Regiment

5th Guard Brigade - Brigadier N.W. Gwatkin
Irish Guards Group - Lt.-Colonel J.O.E. Vandeleur
2nd Battalion - Lt.-Colonel Giles Vandeleur
Grenadier Guards - 2 Battalions(Armor/Infantry)
Coldstream Guards - 2 Battalions(Armor/Infantry)

32nd Guards Brigade - Brigadier G.F. Johnson
Coldstream Guards - 2 Battalions(Armor/Infantry)
Welsh Guards - 2 Battalions(Armor/Infantry)

43rd Wessex Division - Major General G. Ivor Thomas

129th Brigade - Brigadier G.H.L. Mole
4th Somerset Light Infantry - Lt.-Colonel C.G. Lipscomb
5th Wiltshire - Lt.-Colonel W.G. Roberts
4th Wiltshire - Lt.-Colonel E.L. Luce

130th Brigade - Brigadier B.B. Walton
7th Hampshire - Lt.-Colonel D.E.B. Talbot
4th Dorsets - Lt.-Colonel G. Tilley
5th Dorsets - Lt.-Colonel B.A. Coad

214th Brigade - Brigadier H. Essame
7th Somerset Light Infantry - Lt.-Colonel H.A. Borradaile
1st Worcestershire - Lt.-Colonel R.E. Osborne-Smith
5th Duke of Cornwall's Light Infantry - Lt.-Colonel G. Taylor

Royal Netherlands Brigade "Prinses Irene" - Colonel A.de Ruyter van Steveninck

Reserves:

50th Northumbrian (temporary) - Major General D.A.H. Graham

69th Infantry Brigade - Brigadier F.Y.C. Cox
151st Infantry Brigade - Brigadier D.S. Gordon
231st Infantry Brigade - Brigadier A.G.B. Stanier Bart

52nd Lowland (Air Transportable) Northumbrian - Major General E. Hakewill-Smith

155th Infantry Brigade - Brigadier J.F.S. MacLaren
156th Infantry Brigade - Brigadier C.N. Barclay
157th Infantry Brigade - Brigadier A.J.D. Russel

1st British Airborne (Seaborne Tail) - Lt. Colonel G.A. Mobbs

8th Armored Brigade - Brigadier E.G. Prior-Palmer

British Typhoons flying treetop level over the leading vehicles of the Guards Armor.

At precisely 2:15 PM, some 350 guns opened fire with a thunderous roar.

the rolling barrage. Amid the smoke and confusion, there appeared to be few survivors among the lead tank crews. The battle for the road intensified as swarms of British assault vehicles and tanks poured high explosives, purple smoke shells, and machine gun fire into suspected enemy positions only several hundred yards ahead.[6]

Despite the loss of nine tanks, a series of well-coordinated air strikes by the 83rd TAC Typhoons restored the initiative. The deadly Hawker Typhoons suddenly appeared at treetop level firing heavy bursts of rocket and machine guns at enemy defensive positions, while Sherman tank dozers cleared heavily damaged and burning vehicles. Further down the column the 32nd Guards Brigade, which included the Coldstream and Welsh Guards Battle Groups, gathered scores of surrendering enemy troops and escorted them towards the rear. In several instances, captured enemy troops managed to hurl hand grenades into the vehicles of their captors, resulting in additional battle chaos and casualties. The Guards Division commander, Major General Allan Adair, was quite surprised to discover among these hardened captives elements of the 9th SS and 10th SS Panzer Division, 6th Fallschirmjäger Regiment, and troops of General Von Zangen's "trapped" Fifteenth Army.[7]

The Untimely Pause at Valkenswaard
The Guards advanced cautiously as concealed enemy PAK 75mm and deadly 88mm guns fired down the narrow two-lane road. Instead of "thrusting ahead" thirteen miles towards Eindhoven in three to four hours as planned, the Guards only reached Valkenswaard, seven miles north of the staging point at Neerpelt-Bridge, before retiring for the night. The critical ground phase fell behind schedule, yet Major General Adair "stuck strictly" to orders, halting the division at 7:30 p.m. even as the American 506th Parachute Infantry Regiment awaited armor relief a few miles away on the northern outskirts of Eindhoven.[8] Several hours earlier the American 101st Airborne Division had secured key objectives along the main road at Heeswijk, Veghel, and St. Oedenrode, but these initial successes were overshadowed by the destruction of the Son Bridge. A detachment of American troops was annihilated while attempting to secure an alternate route across the Wilhelmina Canal near the town of Best.

Lt.-General Horrocks approved Major General Adair's requests to rest and refit six miles short of Eindhoven, despite having knowledge of the destroyed canal bridge and the need to forward heavy bridge-laying equipment. Meanwhile, the German 59th Infantry Division and powerful 107th Panzer Brigade were quickly amassing along both sides of the Son-Veghel road, awaiting orders from General Kurt Student to counter attack Allied forces.

Along the lower left flank of Horrocks' XXX Corps, Lt.-General Ritchie's British XII Corps attacked Kampfgruppe Chill with the 15th Scottish and 53rd Welsh Infantry Divisions. Poor terrain, tough enemy resistance, and lack of air support resulted in little forward progress and the right flank fell behind. On the right flank, British VIII Corps, commanded by Lt.-General O'Conner, also advanced slowly towards Helmond on a single division front led by the 50th Northrumbian Division. [9]

September 18 (D+2): Liberation of Eindhoven
During the early morning hours a squadron of Daimler armored cars from Lt-Colonel H. Abel Smith's 2nd Household Cavalry reconnoitered ahead of the lead Grenadier Guards tank squadrons from Valkenswaard towards the eastern outskirts of Eindhoven. Lt.-General Horrocks had ordered the 5th Guards Brigade to continue north along the main road towards Son while the 32nd Guards Brigade pursued an alternate road across the Willems Canal eastwards toward Helmond. The 231st Infantry Brigade of the 50th Northumbrian Division remained in Valkenswaard while the Grenadier Guards Group proceeded along the main road. The Grenadiers included the 2nd Armored Battalion, commanded by Lt.-Colonel J.N.R. Moore, and the 1st Motor Battalion, commanded by Lt.-Colonel E.H.Goulburn.

Colonel Robert F. Sink's 506th PIR protecting the flanks of the advancing Guards Armor passing over the Wilhelmina Canal at Zon.

The Allied generals found it hard to understand why the Germans destroyed the smaller bridges instead of the Nijmegen road bridge.

Royal Engineers labored throughout the night until the Type 40 Bailey bridge was completed 19 September, Tuesday morning.

Southeast of Eindhoven the 5th Guards Brigade immediately encountered a series of roadblocks near the town of Aalst, where a single self-propelled gun held up the entire column. The Guards' inability to outflank formidable enemy defenses and harassing fire on its flanks, combined with the "fogging in" of the 83rd TAC Group Typhoons in Belgium, rendered the column further behind schedule.[10]

Meanwhile the 32nd Guards Brigade, commanded by Lt.-Colonel J.C. Windsor-Lewis, pursued an alternate eastward route towards Helmond, but also met stiff enemy resistance and unsuitable terrain for outflanking roadblocks with tanks and assault vehicles. The Welsh Guards fought with enemy troops from the reorganized German LXXXVI Corps, commanded by General Hans von Obstfelder. The enemy force included 7,000 "trainees and invalids" of the 176th Infantry Division and 3,000 Fallschirmjägers of the 7th Parachute Regiment commanded by Colonel Erdman.[11]

After several hours of futility the Welsh Guards were ordered by Horrocks to rejoin the main column, reaching the eastern outskirts of Eindhoven by late evening. Several hours earlier the American 506th PIR had entered Eindhoven, knocked out several 88mm guns, secured the bridges over the Dommel River, and captured a single company defending the entire city.[12]

Enemy Counter Strokes at Son and Best

By 7:00 p.m. the Guards Armored Division had successfully hastened around the eastern outskirts of Eindhoven, crossed the Dommel River, and stopped just south of the destroyed Son Bridge crossing at the Wilhelmina Canal. Royal Engineers immediately set to work erecting a "type 40" Bailey Bridge across the canal.[d]

Further north of the Wilhelmina Canal the American 501st PIR, commanded by Colonel Johnson, protected the main road along a ten-mile stretch reaching the town of Veghel. The adjacent 502nd

PIR, however, encountered serious difficulties west of the Son-Veghel road, which eventually escalated into a series of tough encounters near Best. Lt-Colonel Michaelis, commander of the 502nd PIR, had previously ordered his H Company to secure the secondary crossing along the Wilhelmina Canal near Best, but the Americans suffered heavy losses following an engagement with well-fortified troops of Flak Brigade 18 near the village. Michaelis reinforced the attack with two additional battalions, the 2nd and 3rd, but the second attack also ended with heavy casualties and loss of ground. Michaelis' troops failed to secure the village because of insufficient air and armor support needed to dislodge well-entrenched enemy troops. The 100-foot bridge at Best was eventually destroyed, but enemy pressure increased as reinforcements moved east in an attempt to sever the main road.

The fighting would continue for several days, drawing the entire American 502nd PIR, German Flak Brigade 18, a regiment from the German 59th Infantry Division, and finally the British 8th Armor Brigade into the fray.

Weather delays the arrival of American Reinforcements along the Corridor

Unfavorable weather in England delayed the second lift of the American 82nd Airborne Division, including the 319th and 320th Field Artillery Battalions, the 456th Parachute Field Artillery, and the second half of the 80th Anti-Aircraft Battalion. The much-needed firepower included thirty howitzers, eight 57mm anti-tank guns, and ammunition. The 101st Airborne Division second lift arrived at 1:00 p.m., including two battalions of the 327th Glider Infantry,

---

[d] *Type 40 denotes tonnage carrying capacity of portable bridge constructed by the Royal Engineers..*

At Son, forty-six miles south of Arnhem, Royal Engineers and American troops watched as the first Guards tank trundled across the canal.

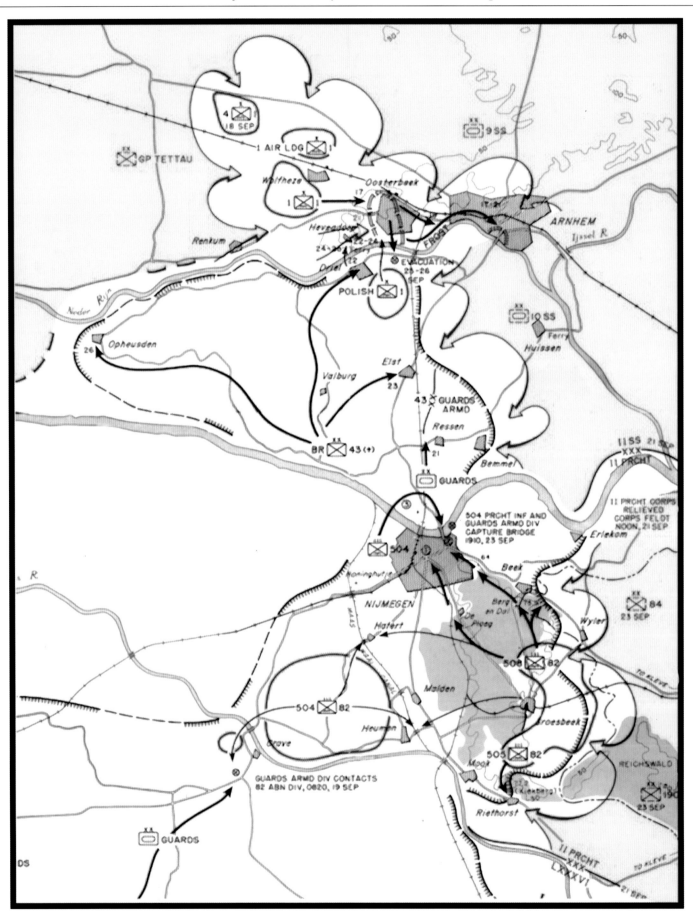

divisional support, and B Battery of the 377th Parachute Artillery.[13] The arrivals strengthened the airborne defenses, but enemy reinforcements also arrived in significant strength, intending to pinch off the already thinly held Allied corridor near Veghel.[14]

By the end of the second day, XXX Corps assumed command of Lt.-General Taylor's 101st Airborne Division, and the British 50th Infantry Division was transferred to the British VIII Corps. Meanwhile, messages from Dutch intelligence had warned Horrocks' staff that the Germans were winning at Arnhem. The British 43rd Wessex Infantry Division remained miles further down the Guards column, placing further burden on the already strained resources of the American 101st and 82nd Division to maintain an open corridor.

September 19 (D+3): Grave and Counter Attacks at Son

The XXX Corps' drive from Son to Grave began at 6:45 a.m. with the 2nd Household Cavalry's armored cars again in the lead. By mid-morning the speed of advance had improved, and the ensuing armored column rumbled thirty-four miles through the towns of St. Oedenrode, Veghel, and Uden. By 8:20 a.m. the 2nd Household Cavalry reached the Grave Bridge, meeting both Lt.-General Browning and Brigadier General Gavin.[15]

Unbeknownst to the British and Americans, a pincer movement was developing under the command of General Student. The formidable 107th Panzer Brigade, commanded by Major von Maltzahn, was fast approaching Son with the intent of establishing a link with General Poppe's 59th Infantry Division already attacking the gritty but weakened American 502nd PIR at Best. The panzer brigade included a company of Panther tanks, a regiment of Panzergrenadiers, and a company of half-tracks.

With some good fortune, Major General Adair had previously ordered a troop of the 8th Armored Brigade, commanded by Brigadier E.G. Prior Palmer, to provide timely assistance to Michaelis' 502nd PIR. The joint forces counterattacked Poppe's infantry, capturing nearly 1,400 enemy troops and forcing the 107th Panzer Brigade to engage, by itself, the improvised American forces near Son. Lacking infantry support, the 107th Panzer's attack was unsuccessful.[16] The panzer brigade penetrated several hundred yards of the American defenses within view of the recently constructed Bailey type 40 bridge, but Major General Maxwell Taylor personally led a successful counterattack with a mixed force of headquarters, glider troops, part of the British 44th Royal tanks, and a single American 57mm anti-tank gun.[17]

XXX Corps' Flanks Weaken

As the battle for the Son-Best perimeter raged, the flanks of XXX Corps weakened as the 50th Infantry Division of British XII Corps

The Guards Armor moving north.

Despite reaching Eindhoven, XXX Corps was now behind schedule nearly twenty-four hours.

lost momentum near the Turnhout-Eindhoven road. The British 7th Armored Division assumed command of the Aart bridgehead, and the 15th Scottish infantry Division passed through the exhausted 50th Infantry Division lines. On the right flank of XXX Corps, the 3rd Infantry Division of VIII Corps reached Weert, with the 11th Armored arriving southeast of Eindhoven. The 4th Armored Brigade continued reinforcing the American 101st until the enemy threat from Best ended.

A Roving FAAA and Idle First Airborne Corps Commander
Appearing amid the traffic jams and confusion in Eindhoven were Lt.-General Lewis Brereton and Major General Matthew Ridgway. Having decided that their FAAA roles in England were completed, both senior officers flew to Holland to personally celebrate an anticipated operational success with the troops. Understandably, as XVIII Airborne Corps Commander Major General Ridgway's essentially training role had ended following the departure of American airborne troops from England. But Brereton mistakenly departed FAAA headquarters, becoming unaware of the increasing difficulties experienced by his transport pilots and fighter support liaison, as well as the severity of enemy resistance against airborne forces on the ground.

In something of an *opera bouffe*, the bemedaled Brereton was forced into a ditch wearing his dress uniform following the unexpected arrival of 120 German Stukas and Ju 88 bombers. Unfortunately, a thousand Dutch citizens were injured and killed during these attacks. [18]

East of Grave, Lt.-General Browning's headquarters had little impact on the battle for Nijmegen. According to the Market Garden Plan the 101st Airborne Division was now under the command of

XXX Corps, and the 82nd would shortly fall under Horrocks' jurisdiction as well. Communications with Urquhart's First Airborne Division were poor, and only snippets of information were obtained indirectly via "Phantom Units." These radio units employed special BBC VHS sets capable of reaching London, and subsequently FAAA Headquarters at Moor Park.

The Dutch Underground (PAN) had bravely provided Browning's staff with vital intelligence via special telephone and coded messages, but distillation and distribution of this vital information to the airborne divisions was difficult to coordinate.

September 20 (D+3): Nijmegen
The Guards Armor Division required an additional forty-two hours to travel from Neerpelt to the southern outskirts of Nijmegen. Movement was continuously hampered by a limited number of TAC support sorties attributed to bad weather, difficulties in coordinating air attacks against close quarters fighting, and severe shortages of American airborne and British ground reinforcements. Meanwhile, the 101st Airborne Division and British 8th Armor Brigade continued resisting enemy attempts to cut the road along the Son-Veghel corridor, now nicknamed "Hells Highway." The 130th Infantry Brigade of the 43rd Wessex Infantry Division finally reached Grave at noon to assist the 82nd Airborne Division.

Following the Guards' arrival in Nijmegen, Adair discovered that the Waal River Bridge remained in enemy control and that Gavin's three exhausted regiments were spread too thinly over a twenty-five mile perimeter facing nearly 6,000 troops and armor of Corps Feldt and II Parachute Corps along the Groesbeek Heights. Adair quickly ordered the Grenadier and Irish Guards to capture the Nijmegen Bridge, the Coldstream Guards to shift eastward and reinforce the beleaguered Americans, and the Welsh Guards to remain in Grave and provide a protective shield against the still formidable 107th Panzer Brigade.[19]

Defending the Heights

Enemy infiltration of the heights intensified, and casualties among Gavin's 505th PIR mounted. The heights were partially overrun, but the Americans cleared the landing zone with a classic bayonet charge. Moments later nearly four hundred gliders arrived with the remaining division artillery, including twelve PAK 75mm howitzers, twelve short-range 105mm howitzers, and eight 57mm anti-tank guns. Unfortunately, heavy fog in England had grounded Colonel Billingslea's 325th Glider Infantry Regiment, delaying further attempts to shift forces towards the Waal River Bridge and reinforce the heights. Major General Adair then ordered several squadrons from the 8th Armored Brigade to reinforce the Groesbeek Heights. Shortly thereafter enemy forces attacked a second time, overrunning American positions and threatening the 82nd Airborne Division rear near the Heumen bridge, but counterattacks by the 508th PIR and Coldstream Guards recaptured the positions by late evening.

Waal River Assault Preparations

After the Americans failed to capture the Nijmegen span on the night of September 17, a second attack was conducted by the Irish Guards Armor and Colonel Reuben Tucker's 504th PIR. The combined force attempted to clear enemy defenses west of the Nijmegen Rail Bridge up to the banks of the Waal, but ended several hundred yards short. The Grenadier Guards and 2nd Battalion of the 505th PIR attacked along the main road, but were halted at Hunner Park just south of the bridge.

Following two failed attempts to secure the southern end of the Waal Bridge, Horrocks, Gavin, and Browning decided to attack the span from both sides. This third plan, proposed by Gavin, included a treacherous river crossing of the Waal and a simultaneous attack against the southern ramp by parachute infantry and British armor. The Irish Guards would provide artillery support while the Grenadier Guards and 505th PIR assault attacked Hunner Park. The 3rd Battalion of the American 504th PIR, commanded by Major Julian Cook, would use assault craft to cross the 400-yard wide Waal and seize the north end of the Nijmegen Bridge. Horrocks immediately issued orders for XXX Corps engineers to rush a number of 19-foot assault boats to Nijmegen for what would be the only "naval action" of Market Garden.[20]

The advance slowed to a crawl as General Adair stuck strictly to orders.

The Grenadier Guards began the slow trundle along a two lane road at eight miles an hour. Many tanks were laden with infantry ready for a fight.

10th SS artillery covered the Allied approaches with deadly accuracy.

"Hail Mary, Full of Grace...."

Early on the morning of September 21st (D+4), the Irish Guards and Major Julian Cook's 3rd Battalion 504th PIR nearly completed preparations for capturing the northern ramp of the Nijmegen Bridge via tactical river crossing. The Grenadier Guards and the 505th Parachute Infantry Regiment planned to simultaneously attack the southern ramp while Cook's troops crossed the Waal in British assault boats. At 2:30 p.m., squadrons of 83rd TAC Hawker Typhoons strafed and rocketed enemy positions on the northern bank of the Waal. Ten minutes later heavy smoke bombardment from Horrocks' XXX Corps medium guns and Vandeleur Irish Guards tanks shrouded the crossing axis as the initial wave of two American airborne companies attempted what many military historians consider one of the bravest and costliest assaults of the war.[21]

Cook's H and I Companies, plus headquarters staff and engineers, desperately struggled across the swift and turbulent Waal, employing any propellant means possible. Many boats became stuck in the shallows or overturned, but eventually the canvas-hulled fleet reached its halfway point. The ruse appeared successful until the white smoke screen evaporated, only to be violently followed by heavy enemy artillery, mortar, and machine gun fire. Enemy shells ceaselessly ripped through the little flotilla, and nearly half were sunk in minutes. Desperate to reach the northern bank, some paratroopers prayed "Hail Mary, Full of Grace" in cadence with each paddle stroke. The maritime slaughter enraged the survivors charging across the exposed northern bank and attacking enemy defenses. No quarter was granted to the enemy defenders desperately attempting to surrender:[22]

> To Vandeleur's amazement the boats turned around and started back for the second wave. Turning to Horrocks, General Browning said, "I have never seen a more gallant action."[23]

At the same time, the Grenadier Guards and the 2nd Battalion 504th PIR attacked Hunner Park and Fort Valkhof, blocking the way to the Nijmegen Bridge. Grenadier armor mounted with American troops advanced through the street while other troops scurried across rooftops, eliminating snipers and locating strong points. Hunner Park was filled with enemy guns of assorted calibers, including self-propelled French 47mm guns and the formidable German 88mm guns. The Americans eventually overran the defenders with bayonets and hand grenades, while the Grenadier armor lined up four abreast and charged the southern approaches of the Nijmegen Bridge.[24] The Grenadier Guards rolled onto the span after mistakenly assuming that an American flag placed on the nearby Waal Railway Bridge signified permission to advance. By 7:10 p.m. Major Cook's surviving troops on the northern banks had linked up with the Grenadier Guards. Standing near the engineer at the detonator box, Brigadeführer Harmel ordered the bridge destroyed, but the charges inexplicably failed to explode.[25]

The Groesbeek Heights were partially overrun by Corps Feldt, but Gavin's troops held firm.

Defense of the Groesbeek Heights

West of Nijmegen, Colonel Ekman's 505th PIR faced another onslaught by hoards of enemy infantry and armor near the town of Mook. Colonel Roy Lindquist's 508th PIR also fought off infantry attacks along the eastern perimeter near Beek and Wyler. The 406th Landesschützen Division with 500 troops led the attack from the north, and General Meindl's II Parachute Corps attacked from the south with nearly 1,200 troops. The Germans recaptured several American positions and threatened the rear of the entire 82nd Airborne Division near Heuman, but Brigadier General Gavin returned to Groesbeek shortly before the Waal crossing to personally take command, in some situations leading squad level counter attacks with his Garand M1 rifle in hand. Gavin would use his last reserves, which included a battalion of Coldstream Guards and three hundred American glider pilots. By late evening every position was recaptured, and the eastern perimeter secured around the Groesbeek Heights.[26]

The battle for the Waal bridges had ended, but Frost's troops were already defeated at the Arnhem Bridge and retreating westwards towards the Oosterbeek pocket. It was not known that only three 10th SS Frundsberg battalions stood between XXX Corps and the besieged British First Airborne Division. Major General Adair's Guards again halted for the night until the 43rd Wessex Infantry Division arrived to provide flanking support. Lt.-General Horrocks concurred with this decision after weighing the difficulties of keeping the main corridor open south of Nijmegen.

During the assault to capture the Nijmegen Bridge, another wave of transports arrived with the balance of the 327th Glider Infantry Regiment (GIF) and artillery. Only 209 of the expected 385 gliders arrived, carrying the 213th and 907th Artillery Battalions, half of the 81st Anti-Aircraft Battalion, and one third of Colonel Bud Harper's 327th GIF. Losses in Allied tugs and gliders exceeded one hundred as anti-aircraft defenses thickened around the drop and landing zones. Lacking sufficient reserves, the American airborne forces remained too thin to protect the vulnerable section of the corridor between Uden and Grave.

Second Enemy Attempt to Recapture Son

The 107th Panzer Brigade attacked Son in daylight for a second time, but withdrew following the British 8th Brigade appearance in force. Major General Taylor quickly ordered counterattacks to widen the corridor but could not exploit the success. Major General Adair's forces in the north were already committed to supporting the undermanned 82nd Airborne Division at Nijmegen and Groesbeek. The VIII and XII Corps continued to move slowly, with the 15th Infantry Division reaching the Wilhelmina Canal near Best, and both the

The Americans furiously counterattacked with fixed bayonets, finally routing the now disorganized enemy troops.

The first wave of H and I Companies, plus headquarters, made a mad dash for the northern bank of the Waal.

None of Major Cook's troops paused, and surviving troops recklessly charged the enemy trenches.

"Paddles were flying like mad, and Major Cook kept yelling Keep Going! Keep Going!"

"The crossing was a scene of mass confusion. Paddles were lost, men fell overboard, and the current caused a number of boats to circle uncontrollably."

"The incoming German shells were intense and concentrated, ripping the small fleet apart. Enemy machine guns raked each boat individually."

50th Infantry Division and 11th Armored reaching the American 101st Airborne near Helmond. Both corps continued experiencing difficulties moving off-road with limited mobility against determined pockets of enemy defenders.

September 21 (D+4): Seven Miles Short of Arnhem

Realizing that further attempts to recapture the Groesbeek Heights and Nijmegen Bridge were futile, Field Marshal Model ordered General Bittrich's II SS Panzer Corps to sieze control of the battle for Arnhem and south of Elst. Model then ordered General der Infantrie Hans Reinhard, commander of LXXXVIII Corps, and

General der Infantrie Hans von Obstfelder, commander of LXXXVI Corps, to continue pincer attacks along the Eindhoven-Veghel corridor. Attacks along the congested Eindhoven-Veghel corridor intensified as roving packs of enemy armor and infantry destroyed dozens of soft-skinned Allied vehicles lined bumper to bumper along the jammed highway. Responding to the carnage, the American paratroopers had nicknamed this corridor "Hell's Highway."

By mid-afternoon, the Irish Guards had led the division across the captured Nijmegen Bridge, followed by the Welsh Guards. Both groups were low on ammunition, troops, and air support. RAF Typhoons flew overhead but were unable to communicate with RASF

None of Cook's troops paused. Despite being sickened and exhausted, the first wave quickly subdued the German defenders and no quarter was granted.

Enemy infantry and armor formations on the western edge of the Allied corridor applied pressure on the American 101st Airborne between Eindhoven and Grave.

ground liaisons attached to XXX Corps. The seven miles to Arnhem were mostly raised roadway, providing ample targets for enemy anti-tank guns. The Guards were halted again, awaiting the arrival of the 43rd Wessex infantry Division that was delayed in Eindhoven. Lt.-General Horrocks had ordered the 43rd Infantry Division to relieve the Guards and Americans holding Nijmegen, then advance across the Waal and link up with the besieged British Airborne near Driel. The arrival of Major General G.I. Thomas' forces allowed the American 504th and 508th PIR to reinforce the Groesbeek Heights and clear out the remaining several thousand troops of Corps Feldt.[27]

A Pole Too Few

At 5:00 p.m. the First Polish Parachute Brigade finally arrived—two days later than planned—on the north side of the Rhine, near Driel. Of the 114 transports departing England, only 60 arrived over the drop zone because of bad weather and heavy flak, delivering fewer than 800 troops and no heavy equipment. Major General Sosabowski's immediate attempts to attack eastwards were checked by a rapidly organized regiment of sailors, airmen, and coastal defense troops under the command of Sperrverband Harzer.[28]

Jagdpanthers attacked and destroyed many British transports stranded bumper to bumper along "Hells Highway."

September 22-25: Checkmate

The British Royal Artillery 64th Medium Regiment was now in contact with Urquhart's forces, providing vital perimeter fire coordinates around the contracting Oosterbeek pocket. The artillery support and late arrival of the 2nd TAC blunted any large-scale enemy attempts to destroy the besieged British paratroopers until their evacuation. However, the Luftwaffe continued to enjoy local air superiority, shooting down a significant number of air transports and strafing the encircled ground troops.

Lt.-General Horrocks ordered another attempt to reach the British First Airborne by sending the Irish Guards and two Wessex Brigades: the 129th Brigade towards Elst and the 214th Brigade towards Driel. Elst was heavily reinforced by Kampfgruppe Knaust, which included thirty Royal Tiger tanks of the 506th Heavy Tank Battalion. The dike roadway rendered many Allied vehicles easy targets, but several armored cars of the 2nd Household Calvary penetrated the enemy roadblocks, reaching the Poles at Driel in late afternoon. Later in the day, the 5th Battalion of the Duke of Cornwall's Light Infantry (DCLI) and a handful of armor reinforced the Poles, completing the "link," albeit a feeble one, between the ground and airborne forces.[29]

Despite the impending failure of the operation, Horrocks ordered Major General Sosabowski to send a token force of Polish paratroopers in four rubber boats across the Rhine to reach Urquhart's shrinking perimeter. Only a handful of troops and supplies managed to reach the Heavesdorp ferry on the other side. Sosabowski would send an additional 200 troops across following the late arrival of assault boats from Nijmegen, but the crossing resulted in heavy losses. [30]

Late Airborne Arrivals

For the first time in nearly a week the weather had cleared, and on September 23 at 3:00 p.m. over one thousand troop transports and gliders arrived with the balance of the 82nd Airborne Division. The airlift included the entire 325th Glider Infantry Regiment, the 101st Airborne's 907th Glider Field Artillery Battalion, and the balance of the 327th Glider Infantry Regiment. The seaborne tail also arrived, bringing the division up to full strength. The remaining troops of the First Polish Parachute Brigade Group arrived near Grave. These troops were immediately sent to reinforce the exhausted American forces at Nijmegen and along Hell's Highway.[31]

The American Paratroopers, along with a troop of Guards tanks, counterattack enemy attempts to sever the main highway.

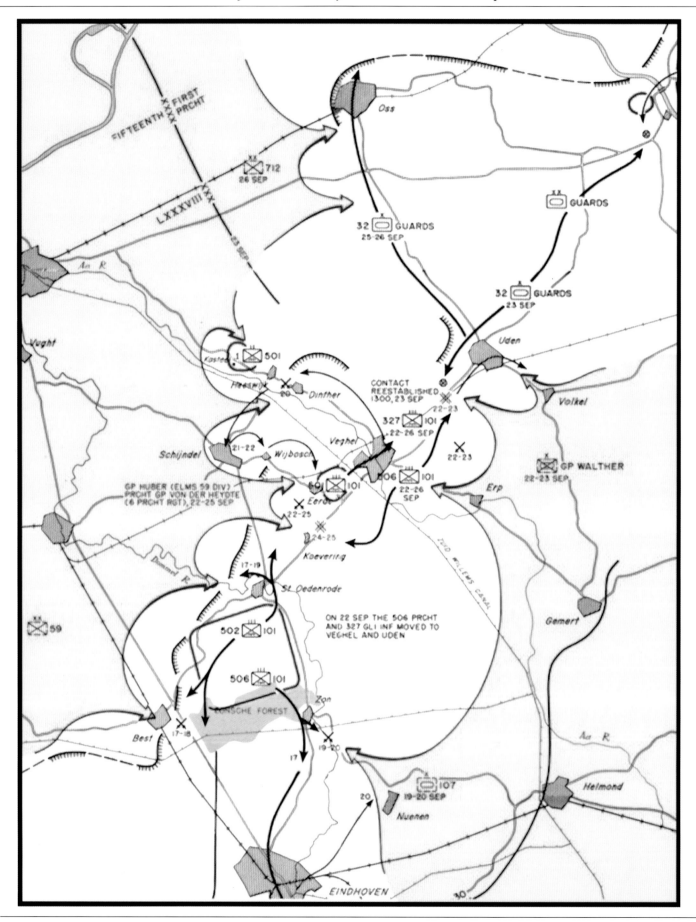

Cutting the Road between Uden and Grave

Another early morning attack by elements of the German 59th Infantry Division and 107th Panzer Brigade severed the road between Uden and Grave, splitting the 69th British infantry Brigade in transit towards the 101st Airborne Division perimeter. The Dutch underground had earlier informed Major General Maxwell Taylor of the impending attack, resulting in his timely ordering of reinforcements. The highway was severed for nearly twenty-four hours, and required nearly eight battalions of Guards and 101st Airborne troops to reopen the road. The entire 32nd Guards Brigade of Coldstream and Grenadier Guards would protect the road near Uden, since the British VIII and XII Corps had halted nearly ten miles south along the Wilhelmina Canal.[32]

Cutting the Road at Koevering

Between September 24-26, the main highway road was cut for a second time as ad hoc formations under the overall command of General der Infantrie Reinhard converged on Koevering, drawing a significant number of XXX Corps forces from the northeast. The kampfgruppes included a company of the 559th Assault Battalion Jagdpanthers and several battalions of Fallschirmjägers.[33] For the next forty-eight hours the main highway remained severed, resulting in scores of destroyed British armor and supply vehicles. The flanking attacks also isolated both Lt.-General Horrocks and Major General Dempsey, who had recently relocated both the British 2nd Army and XXX Corps Headquarters at St. Oedenrode.[34]

Single Jagdpanthers and squads of Fallschirmjägers prowled the main roadway, destroying over fifty stranded vehicles and brewing up nearly fifteen British Shermans that arrived piecemeal into the fray. An Allied counterattack was finally organized that included nearly the entire American 101st Airborne Division, a regiment of the British 50th Infantry Division, and tanks from the British 44th Royal Armored Tank Battalion.

The road was not reopened for traffic until 2:00 p.m. on September 26, following the removal of mines and destroyed vehicles. Even though German forces were too exhausted to continue, indirect artillery fire continued and British reinforcements needed in the north were seriously delayed.[35]

Closing Attempt to Relieve Urquhart

Despite the tremendous difficulty in keeping the lower road open, Horrocks approved a final river "assault" with two companies of the 4th Battalion of the Dorsetshire Regiment. The crossing took place the night of September 25 using a combination of assault

Futile attempts were made to reach the British First Airborne using DUKWs, but the combination of strong currents and steep embankments along the Lower Rhine severely hampered efforts.

British engineers and Polish troops attempt to send supplies and ammunition across the Lower Rhine.

boats and DUKW amphibious craft. Over 300 Dorsets reached the far bank, but only half joined the defensive perimeter intact.[36] Several hours following the futile efforts of the Dorsets, Major General Urquhart signaled Major General Thomas to begin evacuation of the remaining British airborne forces trapped inside the Oosterbeek perimeter.

Notes:
1 Oliver Lindsay, ed., *A Guards' General: The Memoirs of Major General Sir Allan Adair* (London: Hanish Hamilton, 1986), p.150.
2 Anthony Farrar-Hockley, *Airborne Carpet Operation Market Garden* (New York: Ballantine Books, 1969), pp.102-103. *Interview with Lt.-General Sir Brian Horrocks.*
3 Cornelius Ryan, *A Bridge Too Far* (New York :Simon and Shuster, 1974), pp.245-246.
4 Stephen Badsey Arnhem 1944: Operation Market Garden (London: Osprey Publishing Ltd., 1993), pp.40-41.
5 *Term used by the Germans to describe the tendency of the American built tank to catch fire after scoring a hit.*
6 Ryan, op.cit., p.246.
7 Farrar-Hockley, op.cit., pp.104-105.
8 Badsey, op.cit., p.40.
9 Ibid. p.41.
10 Geoffrey Powell, *The Devil's Birthday: The Bridges to Arnhem 1944* (London: Leo Cooper, 1992), p.113. *First printed by Buchan and Enright, Publishers Ltd. in 1984.*
11 Robert J. Kershaw, *It Never Snows in September* (Ramsbury: Crowood Press, 1990), pp.249-250.
12 Badsey, op.cit., p.46.
13 Clay Blair, *Ridgway's Paratroopers: The American Airborne in World War II* (New York: William Morrow, 1985), p.336.
14 Charles MacDonald, *The Siegfried Line Campaign* (Washington, DC, Center of Military History, 1993),pp.151-152.

15 Badsey, op.cit., p.56.
16 Powell, op.cit., p.115.
17 Farrar-Hockley, op.cit. p.127.
18 Gerard M. Devlin, *Paratrooper!: The Saga of U.S. Army and Marine Parachute and Glider Combat Troops during World War II* (New York: St. Martin's Press, 1979), p.503.
19 Badsey, op.cit., p.60.
20 Russell F.Weigley, *Eisenhower's Lieutenants* (Bloomington: Indiana University Press, 1990), p.313.
21 Ryan, op.cit.,p.461.
22 Ibid., pp.314-315.
23 Ibid., p.463.
24 Donald Featherstone, *Wargaming Airborne Operations* (New York, A.S. Barnes and Company, 1979), p.179.
25 Ryan, op.cit.,p.473.
26 Bair, p.341.
27 Weigley, p.315.
28 Kershaw, op.cit., p.243.
29 Badsey, p.73.
30 Martin Middlebrook, *Arnhem 1944* (Boulder: Westview Press, 1994), p.411.
31 Huston, op.cit., pp.34-37.
32 Ibid., p.74.
33 Kershaw, op.cit., p.280.
34 Horrocks, op.cit., pp.229-230.
35 Kershaw, op.cit., p.287.
36 Middlebrook, op.cit., p.422.

7

"The Last Charge of the Light Brigades"

"Tell them to go to hell...."

-Lt.-Colonel John Frost, Arnhem - September 19, 1944[1]

First British Airborne Operational Summary

The arrival of the British First Airborne Division on Sunday September 17 was virtually unopposed until the 1st Parachute Brigade, under the command of Brigadier Lathbury, marched eastward towards Arnhem. Within hours the three-battalion advance was halted along two of three roads amid unanticipated sniping, roadblocks, roving enemy armor, and shelling. The surrounding heavy woods and tall buildings of Arnhem hampered attempts to maintain brigade, battalion, and company level communications, including both radio and courier contact. The streets of Arnhem had quickly become a deadly maze of street fighting, dissipating British attempts to reach the road bridge in force. By early dusk brigade and battalion integrity was seriously challenged, and less than one-third of the original 2,400 troops had reached Arnhem.

Following the completion of the second lift on September 18, the First Airborne Division had amassed nine battalions against fourteen *ad hoc* German battalions, or kampfgruppes, supported by numerous artillery and armor. It required hours to establish sufficient local superiority to punch through a formidable *Sperrlinie* wedged between the British forces approaching from the west and Frost's perimeter isolated near the Arnhem Bridge. Over the next three days nearly 4,000 British airborne troops were channeled into a maelstrom of destructive close-quarter fighting. In General Urquhart's absence, acting division commander Brigadier Hicks adhered to the original Market Garden plan of pushing towards the bridge, despite having knowledge of the increasing buildup of enemy forces. Fog of war, heavy casualties among officers and NCOs, a hardened enemy, and the inherent vagaries of street fighting precluded sufficient command to prevent the destruction of the First British Airborne Division.

Seizure and Defense of the Arnhem Bridge

On Sunday afternoon, Lt.-Colonel John Frost's 2nd Parachute Battalion had assembled near the eastern corner of Drop Zone X, located less than a mile north of Heelsum. The battalion, which included four companies (A, B, C, and Headquarters), set out at 2:45 p.m. along a seven-mile southern route code-named "Lion." The 2nd Battalion originally numbered less than 500 troops, but was re-

inforced by partial units of the 1st Parachute Squadron and 9th Field Company/Royal Engineers, along with five six-pounders of the 1st Airlanding Anti-Tank Battery.[2]

Frost's troops had marched past the well kept Dutch homes and gardens and tree shrouded brick roads, later ambushing several enemy vehicles approaching Major Digby Tatham-Warter's lead A Company. Sniping intensified and several armored cars appeared, but Frost's column kept moving along the lower road towards Arnhem. Frost later dispatched Major Dover's C Company, along with a number of 9th Field Company engineers, to capture the Railway Bridge, but the enemy destroyed the center span moments following their arrival. A short time later, heavy machine gun fire erupted near a rise called Den Brink, forcing sections of Tatham-Warter's A Company to counterattack.

As darkness fell A Company and Headquarters Company reached the large Arnhem Bridge ramp alongside the Eusebiusplein. Infantry sections from A Company quickly took positions alongside the embankment leading up to the bridge, and Headquarters Company took over a large government building across the street. Shortly thereafter 1st Brigade Headquarters arrived without Brigadier Lathbury and established themselves in the attic of the government building. Several other groups arrived, including Major Freddie Gough with a number of his armed reconnaissance vehicles, a platoon of R.A.S.C., several sections of Royal Engineers, and a captured lorry fortuitously filled with ammunition transported from the drop zone.[3]

A platoon from A Company moved across the bridge but encountered heavy machine gun fire from a pillbox situated on the northern end and an armored car positioned on the southern approaches. Later that evening the pillbox was destroyed in spectacular fashion by Captain Mackay's sappers following a flame-thrower and PIAT attack, which ignited a small munitions building behind the pillbox. The ensuing explosions and flames illuminated the entire perimeter, making it quite difficult to maneuver without attracting enemy counter fire. Further attempts to capture the southern ramp proved costly, forcing the small British force to establish a tight semicircular defensive perimeter. The enemy counterattacked throughout the night by firing illuminating flares over the perimeter, then several rounds of mortar fire followed by squads of attacking infantry. The enemy attempts to eradicate the British proved futile, and casualties were heavy. Frost had ordered a final attempt to reach the southern banks, but was unable to locate any boats or barges capable of carrying a company across.

By early Monday morning several additional enemy vehicles were destroyed while attempting to cross the span, and nearly one hundred prisoners were held captive.[4]

Frost would eventually assume command of the entire bridgehead of nearly seven hundred troops; a significantly smaller force than the original brigade planned by Brigadier Lathbury. Airborne troops reaching Arnhem on September 17, 1944:[5]

2nd Parachute Battalion (A, B [less No.4], HQ) - 340 troops
1st Parachute Brigade HQ - 110 troops
1st Parachute Squadron/R.E. - 75 troops
3rd Parachute Battalion - 45 troops
1st Airlanding A/T Troop - five guns and 30 troops
250 Light, RASC - 40 troops
9th Field Company - 30 troops
Glider Pilots, Recce, Royal Artillery Observers, Other - 59 troops

Despite its diminutive size in troops and guns, Frost's command had effectively severed the Arnhem-Nijmegen road, preempting attempts by II SS Panzer Corps to move any heavy armor towards Nijmegen. Field Marshal Model and Obergruppenführer Willi Bittrich, though unable to determine the relative strength of the airborne forces, quickly assessed the criticality of removing the British at the bridge in order to counterattack British XXX Corps and the American 82nd Airborne Division. Bittrich immediately ordered ferrying operations of the 10th SS Frundsberg several miles east near Pannerderm to reinforce the weak blocking force at Nijmegen.[6] Harzer would build sufficient forces to eventually exhaust and overwhelm the British forces defending the bridge.

The Assault by Haupsturmführer Viktor Gräbner
Monday morning the Arnhem perimeter remained quiet until three truckloads of enemy infantry drove slowly towards Frost's headquarters on the Eusebius Binnensingel. The alert British quickly poured a stream of bullets into the vehicles, then escorted the few survivors into one of the nearby buildings. A short time later several Mark III/IV tanks and supporting infantry probed the perimeter from the east, but a six-pounder destroyed one tank, forcing a hasty retreat.

At 11:30 a.m., heavy vehicles were heard approaching from the south. Many British troops optimistically expected the arrival of the Household Cavalry followed by Horrocks' powerful XXX Corps, but as the darkened images grew it became quickly apparent that the vehicles were part of a large enemy column. The fast approaching vehicles included six half-tracks followed by a dozen armored cars and camouflaged lorries spaced between fifteen to twenty yards apart.[7] One of the lead vehicles, a mottled British Humber I, carried the assault commander Captain Viktor Gräbner. Only the previous day Standartenführer Harmel had presented

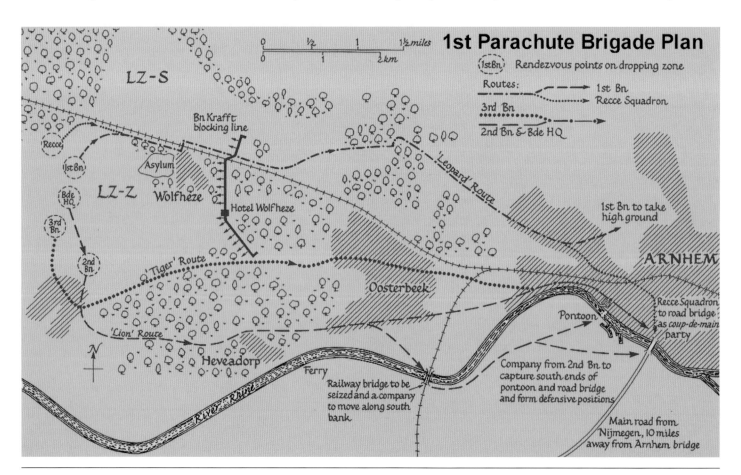

Frost's 2nd Battalion immediately marched along a seven-mile southern route code named "Lion."

Gräbner with the Knights Cross (with emblem and ribbon) for leading a successful counterattack against the British in Normandy.[8] Gräbner had earlier received a radio message from Harzer's headquarters that the bridge was merely held by "advance units" of British paratroopers.[9]

Frost's troops withheld their fire until the lead half-tracks of Gräbner's 9th SS Panzer Recce trundled unabated over the necklace of airborne laid street mines and finally past their positions overlooking the ramp. British artillery observers awaited the command to direct Sheriff Thompson's Light Regiment to open fire from nearby Oosterbeek. The PAK 75mm gunners had previously registered the northern ramp in order to lob high explosive shells onto any onrushing armored columns with relative precision.

As the main enemy column crossed the ramp a tremendous hail of fire erupted from both sides. The British employed every available weapon, including Enfields, Brens, Stens, PIATs, mortars, six-pounders, and the distant PAK 75mm artillery. Several airborne troops, located only several feet above the passing enemy vehicles, lobbed hand grenades into open top half-tracks, setting them ablaze and cutting down panicked troops spilling out to escape. Many vehicles had abruptly and uncontrollably collided with one another, burning fiercely for several hours. Scores of enemy troops collapsed into dark heaps alongside their flaming vehicles as the deadly defensive crossfire engulfed the entire ramp. The battle lasted nearly two hours, and enemy losses totaled seventy dead, including the assault commander Gräbner. The first large-scale attempt by Bittrich to eradicate Frost's troops had ended in a pyre of death and destruction.[10]

Following Gräbner's attack a pattern developed, whereby intensive mortar and artillery fire was immediately followed by tank and infantry probes from the east, many of which ended inconclusively with heavy enemy losses. Harzer's divisional artillery targeted any building suspected of being a British stronghold. Throughout the next sixty hours, Frost's troops engaged in dozens of counterattacks necessary to keep the enemy off balance, but the perimeter eventually contracted as the scale of enemy infiltration intensified and irreplaceable airborne losses mounted.

Divisional reinforcements and ammunition from the west were virtually cut off, and much-needed 2nd TAF support would never arrive. Frost was later informed that both the 1st and 3rd Parachute Battalions had failed to penetrate enemy roadblocks east of St. Elizabeths Hospital, but would make a second attempt the following day. The battalion, facing nearly an entire armored division, remained isolated from the main body of airborne troops west of Arnhem.

The fateful charge of Haupsturmführer Viktor Gräbner.

One of the lead vehicles appeared to be a mottled British Humber Mark I carrying the assault commander Viktor Gräbner.

German armor and infantry fell prey to pockets of Frost's troops, which included a number of six pounder anti-tank guns.

The battle was fought savagely, as each house was attacked individually with explosives, followed by enemy infantry and armor.

Gunners of the 1st Airlanding Light Artillery Brigade at Oosterbeek engaged enemy targets in Arnhem with 75mm PAK howitzers.

Monday night was fraught with piecemeal enemy infantry and armor attacks seeking to infiltrate the perimeter.

First Attempt to Reach Frost at the Bridge

3rd Battalion

On Sunday the 3rd Battalion, commanded by Lt.-Colonel J.A.C. Fitch, had advanced from Drop Zone X north of Heelsum towards Arnhem along the Utrechtseweg, code-named route "Tiger." The 3rd Battalion (A, B, C, and HQ Companies) included three anti-tank guns of C Troop, sections from the 9th Field Company/Royal Engineers, an RAMC section, artillery observers, Dutch commandos, and Brigadier Lathbury. Employing infantry tactics similar to its sister battalions, the 3rd Battalion marched off in single file on alternate sides of the narrow Dutch streets, with fifty-foot intervals between each platoon.[11] Several hours later, Major General Urquhart, the First Airborne Divisional commander, would join the battalion after failing to reach the battalions through the brigade and division radios.

Major Peter Waddy's B Company led the column, making steady progress for nearly two hours until Sturmbannführer Krafft's troops, along with several armored cars, opened fire from a wooded area near the Wolfheze-Doorwerth crossroads. Fitch quickly dispatched Company C, commanded by Major Pongo Lewis, to outflank the defenders, but it became separated and eventually reached the 2nd Battalion in Arnhem late Sunday night with fewer than fifty

troops. At the rear of the column, harassed by machine gun and mortar fire, Major Dennison's A Company and Headquarters quickly fell behind. Despite relatively light casualties the remaining companies lost forward momentum, and by 9:30 p.m. Brigadier Lathbury altered the original plan of reaching Arnhem on D-Day, ordering the 3rd Battalion to regroup near the Hartenstein Hotel for the night.

On Monday at 4:30 a.m. the advance resumed, less C Company, for nearly two and a half miles along the lower road through the Oosterbeek-Laag overpass, until the leading troops reached the outskirts of Arnhem. The rear companies again became separated as enemy sniping and mortar fire held up the column, forcing many troops inside dwellings lining the narrow urban streets. Confused fighting ensued, as enemy armor and self-propelled guns intermingled with exposed forward sections lacking anti-tank weapons. By 7:00 a.m., only several platoons of B Company, some Royal Engineers, and a single anti-tank gun had reached positions near the Rhine Pavilion, located less than 2,000 yards from the trapped 2nd Battalion. Heavy casualties among officers and NCOs hampered attempts to organize a concentrated push, and by late Monday evening the battalion was reduced to 140 troops. In the midst of this melee, both Major General Urquhart and Brigadier Lathbury became isolated from their command, ignominiously forced by street fighting into the attic of a Dutch row house for thirty-six hours.[12]

Frost's troops counterattacked with deadly accuracy.

Attempts to dislodge Frost's forces intensified with the arrival of King Tigers attached to the 506th Heavy Tank Battalion.

Frost's troops were defenseless against the nearly impregnable sixty-ton Royal Tigers.

1ˢᵗ Battalion

On Sunday, Lt.-Colonel David Dobie's 1ˢᵗ Battalion (R, S, T, and HQ Companies) had followed the northern route code-named "Leopard," but was halted following heavy fighting near a wooded area off the Wolfhezerweg. The lead R Company, commanded by Major Timothy, suffered heavy casualties, and flanking attacks by troops and armor of Kampfgruppes Weber and von Allworden disrupted the rest of the column. Throughout the first night Dobie's troops continued attacking in a southeastward direction through heavy woods, losing nearly one hundred troops.

By Monday morning, Major Stark's S Company had reached the middle route, or Utrechtseweg, used by the 3ʳᵈ Battalion in Oosterbeek. The British encountered heavy fire along the Utrechtseweg near the Oosterbeek-Laag overpass, forcing the battalion further south along the lower road followed by the 2ⁿᵈ Battalion. The 1ˢᵗ Battalion was later joined by detached elements of Fitch's 3ʳᵈ Battalion, and proceeded nearly a quarter mile beyond the underpass until enemy infantry and armor opened fire on the column. Heavy fighting ensued, and by late afternoon Dobie's troops had reached the outskirts of Arnhem, but many officers and NCOs were either dead or wounded. A number of surviving troops sought refuge in Dutch homes near the Rhine Pavilion and St. Elizabeths Hospital.

The 1ˢᵗ Battalion had unknowingly halted alongside the remnants of the 3rd Battalion only several hundred yards away. The combined strength of both assault battalions had been reduced from nearly 1,300 troops to several understrength companies.

The 2ⁿᵈ South Staffordshires

The 2ⁿᵈ South Staffordshires, commanded by Lt.-Colonel W.D.H. McCardie, had arrived on Sunday and established defensive positions near the Reyerscamp landing zone.[13] The battalion was understrength by nearly two companies, which were scheduled to arrive in the second lift on D+1. Early Monday morning, McCardie received orders from Brigadier Hicks to proceed immediately to Arnhem. By 10:30 a.m. the battalion set out along the Utrechtseweg, sidestepping heavy resistance near the Oosterbeek Railway towards the lower road previously used by Frost. The battalion encountered snipers and mortar fire, but casualties remained light. By 5:30 p.m. the South Staffs arrived at an assembly area west of St. Elizabeths Hospital and reached full strength following the arrival of its two missing companies.[14]

By Wednesday evening, all but a handful of British troops remained near the span.

Out of ammunition, food, and sleepless for nearly seventy-two hours, Frost's remaining troops surrendered in small pockets or attempted to exfiltrate towards Oosterbeek.

Street fighting slowed Lt.-Colonel Fitch's 3rd Parachute Battalion's advance along the Utrechtsestraatweg.

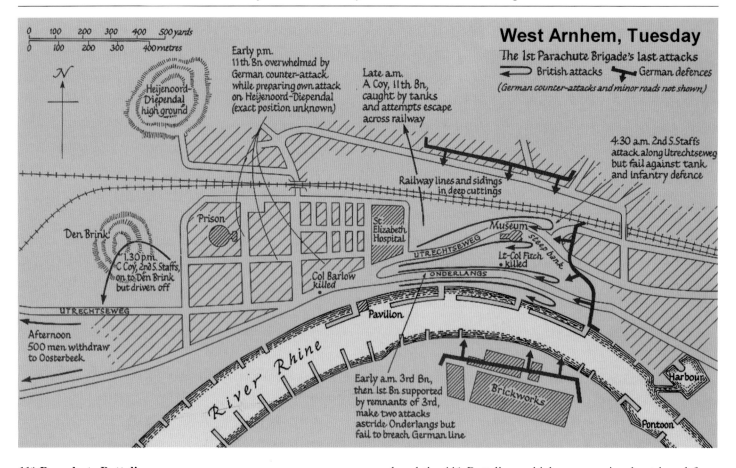

West Arnhem, Tuesday
The 1st Parachute Brigade's last attacks
British attacks   German defences
(German counter-attacks and minor roads not shown)

Early p.m.
11th Bn overwhelmed by German counter-attack while preparing own attack on Heijenoord-Diependal (exact position unknown)

Late a.m.
A Coy, 11th Bn, caught by tanks and attempts escape across railway

4:30 a.m. 2nd S.Staffs attack along Utrechtseweg but fail against tank and infantry defence

Railway lines and sidings in deep cuttings

Heijenoord-Diependal high ground

Den Brink

1.30 p.m. C Coy, 2nd S.Staffs, on to Den Brink but driven off

Prison

St Elizabeth Hospital

Museum

Lt-Col Fitch killed

steep bank

UTRECHTSEWEG

ONDERLANGS

Col Barlow killed

UTRECHTSEWEG

Afternoon 500 men withdraw to Oosterbeek

Pavilion

River Rhine

Early a.m. 3rd Bn, then 1st Bn supported by remnants of 3rd, make two attacks astride Onderlangs but fail to breach German line

Brickworks

Harbour

Pontoon

11th Parachute Battalion

The 11th Parachute Battalion, commanded by Lt-Colonel George Lea, had departed Drop Zone Y along the Amsterdamseweg, but was delayed near the Hartenstein for nearly two hours while the 4th Parachute Brigade Commander, Brigadier John Hackett, and temporary Divisional Commander, Brigadier Hicks, quarreled over tactical plans. The full-strength battalion eventually arrived in the late afternoon with few casualties west of St. Elizabeths Hospital. The relative speed of advance was attributed to the commander's decision to utilize Dutch guides.[15]

Second Attempt to Reach Frost

By late Monday night the 11th Battalion and 2nd South Staffordshires were positioned several hundred yards west of St. Elizabeths Hospital, amounting to nearly two fresh battalions of 1,000 troops, together with 500 battle-weary troops of the 1st and 3rd Battalions. Despite this seemingly formidable force, both Urquhart and Lathbury were isolated somewhere forward and the battalions lacked unified command. Major General Urquhart had earlier sent his adjutant, Colonel Hilary Barlow, to oversee the attack, but Barlow was killed while attempting to reach the battalions.[16]

In Urquhart's forced absence, Brigadier Hicks adhered to the original Market plan, sending the 4th Parachute Brigade and reinforced 1st Parachute Brigade to Arnhem. Brigadier Hicks augmented the 1st Parachute Brigade with three companies of the 2nd South Staffordshires and the recently airdropped 11th Battalion. The exhausted 7th KOSBs defending the drop zones north of Wolfheze

replaced the 11th Battalion, which was previously stripped from Brigadier Hackett's 4th Parachute Brigade.

Lt.-Colonel Dobie, commander of the 1st Battalion, initially planned a Monday 9:00 p.m. breakthrough to the bridge with Lt.-Colonel McCardie, but conflicting information that Frost's position had been overrun postponed the attack. The delay continued for several hours until the regimental artillery net confirmed that Frost's troops were still putting up a stiff fight at the bridge. With the unexpected arrival of the 11th Battalion at midnight the plan now expanded to a three-battalion advance, but was again delayed by the late arrival of the second lift South Staffords, resulting in a 4:00 a.m. attack with only one hour of darkness remaining.

Unbeknownst to the three battalion commanders near St. Elizabeths Hospital, Lt.-Colonel Fitch's half-strength 3rd Battalion lay stranded several hundred yards to the south near the Rhine Pavilion following an unsuccessful attempt to reach Frost on Monday.

Moments after the British attack began Dobie would discover the missing battalion, but the advance continued along the lower road with Fitch's troops following immediately behind.[17]

The overall plan included an advance by the 2nd South Staffordshires along the "upper road," or Utrechtseweg, east of St Elizabeths Hospital towards the Municipal Museum less than a mile ahead at the crest of the road. The 1st Battalion would advance in tandem along the "lower road," or Onderlangs, which was parallel to the upper road along the Lower Rhine. The 11th Parachute Battalion would advance behind the South Staffords and provide cover

The 2nd South Staffords advanced towards St. Elizabeths Hospital to reinforce the 1st Parachute Brigade...

...Only to be savagely beaten back by Kampfgruppe Spindler.

on the left flank. The key objective was to reach Frost before daylight and avoid exposing the vulnerable airborne infantry to enemy troop concentrations defending both sides of the roads. The attack frontage would vary from forty to two hundred yards in width. The British force of less than 1,500 troops would engage nearly five enemy battle groups of equal size, but superior in both heavy weapons and defensive positioning.[18]

The Last Charge of the Light Brigade

The Lower Road
Dobie and Fitch's half-strength battalion attacked along the unreconnoitered flat lower road near the Neder Rhine at 4:00 a.m., fighting hard and making good progress across a forty yard wide front. The lead T and S Companies overran a number of enemy defenses blocking the road until SS Engineers occupying nearby houses and 9th SS Recce guns across the river began raking the column with heavy fire. The SS Engineers, commanded by Captain Hans Möller, fired heavy weapons and dropped hand grenades onto the charging British troops, breaking up the advancing sections into small clusters of troops. As dawn quickly approached, the heavy 20mm and 37mm cannons of Gräbner's surviving 9th SS Recce fired "open sights" with "uninterrupted traverse" from the brickworks

across the Lower Rhine, straddling the slow moving targets with concentrated bursts of high-velocity shells.[19]

Despite such violent opposition from three sides, the British troops valiantly pushed on with bayonet charges, only to be cut down or forced into whatever shelter or slit trenches became available. Within an hour both the 1st and 3rd Battalions were reduced to desperate pockets of survivors fighting to reach Frost's troops at the bridge. By 7:30 a.m. only a handful of exhausted troops remained from the 1st and 3rd Battalion, reaching the old harbor located less than a mile from the Arnhem Bridge.[20] Lt.-Colonel Fitch, commander of the 3rd Battalion, would die while vainly attempting to command an orderly retreat westward towards the Rhine Pavilion.

The Upper Road
At 4:30 a.m. the South Staffordshires, commanded by Lt-Colonel Derek McCardie, had gotten off to a late start along the darkened Utrechtseweg, passing the well-illuminated St. Elizabeths Hospital with its large Red Cross flags as they moved towards the Municipal Museum. Many of the advancing troops in the lead A Company could see the silhouette of the Arnhem Bridge as the surrounding buildings at its northern end burned fiercely. The troops advanced, not realizing that the upper road diverged from the lower road, ef-

The counterattacking 280th Assault Gun Brigade and 9th SS Panzer Grenadiers quickly decimated the ranks of the 2nd South Staffords and 11th Battalion.

The four uncoordinated British battalions were overwhelmed within several hours, and exhausted pockets were forced to surrender.

A number of Red Devils and 9th SS Grenadiers became embroiled in heavy street fighting while withdrawing towards Oosterbeek.

fectively splitting the eastward attack by the four battalions. The South Staffs moved cautiously, but flanking fire from SS Lt. Gropp's Flak Kampfgruppe in houses on the left and Möller's SS Engineers on the right intensified, inflicting heavy casualties. By 6:30 a.m. the Staffs' lead A Company, commanded by Major T. Lane, along with some troops from Headquarters Company, occupied the Municipal Museum and several adjacent buildings.[21]

By 8:00 a.m. any semblance of company or battalion order evaporated, and the advance was halted following counterattacks by Sturmgeschutz III SPs of the 280th Assault Gun Brigade and scores of panzer grenadiers, forcing many South Staffs into nearby buildings along the crest of the Utrechtseweg. British troops in the rear failed to appear following the death of C Company commander Major Phillip Wright along the Utrechtseweg.

At 8:30 a.m. Lt.-Colonel McCardie requested that Lt.-Colonel Lea support his left flank along the southern edge of the railroad marshalling yards. This plan was countermanded by Major General Urquhart, who had recently escaped the confines of the Dutch rowhouse only to discover that his battalions were being fed piecemeal into the battle. McCardie was ordered to pivot the 11th Battalion northwest, occupy the high ground near the Heyenoord-Diependaal, and await the arrival of the 4th Parachute Brigade.[22]

As the 11th Battalion withdrew and turned westwards beyond the railway yard near the hospital, enemy assault guns converged on the besieged South Staffs, firing directly into the museum and adjacent buildings. By 12:30 p.m. the South Staffs were nearly out of ammunition, especially PIAT shells, forcing A Company to disengage and a large number of Staffs to surrender. Sensing that the British attack had lost momentum, Spindler's troops and tanks stormed down the Utrechtseweg, scattering the remaining South Staffs and driving into the rear of the 11th Battalion and support troops facing the wrong direction. By 2:30 p.m. the confused street fighting had ended in a rout of the 2nd South Staffordshires and 11th Battalion, with their combat effectiveness reduced by nearly two-thirds.[23]

By late afternoon the final attempt to reach the 2nd Battalion ended with nearly three hundred casualties and the destruction of four British battalions.[24] Many of the escaping troops retreated westward along the lower road, but nearly a thousand fell into captivity until the end of the war.

The Destruction of the Arnhem Perimeter – September 18-21
Monday night at the northern ramp was fraught with continual enemy infiltration into the eastern side of the British perimeter. Costly tank and infantry attacks were repelled following hours of deadly close quarter fighting using grenades, rifles, and bayonets. Casualties mounted on both sides, and the cellars near the bridge overflowed with wounded British and German troops. Renewed assaults

At times quarter was granted, as 9th SS Panzer Grenadiers rounded up exhausted Red Devils attempting to relieve Frost's forces at the bridge.

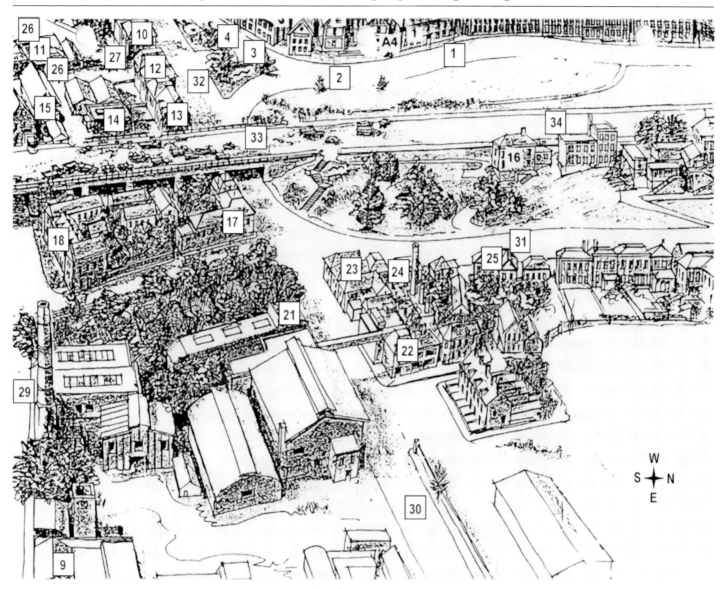

Dispositions of 1st Parachute Brigade Group at the Northern end of the Arnhem Bridge Commanded by Lt.Colonel John Frost

1.	1st Parachute Brigade Defense Platoon
2.	HQ 1st Parachute Brigade
3.	HQ 2nd Parachute Brigade
4.	Mortar Platoon 2nd Parachute Battalion
5.	HQ/Sp Company 2nd Parachute Battalion
6.	HQ/SPCompany 2nd Parachute Battalion
7.	HQ 1st Anti-Tank Battery Royal Artillery
8.	RASC Platoon
9.	B Company 2nd Parachute Battalion
10.	B Company 2nd Parachute Battalion
11.	Platoon A Company 2nd Parachute Battalion
12.	A Company HQ/PL 2nd Parachute Battalion
13.	Platoon A Company 2nd Parachute Battalion
14.	9th Field Company Royal Engineers
15.	Platoon A Company /MMG 2nd Parachute Battalion

16.	C Company HQ/9PL 3rd Parachute Battalion and A Troop 1st Parachute Squadron RE
17.	Platoon A Company 2nd Parachute Battalion
18.	A/B Company 2nd Parachute Battalion
19.	8PL C Company 3rd Parachute Battalion
20.	8PL C Company 3rd Parachute Battalion
21.	8PL C Company 3rd Parachute Battalion
22.	Brigade HQ Defense Platoon
23.	Signals/RASC/Ordnance
24.	Signals/ Royal Engineers
25.	Signals/ Royal Engineers
26.	6 pdr. Anti-Tank gun/jeep park (17th)
27.	6 pdr. Anti-Tank gun (18th/19th)
28.	6 pdr. Anti-Tank gun (18th/19th)
29.	6 pdr. Anti-Tank gun (18th/19th)
30.	6 pdr. Anti-Tank gun (18th/19th)

by Mark III/IV Tanks and self-propelled guns were halted after six-pounder guns destroyed several of them. A number of buildings near the ramp burned fiercely throughout the night, forcing many British troops to relocate to safer positions.

By Tuesday the battle raged as sniping, mortaring, shelling, and infiltration intensified, but any coordinated large-scale enemy attack failed to materialize. Neither the Poles nor XXX Corps arrived to relieve the airborne troops. The exhausted British bravely counterattacked any suspected enemy buildups, hunting down isolated enemy tanks with PIATs and Gammon bombs. By midday General Bittrich sent an emissary to Frost requesting that surrender be arranged, but Frost's somewhat laconic response was simply "tell them to go to hell."[25]

Following a brief respite, street fighting resumed with well-directed heavy artillery and tank fire targeting British strong points along the northern ramp. The commander of the 10th SS Panzer Division, Standartenführer Heinz Harmel, ordered artillery to destroy suspected buildings using high explosives and phosphorous shells, beginning with the top floors and whittling each structure down to rubble. Further attempts to dislodge stubborn British airborne troops intensified with the arrival of King Tiger II tanks attached to the 506th Heavy Tank Battalion. By the end of the day the entire perimeter was aflame, with nearly every structure damaged

or destroyed and thirty percent of Frost's force either dead or wounded. Despite these heavy losses, Frost ordered two platoons to probe westward in the direction of St. Elizabeths Hospital to locate any relief forces attempting to break through the enemy defenses. Instead, the platoons encountered a powerful force of tanks and self-propelled guns attacking eastwards towards the Arnhem perimeter. The approaching armor had previously assisted in the destruction of the four British battalions attempting to reach Frost's positions only 2,000 yards to the west.

By Wednesday most food and ammunition was spent, and only small pockets of British troops remained, seeking protection on the western side of the ramp behind what few defensible buildings or slit trenches could be found within the perimeter. The only movement permitted by each side was British and German medics searching for wounded among the rubble-strewn streets. By mid-afternoon, heavy enemy attacks by armor, infantry, and artillery intensified around the entire perimeter. As the perimeter collapsed Frost finally reached Urquhart at Divisional Headquarters, only to be informed that relief could only arrive from Nijmegen. The tattered force was now reduced to less than two hundred; enemy snipers now prevented effective use of the two remaining anti-tank guns.

It became quite apparent to Harmel that the British were exhausted, so he pressed forward a heavy attack from the east that

It would take weeks before many were captured.

would last until Thursday morning. Frost's troops continued fighting, but the effort was hopeless, with nearly seventy percent of the British defenders eventually killed or wounded. Harmel's tanks and heavy artillery now poured high explosives into the perimeter at will, even firing selectively at individual British troops caught exposed on the streets. Nearly every building inside the collapsing defensive perimeter was ablaze, and by the morning of Thursday, September 21, surviving pockets of British troops broke into small groups attempting to disappear into the debris-clogged streets of western Arnhem.

The battle for the Arnhem Bridge ended as Panzergrenadiers of the 9th SS Hohenstaufen cautiously entered the perimeter, clearing every suspected holdout with tank fire and hand grenades to ensure that its defiant occupants were gone. Eventually the battle exhausted Panzergrenadiers discovered hundreds of wounded British and German troops hidden in the basements of destroyed buildings, including the severely wounded Frost. The last radio transmission sent from Frost's position was "Out of Ammunition, God save the King."[26]

Notes:

[1] Martin Middlebrook, *Arnhem 1944* (Boulder: Westview Press, 1994), p.303.

[2] Ibid., p.143.

[3] Major General John Frost, *A Drop Too Many* (Leo Cooper, Ltd., London, 1994), p. 216.

[4] Ibid., p. 217.

[5] Middlebrook, op.cit., p.287.

[6] Donald Featherstone, *Wargaming Airborne Operations* (A.S. Barnes and Company, New York, 1979), p.179

[7] *By Air to Battle: The Official Account of the British Airborne Divisions* (London: HMSO, 1945), pp.102-103.

[8] Robert J. Kershaw, *It Never Snows in September* (Ramsbury: Crowood Press, 1990), p.60.

[9] Cornelius Ryan, *A Bridge Too Far* Popular Edition (New York, Simon and Shuster, 1974), p. 350.

[10] Middlebrook, op.cit., p.294.

[11] Ibid., p.130.

[12] Ibid., pp.174-175

[13] Cornelius Bauer, *The Battle of Arnhem* (Hodder and Stoughton, 1966, London), p.173.

[14] Middlebrook, p.188.

[15] Ibid., p.188.

[16] Geoffrey Powell, *The Devils Birthday* (London, Leo Cooper, 1993), p.126.

[17] Bauer, op.cit., p.179.

[18] Ibid., pp.174-175.

[19] Kershaw, op.cit., p.169.

[20] Bauer, op.cit., p.180.

[21] Kershaw, op.cit., p.170.

[22] Bauer, op.cit., pp.181-182.

[23] Middlebrook, op.cit., p.209.

[24] Anthony Farrar-Hockley, *Airborne Carpet: Operation Market Garden* (New York: Ballantine Books, 1969), p.140.

[25] Middlebrook, op.cit., p.303.

[26] Ryan, op.cit., p.486

8

"Landing on a Hornets Nest"

"That's live ammunition–and the Tommies have landed."[1]
"The 9ᵗʰ SS Panzer Division Kampfgruppe is immediately to mount concentric attacks against the remainder of British Airborne Division, and annihilate them as soon as possible...."
- SS Lt.-Colonel Walter Harzer[2]

German Forces: II SS Panzer Corps, Division von Tettau, and Wehrkreis VI

Allied intelligence had erroneously concluded that British airborne forces would quickly subdue a relatively weak garrison in Arnhem. Much to Major General Urquhart's surprise, the assault battalions of Brigadier Lathbury's 1st Parachute Brigade encountered stiff opposition east of Wolfheze, compounded by a temporary yet crucial breakdown of airborne divisional command and control. Despite Lt.-Colonel Frost's success in seizing the northern ramp of the Arnhem Bridge, the British airborne forces lost offensive momentum only hours following a near perfect arrival.

Immediately after receiving situation reports of Allied landings by Luftwaffe radar air controllers, Field Marshal Model issued orders to simultaneously check the British and American airborne forces with every scratch formation available until reinforcements arrived from Germany and Central Front of Army Group B. SS General Willi Bittrich, commander of the II SS Panzer Corps, subsequently ordered the 9ᵗʰ SS Hohenstaufen to counter attack British forces assembling near Oosterbeek and the 10ᵗʰ SS Frundsberg to block the American 82ⁿᵈ Airborne Division and British XXX Corps at the Nijmegen bridgehead. Model also ordered General der Flieger Friedrich Christiansen, Commander of German forces in Western Holland, to commence a series of probing counterattacks against British airborne troops near Wofhezen. However, an initial lack of tactical coordination among Christiansen's formations and Bittrich's II SS Panzer Corps—each located on opposite sides of the British airhead—afforded Urquhart's forces valuable time to reorganize and establish a defensive pocket north of the Rhine until the closing week of September 1944.

Model the Defensive Specialist

Field Marshal Model had previously commanded troops on the Eastern Front, where he established a reputation as an effective defensive specialist. Model was well respected by his troops and considered a "soldier's friend"—always visible on the front. As Commander and Chief of Army Group B, Model unknowingly positioned Army Group B Headquarters less than two miles east of

the primary Wolfheze drop zone at the Hotel de Tafelberg in Oosterbeek.[3] Ironically, the location of Army Group B Headquarters was based upon expectations that Allied air landings were imminent, but forty miles to the south near the city of Eindhoven. Only after experiencing first-hand the sound and spectacle of hundreds of Douglas Dakota C-47s flying overhead did the Field Marshal realize that the front lines were now in Arnhem.

Model hastily relocated headquarters eastward, momentarily pausing at General Kussin's Arnhem garrison headquarters to radio the Führer of the invasion before arriving at General Bittrich's II SS Panzer Corps command post in Doetinchem. By the evening of September 17, having distilled a sufficient number of intelligence reports to determine overall Allied intentions, Model ordered every available scratch formation to attack the invasion corridor and landing sites, assigning specific tasks along geographic boundaries. A number of additional formations, mostly artillery and anti-aircraft battalions, would converge on the Allied forces, providing critical support in halting the British Second Army advancing from the south.

The First Parachute Army: Swift and Immediate Action

The First Fallschirmjäger (Parachute) Army, commanded by General der Fallschirmtruppen Kurt Student, was ordered by Model to immediately contain the advancing British XXX, XII, and VIII Corps now crossing the Maas-Escaut bridgehead and destroy the recently landed American 101ˢᵗ Airborne Division north of Eindhoven. Kampfgruppe Chill, located several miles west of the Neerpelt-Arnhem invasion corridor, would attack the thinly stretched British columns advancing along the main road, while the 59ᵗʰ Infantry Division and the 107ᵗʰ Panzer Brigade supported the First Parachute Army in the vicinity of Son-St. Oedenrode.[4] Model had also ordered Regional German Command Wehrkreis VI to send the ad hoc "Corps Feldt" to recapture the high ground occupied by the American 82ⁿᵈ Airborne Division south of Nijmegen. General der Kavallerie Kurt Feldt was commander of this mixed force, which included armor replacements, quick reaction units, "stomach and ear" troops, Fliegerhorst and Luftwaffe NCO training personnel, and the 406th Landesschützen Division.[5] These makeshift units were also expected to hold the Waal River bridges until the arrival of Harmel's 10th SS Panzer Division from Pannerden.

Model eventually shifted the II Fallschirmjäger Corps, commanded by General Eugen Meindl, to support the weaker Wehrkreis VI forces attacking from the Reichswald. Unfortunately for the British First Airborne, Bittrich's II SS Panzer Corps were pre-positioned closely to Arnhem, and Model remained "in situ," commanding nearly every significant tactical movement of German forces. General Christiansen, Armed Forces Commander Netherlands in the west, was ordered by Model to mobilize his crazy quilt mob of regional training and alarm battalions under the command of his subordinate, Generalleutnant Hans von Tettau. Despite a number of severe setbacks Division Tettau would eventually place heavy pressure on the isolated British airborne forces. Insufficient Allied tactical support would allow armor and infantry reinforcements to move quickly westwards, including the 280th Assault Gun Brigade, 506th Heavy Tiger Tank Battalion, and infantry replacements from Wehrkreis VI.[6]

The Wounded Lion - II SS Panzer Corps

The II SS Panzer Corps, commanded by Obergruppenführer und General der Waffen SS Willi Bittrich, included: Kampfgruppe 9th SS Hohenstaufen, commanded by Obersturmbannführer Walther Harzer; and Kampfgruppe 10th SS Frundsberg, commanded by Standartenführer Heinz Harmel.[7] Bittrich had previously ordered Harzer and Harmel to reposition both formations close to Arnhem during the early days of September. Though weakened from previous battles in France, both formations remained relatively formidable fighting brigades, or kampfgruppes, and included a significant number of veterans and logistical personnel who had survived the arduous retreat through France and Belgium. Field Marshal Model had fortuitously planned to replenish both former panzer divisions at the front while retaining the fighting units in a state of local readiness:[8]

> The whole II SS Corps was especially trained over the previous fifteen months via classroom and radio exercises— all directed to countering a landing supported by airborne forces in Normandy. This training benefited us enormously during the Arnhem operation. At the lower end, NCO's and officers were taught to react quickly and make their own decisions. NCO's were taught not to wait until an order came but to decide for themselves what to do. This happened during the fighting (Arnhem) all the time."[9]

9th SS Hohenstaufen

Following the Battle for Normandy, the 9th SS Hohenstaufen Division, now reduced to a weak brigade (kampfgruppe) of 2,500 troops, had relocated in the vicinity of Arnhem during early September for rest and refitting. The division was parceled into nineteen assault ("alarm") companies and positioned within thirty minutes of the city by motor vehicle.[10] The assault units included Haupsturmführer Viktor Gräbner's 400 troop 9th SS Reconnaissance (Recce) Battalion of nearly thirty armored vehicles and a number of self-propelled

20mm and medium artillery guns, but the division lacked heavy tanks and weapons.[11]

The commander of the 9th SS Hohenstaufen, Obersturmbannführer Walther Harzer, reorganized the largest formation in the division, the 9th SS Panzer Grenadier Regiment, into several undersized alarm battalions. These infantry battalions were located in Deventer, Diepensen, and Rheden, the medium armor (mostly Mark III/IVs) in Vorden, and the artillery near Dieren.[12]

On Sunday afternoon September 17 at 1:30 p.m., situation reports of airborne landings began pouring into II SS Panzer Corps Headquarters from the Flugmeldezentrale (aircraft warning center) at Deelen. Without delay Bittrich quickly ordered the 9th SS Hohenstaufen to isolate and eliminate any British airborne troops in the vicinity of Arnhem. Bittrich also placed the II SS Panzer Corps immediately subordinate to the command of Army Group B.[13]

Many officers and NCOs under Bittrich's command were well instructed in anti-airborne warfare and keenly aware that the key to defeating airborne forces was by "driving into the teeth of the landings" before unit cohesion could be established. The sharp end of Hohenstaufen, Gräbner's 9th SS Recce, had quickly assembled and proceeded west along the Ede-Arnhem road to the town of Wolfheze to engage any airborne troops in the vicinity.[14]

As the fighting escalated over the following seventy-two hours, Harzer would command a total of seven battlegroups, equivalent to an oversized British airborne brigade. The formation would include battalion and company level units commanded by: SS Lt.-Colonel Spindler; SS Captain Klaus von Allworden; SS Leutnant Harder; SS Major Brinkman; SS Captain Hans Knaust; SS Captain Sepp Krafft; and SS Captain Viktor Gräbner.

Bittrich ordered the 10th SS Recce, commanded by Major Brinkman, to reinforce the 9th SS Hohenstaufen. Brinkman's force attacked Frost's troops, who were defending the northeastern side of the Arnhem Bridge ramp, with infantry and Mark III/IV medium tanks. Kampfgruppes Von Allworden and Harder attacked the British with infantry from the western side of the ramp. Kampfgruppes Knaust and Gräbner eventually attacked the British positions from the north and south with a combination of tanks, infantry, and armored assault vehicles. Spindler established a blocking line, or "Sperrlinie," in the western suburbs, eventually isolating Frost's forces in the east from the 1st Parachute Brigade attacking through Oosterbeek from the west. By the third day of the battle, Captain Sepp Krafft's companies would link up with Harzer's forces, completing an enveloping box of the British First Airborne Division.[15]

Haupsturmführer Sepp Krafft

As Harzer's forces hurriedly prepared a series of counterblows against airborne troops east of Oosterbeek, two companies of veteran SS troops, commanded by Captain Sepp Krafft, provided a desperately needed interval to slow the forward progress of Brigadier Lathbury's 1st British Parachute Brigade.

Originally under the command of Generalleutnant Hans von Tettau, Captain Krafft's 16th SS Ausbildung und Ersatz (Training and Replacement) Battalion was the largest formation nearest to the British landing zones between Wolfheze and Heelsum during the early hours of the air invasion. After observing British landings west of the town Krafft sent patrols, then established a number of platoon-size roadblocks along the Wolfheze Road, main Ede-Arnhem railway cut, and Wageningen-Arnhem Road. These well-positioned troops and supporting armor eventually disrupted the entire British First Airborne timetable of advancing nearly 2,000 troops to Arnhem by nightfall. Throughout late Sunday afternoon, September 17, Krafft's forces inflicted many casualties—mostly on Brigadier Lathbury's 1st and 3rd Parachute Battalions—with less than 450 troops supported by a handful of mortars, anti-tank guns, and Haupsturmführer (Captain) Viktor Gräbner's armored cars and half-tracks. Krafft's command also ambushed a number of Major Freddie Gough's heavily armed assault jeeps attempting to rush the Arnhem Bridge. Krafft's forces were later reinforced by several companies of the 9th SS Panzergrenadiers and the 213th Nachrichten Company, but eventually withdrew eastwards to strengthen the blocking line formed east of Oosterbeek by 9th SS Lt.-Colonel Spindler.[16]

SS Kampfgruppe Spindler - "Touch Them and They React"[17]
While Krafft's forces hampered the advance of the British 1st Parachute Brigade, the resourceful commander of the 9th SS Armored Artillery Regiment, Lt.-Colonel Ludwig Spindler, formed an effective defensive line further east spanning the Ede-Arnhem Road to-

wards the lower Rhine. Similar in many ways to officers within the ranks of Hohenstaufen, Spindler was a hardened campaigner, decorated with the Iron Cross and well respected by his troops. Throughout the next twenty-four hours, Kampfgruppe Spindler expanded from a handful of several quick-reaction companies to nearly 1,000 troops.[18] The core of Spindler's forces were his two companies, reinforced by several companies of Kampfgruppe Möller, including a number of armored cars and half-tracks.

By Monday, September 18, a continuous north-south defensive *Sperrlinie*, or blocking line, prevented further eastward movement of Lathbury's forces. The defensive line included Krafft's 300 surviving troops anchoring the Ede-Arnhem Road, followed by Gropp's and Möller's troops covering the railway cut and junction to the Utrechtseweg, and Spindler's troops connecting the line to the Rhine. Additional reinforcements sent by Harmel were ordered to attack the British as soon as they arrived in Arnhem from the east.

To maintain command of inexperienced reinforcements from the east, two additional kampfgruppes were formed. These units, equal to weak battalions, included a number of armored vehicles and anti-tank guns. Kampfgruppes von Allworden and Harder were formed from Panzer Regiment 9 and Panzerjäger Abteilung 9 (tank destroyer), and included dismounted tank crewman, support troops, and former naval personnel. Kampfgruppe von Allworden also stopped the 1st and 3rd Parachute Battalions near the Dreyenseweg,

The 10th SS Frundsberg retained a number of formidable Panther tanks east of Arnhem.

Harmel's forces converged on Frost's shrinking perimeter from three sides.

Street fighting was continual, and casualties heavy on both sides.

Street fighting intensified, and each building was attacked individually.

Tuesday ended with Frost commanding less than two hundred and fifty troops, and the remaining four hundred dead, wounded, or missing.

and later attacked the landing zones along the Ede-Arnhem road. Surviving armored vehicles from Gräbner's reconnaissance battalion assisted in attacking surviving pockets of British paratroopers. The combined firepower of armored half-tracks, anti-aircraft guns, and assault vehicles eventually pushed the entire British formation westwards into Oosterbeek.

Kampfgruppe Harder formed a second blocking line from the high ground in central Arnhem, southward through the Nieuwe and Roermands Plein, and down to the Lower Rhine, effectively cutting off Lt. Colonel Frost's troops east of the Arnhem bridge.

In less than twenty-four hours Spindler's eight battalions, reinforced with artillery and armored vehicles, had effectively halted the 1st Parachute Brigade's attempts to capture and reinforce the Arnhem Bridge. Less than a third of the British 1st Airborne Brigade would reach the northern ramp of the Arnhem Bridge. On Tuesday, September 19, four British battalions had conducted a final attempt to penetrate the Sperrlinie near St. Elizabeths Hospital, only to be decimated within a matter of hours by the more powerful and entrenched German defenses. In the northwest, Haupsturmführer Krafft's augmented forces attacked the British 4th Parachute Brigade below Johannahoeve and along the Ede-Arnhem railway line. Krafft's forces would eventually become the "lid on the box" of trapped British airborne forces formed by Division von Tettau in the west and Sperrlinie Spindler in the east.

Spindler's Sperrlinie Facing the British Relief Assault
September 19, 1944

Central Arnhem Breakthrough:

1st British PARA Regt. (1,200 troops)	9thSS Hohenstaufen (1,500 troops, armor)
1st & 3rd PARAS (lower road)	SS Panzergrenadier Regt. 19 (lower road)
2nd South Staffs (Utrechtseweg)	SS Panzergrenadier Regt. 20 (lower road)
11th PARAS (Utrechtseweg)	SS Artillery Regiment (Utrechtseweg)
	SS Eng. Battalion Möller (Utrechtseweg)
	SS Reconnaissance 9 (brickworks)
	Kampfgruppe Groppe (marshalling yards)
	Kampfgruppe Harder Assault Brigade 280 (StuGIII 75/105mm)

Northern Arnhem Breakthrough:

British (450 troops)	German (900 troops, armor)
156th, 10th Parachute Brigade	SS Training/Replacement Battalion Krafft
7th KOSB	Kampfgruppe Bruhn
	Kampfgruppe Allworden (partial)

Frost's exhausted troops fought until they ran out of ammunition or were overwhelmed by the converging forces of the 9th SS Panzer Brigade.

One SS Panzer Grenadier officer was overheard saying, "Good fight Tommy."

Defeat of Frost's Troops at Arnhem

Almost simultaneously with British air landings near Wolfheze, General Bittrich issued a series of countermeasures, ordering Gräbner's 9th SS Reconnaissance Battalion towards Nijmegen and Haupsturmführer Brinkman's 10th SS Reconnaissance towards the Arnhem Bridge. Much to Bittrich's surprise, Frost's troops used the lower road and reached Arnhem Bridge by late evening, occupying key defensive positions within ten hours after landing.

Night skirmishes with Frost's forces were fraught with wild and deadly confusion. SS companies were fed piecemeal into the formidable British defensive perimeter, resulting in heavy casualties. Several of Kampfgruppe Brinkman's armored cars had prevented Frost's advancing platoons from capturing the southern ramp, but the main bunker defending the northern ramp caught fire and exploded. Numerous German transport vehicles were destroyed while attempting to cross the main span. Other vehicles were riddled along the streets below the bridge as quick-reaction Hohenstaufen companies unwittingly entered the deadly British killing zone. SS Captain Heinz Euling's forces arrived at the northern ramp, encountering intensive small arms and anti-tank gunfire from the British. Frost's airborne troops appeared to fire from every building, pushing Euling's infantry away from the perimeter until daylight. By the close of Sunday evening, wrecked and abandoned vehicles blocked the main roadway and streets below the northern ramp.

On Monday, September 18, the situation remained confused and the size of the British bridgehead unknown. Bittrich ordered a series of coordinated attacks, with Brinkman's forces approaching from both the north and east reinforced by four companies of "convalescent" infantry and the obsolete Mark III and Mark IV Panzers commanded by SS Captain Hans-Peter Knaust. Knaust—invalided with a wooden leg yet tenacious in battle—was emblematic of the strong leadership prevalent among many veteran elite German commanders. Meanwhile, a company of the 21st SS Panzergrenadier Regiment attacked the perimeter, while divisional artillery engaged individual buildings sheltering the British defenders.[19]

Street fighting was reminiscent of close quarter fighting in Russia

The battle savagely continued, as every house defended by the British was attacked individually with explosives, followed by infantry and armor attacks. Casualties were heavy on both sides as the British forces held and the German attacks slowly melted away. The highpoint of the valiant but outnumbered British defense was the destruction of a dozen 9th SS Recce vehicles returning from Nijmegen. The column was nearly wiped out, and Gräbner was killed during the fighting.

By Tuesday, September 19, coordination among the SS battalions improved as infantry and panzers methodically squeezed the British perimeter from three directions. Bittrich's forces cautiously moved amid destroyed buildings and burned out vehicles, grinding down the exhausted pocket of British defenders. Additional German reinforcements arrived from the west following the destruction of the four-battalion British relief force near St. Elizabeths Hospital. Heavy artillery arrived, including Flak Brigade "von Swoboda," taking an additional toll on British strong points and compressing the perimeter to half its original size. Infantry attacks followed the systematic destruction of British strongholds, with the axis of German attacks running parallel to the northern ramp along the Eusebius Binnen and Buiten Singel. It became acutely apparent to Bittrich that Frost's forces were low on anti-tank PIAT and six-pounder shells, allowing heavy tanks to cross the Arnhem Bridge from the southern approaches. Assault Gun Brigade 280, which had earlier repulsed the British along the Utrechtseweg, attacked Frost's forces from the west.[20] The day ended with Frost's command numbering less than two hundred and fifty troops; the remaining four hundred were dead, wounded, or captured.

By Wednesday, September 20, the operation became a combination of mopping-up efforts against small pockets of British resistance and capturing evaders. The British commander Frost did not formally surrender, and individual British troops spent every rifle shell available until overwhelmed by Bittrich's troops. Many buildings now lay in ruins, and nearly every street within a quarter mile of the bridge was rendered impassible.

On Thursday, September 21, the battle for the Arnhem Bridge ended as Knaust's Mark III Panzers rumbled across the Arnhem Bridge towards Nijmegen and Elst. Several hours following Knaust's crossing, the Allies captured the Nijmegen Bridge. Lt.-Colonel Frost's seven hundred troops had sustained a bridgehead for nearly four days, holding up an entire panzer division while futilely awaiting the arrival of Horrocks' XXX Corps.

German Attack of British 1st PARA Brigade – Arnhem Bridge: September 18 / 21

1st British PARA Regt. (650 troops)	10thSS Frundsberg (1,500 troops, armor)
2nd Parachute Battalion (9/17-21)	KGr SS Brinkman (east 9/18) – 6 x Panthers
3rd Parachute Battalion (9/17-21)	SS Artillery Regiment (north 9/18)
1st Parachute Brigade HQ	506th Heavy Tank Company (9/18) – Tiger II
1st Squadron/R.E.	
1st Airlanding A/T Troop	

KGr SS Knaust (north 9/18) 4 comp, 8 tanks

250 Light, RASC	SS Euling Battalion (north 9/18, withdrawn)
9th Field Company	SS von Swoboda Bn (north 9/18) –
Glider Pilots, Recce, R.A.,Observers 40X88/20mm	SS Panzer Grenadier Regt 21 (9/17-19)
	KGr SS AA9th Gräbner (south 9/18) SS Recce (north 9/18) - 30 armored vehicle
	KGr SS Euling Coy. (9/18)

Mielke's Tank Company moves towards the northern ramp.

10th SS Frundsberg

The 10th SS Division, commanded by SS Brigadeführer (Colonel) Heinz Harmel, was reduced to a brigade (kampfgruppe) of less than 3,000 troops following the Battle for Normandy. By early September the remnants of the division were withdrawn into a rear guard position northeast of Arnhem. Colonel Harmel retained a core of divisional troops near the town of Ruurlo, three weak Panzer Grenadier battalions at Deventer, Diepensen, and Rheden, a company of Mark IV tanks near Vorden, and artillery in Dieren.[21] The Frundsberg Division was also well versed in anti-airborne operations and reacted aggressively when engaging British troops. Harmel had redistributed his limited resources into quick reaction companies located along the Arnhem-Velp-Zutphen road.[22] Throughout the entire Market Garden campaign, small battle groups from Frundsberg continuously attacked American and British positions along the corridor between Veghel and Overloon with infantry and armor.

On Sunday September 17, General Bittrich ordered Harmel to occupy the Nijmegen Bridge, secure a bridgehead south of the Waal, and counterattack the American 82nd Airborne Division. The key objective was to prevent a linkup between the British First Airborne Division and the vanguard of XXX Corps. However, reaching Nijmegen remained a difficult task, since British airborne troops blocked the main roadway at Arnhem by late evening.

On Tuesday, September 18, Harmel ordered SS Captain Reinhold to oversee the movement of armor and troops southeast of Arnhem at the Pannerden ferry crossing, while a number of 10th SS Battalions attacked Frost's blocking force at the northern ramp. The effect of Frost's troops commanding the main highway remained apparent, as 10th SS engineers slowly struggled to construct ferries capable of carrying 40 ton Mark IV Panzer tanks and heavy vehicles across the Lower Rhine. Movement was confined at night because of heavy Allied fighter-bomber activity. As the ferries reached the southern banks of the Lower Rhine, troops and vehicles immediately sped towards the Nijmegen Bridge to prevent the XXX Corps linkup with the American 101st Airborne Division.

Defense of Nijmegen

Hours following the arrival of the American 82nd Airborne Division, the first German troops—a company of the 10th SS engineers commanded by SS Captain Karl Euling—arrived at Nijmegen on bicycles and transports. By midday a battalion of five hundred SS troops commanded by SS Captain Reinhold reinforced the southern approaches of the main Nijmegen road and rail bridges.[23] A series of costly company-level attacks ensued at the southern end of the Nijmegen Bridge ramp as newly arrived German troops clashed with the American 508th Parachute Infantry Regiment of the 82nd

General Tettau haphazardly assembled every soldier and vehicle available, including bicycles, buses, fire trucks, and captured French tanks previously held in reserve.

Mobile flak intensified around the British perimeter, inflicting heavy casualties among the slow moving resupply aircraft.

Airborne Division. The German defenses stiffened as batteries of 10th SS artillery commanded by SS Lt.-Colonel Zonnenstahl fired onto suspected concentrations of American paratroopers. Several hundred yards south of the road bridge a firm semicircular defensive base was established, anchored at Hunner and Kronenburger Parks. After a series of costly attacks, the American paratroopers withdrew to await the arrival of additional infantry and armor support. During this lull several Mark IV SPs and towed 88mm flak guns arrived and were sited across the Maas River.

By September 19, Harmel's forces had established a firm defensive cordon several hundred yards south of the Nijmegen road and rail bridge. However, the strength of the Allied forces improved as XXX Corps linked up with Gavin's 82nd Airborne Division at the southern edge of Nijmegen.

On the afternoon of September 20, Colonel Vandervoort's 2nd Battalion/505th PIR, combined with a troop of Grenadier Guards tanks and infantry, attacked the main traffic circle south of Hunner Park. Further west, several dozen assault boats began crossing the Waal as smoke shells fired by XXX Corps exploded on the northern banks. Harmel's troops poured 20mm cannon, mortar, and artillery shells onto the little fleet, which disappeared in the smoke

and haze. Eventually half of the assault boats, commanded by Major Julian Cooke, reached the north shore. The miraculous success of the American crossing unhinged the exhausted defenders, already under heavy pressure from simultaneous attacks against the southern ramp of the Nijmegen Bridge. By early evening the American troops had seized Fort Hof van Holland and Oosterhout on the northern banks, and the Grenadier Guards crossed the Nijmegen Bridge. Further attempts to detonate the bridge failed, and the remaining artillery defenses were destroyed by effective Allied counterbattery fire. Hundreds of German troops were slain while attempting to flee north across the railway bridge. By late evening both the road and rail bridge were captured, the Groesbeek Heights secured by the 82nd Airborne, and the routed German forces rushing northwards towards Arnhem.

On the morning of September 21, Harmel's new defensive line was established near the town of Elst, situated in an area several miles north of Nijmegen called the Betuwe. Much to Harmel's surprise XXX Corps lost momentum, providing Harmel additional time to strengthen positions near the town. Over the next several days the defenses were reinforced by the arrival of Tiger tanks and infantry, contributing to the eventual Allied stalemate and withdrawal of surviving British First Airborne forces across the Lower Rhine.

Bittrich sent Panzerkompagnie 224, which included six captured French Renault Char Bs.

Von Tettau's troops were unpleasantly surprised by several deadly 17-pound anti-tank guns defending the landing sites.

Division von Tettau

As Bittrich's II SS Panzer Corps regained the initiative and halted the British 1st Parachute Brigade east of Oosterbeek, a number of weaker German troop concentrations west of Wolfheze remained at a virtual standstill. Wermacht Generaleutenant Hans von Tettau now commanded a mixed force of varied quality, including several SS training units, Schiffstammabteilung (naval manning) companies, Fliegerhorst (former Luftwaffe) ground personnel, and coastal artillerymen without their heavy guns.[24] Many of von Tettau's troops were "voluntarily" collected from reception centers located at key water and road crossings. A large number of these forces were of low fighting caliber, characteristic of the weak enemy troops expected in previous Second British Army intelligence estimates.

Throughout the first crucial twenty-four hours, several of "Division" von Tettau's elite formations—including SS Colonel Hans Lippert's NCO School "Arnheim," SS Captain Krafft's 16th SS Supply and Replacement Battalion, and SS Captain Helle's Dutch SS Surveillance Battalion—would conduct a series of costly but successful attacks against British glider and parachute forces. Their objective was to seal off the landing sites and eventually form the left side of a defensive box surrounding the British forces.

Scraping the Barrel

"Division Tettau" was hastily assembled for battle employing any vehicular means available, including bicycles, horse drawn carts, buses, and confiscated fire trucks. Despite attempts by veteran officers and NCOs to establish good fighting order, one witness best described von Tettau's counteroffensive against the British as "more like Napoleon's retreat from Moscow than a military operation."[25] However, Field Marshal Model would supplement von Tettau with additional troops and armor, including battalion reserves from Training and Replacement Regiment "Herman Göring," the Waffen SS Police School, and Panzerkompanie 224 of the II Panzer Corps.[26]

Several hours following the British landings near Wolfheze, von Tettau ordered Dutch SS-Wachbattalion 3, commanded by SS Captain Helle, to engage the airlanding forces east of Ede along the Ede-Arnhem road. The force of less than two hundred troops was composed of Nazi sympathizers and musicians. Helle's two companies crossed the Ede Arnhem road onto Ginkel Heath (Drop Zone Y), only to suffer heavy casualties inflicted by the 7th Kings Own Scottish Borders.[27] The Borders, commanded by Lt.-Colonel Payton Reid, were responsible for defending the landing and drop zones until the second wave arrival of Brigadier Hackett's 4th Parachute Brigade.[28]

The Plan to Attack the Landing Sites

As Helle's companies unsuccessfully attacked the British 1st Airlanding Brigade near Ginkel Heath, Generalleutnant von Tettau continued plans for a six-battalion attack against a significantly smaller yet determined British force within a six square mile triangular shaped area of Ginkel Heath-Renkum-Wolfheze. On the morning of September 18, "Division Tettau" attacked the 1st British Airlanding Brigade, which included the 7th KOSB at Ginkel Heath (Drop Zone Y) and 1st Borders at Renkum-Heelsum-Wolfheze (Drop Zone/Landing Zone X and LZZ). Brigadier Hicks, acting British

First Airborne Division commander, had weakened the 1st Airlanding Brigade by ordering half of the 2nd Battalion South Staffordshires eastwards to assist the 1st Parachute Brigade fighting through Oosterbeek. The 1st and 3rd Parachute Battalions were unable to break through Lippert's Sperrlinie, which was blocking attempts to reach Frost's 2nd Parachute Battalion at Arnhem. Colonel Lippert's SS NCO Regiment would spearhead the eastern attack towards the drop zones defended by the 1st Borders. The Fliegerhorst (Luftwaffe) "infantry," commanded by Major Liebsch, would support Lippert by advancing from the east towards the center of DZX near Wolfheze while the 10th Naval Manning Battalion and 184th Artillery Regiment attacked Renkum Heath. Eberwün's SS Battalion would advance from the town of Bennekom towards the northwest corner of LZZ.

Capturing the British Landing Zones

In the early dawn hours of Monday, September 18, SS Battalion Helle attacked the 7th KOSB from the northwest along the Ede-Arnhem road, while SS Kampfgruppe Lippert's forces attacked the center of DZX and LZZ. Lippert's forces penetrated the western edges of Renkum and Heelsum, eventually breaking through the thinly held British defenses onto Landing Zone Z northeast of Heelsum. Despite valiant resistance by the exhausted 1st Borders, by 3:00 p.m. the naval battalion captured the vital brickworks at Renkum.

SS Captain Lippert's veteran troops made considerable progress, but the center of the attack at DZX by the Fliegerhorst Battalion lost momentum after sustaining heavy casualties. Lippert reinvigorated the faltering attack by valiantly driving his Kubelwagen onto DZX, firing signal flares, confusing the British defenders, and inspiring the inexperienced infantry into storming the 1st Border positions.[29]

The battle for the landing sites intensified as the 4th Parachute Brigade descended onto Ginkel Heath in the middle of the afternoon melee, minutes following Lt.-Colonel Payton-Reid bayonet charge against SS Battalion Helle. The heroic charge by Payton-Reid and the arrival of additional reinforcements disrupted Helle's attacking forces, resulting in a rout. Despite the confusion on the ground, Brigadier Hackett's 4th Parachute Brigade quickly assembled and proceeded to the originally planned rendezvous points. The second echelon of the 1st Air Landing Brigade Group also arrived at LZS and LZX.

By early evening the British would conduct a fighting withdraw from the three landing areas, only to be pursued by Tettau's forces. Hundreds of gliders were abandoned, including equipment, jeeps, and supplies. Brigadier Hackett's 4th Parachute Brigade, which now included the exhausted 7th KOSB along with the recently landed 156th and 10th Parachute Battalions, conducted a fighting withdrawal east of Wolfheze along the Ede-Arnhem Road beyond the Polish Landing Brigade (LZL) area. The 1st Borders eventually reached the Oosterbeek pocket with heavy losses. Hackett's 4th Parachute Brigade conducted a series of company-level engagements with the now entrenched Sperrlinie to the east along the Dreyenseweg, also suffering heavy losses before withdrawing southward into the newly formed Oosterbeek pocket.

By the end of Tuesday, September 19, General von Tettau's command numbered ten battalions facing two exhausted British 1st Airlanding Battalions, two Parachute Battalions, and various divisional support troops

Destruction of the 4th Parachute Brigade

As Division von Tettau's forces pursued the withdrawing British forces from the west, Brigadier Hackett's 4th Parachute Brigade marched eastwards toward the Wolfheze railroad crossing. Hackett conducted a series of costly company level attacks against Lippert's Sperrlinie along the Dreyenseweg between the Ede-Arnhem Road and the Ede-Arnhem Railroad, resulting in heavy casualties. Krafft's seemingly ubiquitous 16th SS Training and Supply Battalion attacked from the north, taking an additional toll on Hackett's forces. Krafft's two companies, which had previously halted the advance of Lathbury's 1st Parachute Brigade twenty-four hours earlier, had expanded to nearly five hundred troops under Lippert's command and were repositioned along the Ede-Arnhem Road.

Turning Point

By the end of September 19th, all surprise and initiative expected of Market Garden was lost. Field Marshal Model's forces had surrounded the British First Airborne Division, effectively outnumbering Urquhart's by nearly three to one. Generalleutnant von Tettau's ten battalions in the west and Harmel's eight battalions in the east had slowly converged on Urquhart's weakened equivalent of five battalions. The British were isolated into two pockets: boxed-in by von Tettau's forces on the left; Lippert's forces on the right; and Krafft's augmented forces closing the lid on the box. Frost's forces at the Arnhem Bridge were eventually eliminated by Thursday morning, September 21, and the remaining Oosterbeek Pocket evacuated by September 26.

VICTORIA CROSS: Flight Lt. David S.A. Lord. Despite knowledge of his impending doom, Lt. David Lord made a second low level pass over the drop zone with a furiously burning engine. He completed delivery of the much-needed supplies on a straight and level course at 500 feet. Seconds later, Lt. Lord's burning wings collapsed, and the plane crashed and exploded.

Estimated German Casualties September 17-26[30]

Arnhem-Oosterbeek:

Units	Troops	Casualties
Von Tettau	8,200	17%
9th SS Hohenstaufen	2,700	51%

Market Garden Corridor:

Units	Troops	Casualties
Kampfgruppe Walther (w/107 Pz. Bdg.von Malzahan)	3,000	25%
10th SS Frundsberg	3,000	25%
Corps Feldt	6,000	25%
59th Infantry Division (Poppe)	4,000	25%
Total [31]	26,860	24%

Estimated German Strength at Arnhem (9/17- 9/24, 1944)[32]

SS Units Battalions/Commanders	Troops	Vehicles/Armor/Heavy Guns	Total
Helle	600		
9th SS Recce/Gräbner	400	Sdkfz 232, 222 armored car Sdkfz 250/9, 251/9 half-tracks transports	40
Petersen	250		
Knaust - Heavy Tank Detachment	200+	Panzer III, IV, transports Tiger I	25
Krafft	600	transports, 81mm mortars, 75mm PAK 40 anti-tank guns 20mm anti-aircraft	20
Müller	120		
Panzerjäger	120		
9th SS Headquarters	280		
9th Engineering/Artillery/Support	250+		
10th SS – Brinkman	700	Sdkfz 250, 251/9, 251 half-tracks Sdkfz 232 20mm armored car transports, 120 mm mortars Tiger II- Heavy Tank Detachment	50
Regiments/Commanders			
NCO School – Lippert	3,000		
Lt. Col. Ludwig Spindler	1,000+	Sdkfz 251 half-tracks, 20mm S.P.AA, light armor, transports Heavy 88 AA, Self propelled quad 20mm	100
- Assault Brigade	280	StuG III (75mmand 105mm)	
Wermacht/Attached Units Division/Commanders			
Von Tettau	3,000+		5
Total Forces	**9,820**		**200**

Notes:

1. Robert J. Kershaw, *It Never Snows in September* (Ramsbury: The Crowood Press, 1990), p. 75.
2. Ibid., p. 263.
3. Cornelius Bauer, *The Battle for Arnhem* (London: Hodder and Stoughton Ltd., 1966), p. 49. *Bauer somewhat sardonically describers Model's departure in a state of panic dropping his personal belongings on the steps of the Hotel Tafelberg while rushing towards his awaiting staff car.*
4. Kershaw, op.cit., p.76.
5. Ibid., p.37.
6. Ibid., p.77.
7. *The term Kampfgruppe was used to describe a weak brigade of less than 3,000 troops and heavy equipment.*
8. Tieke, Wilhelm, *In the Firestorm of the Last Years of the War: II SS-Panzerkorps with the 9.and 10. SS-Division "Hohenstaufen" and "Frundsberg"* (Winnipeg, J.J. Fedoricz, 1999), p.272.
9. Kershaw, op.cit., pp.38-40. *Comments from interview with Heinz Harmel October 27, 1987.*
10. Ibid., p.41.
11. Ibid., p.327.
12. Ibid., p.34.
13. Tielke, op.cit., pp.231-233.
14. Kershaw, op.cit., p.73
15. Geoffrey Powell, *The Devils Birthday* (London, Leo Cooper, 1993), p.142.
16. Cornelius Bauer, *The Battle of Arnhem* (Hodder and Stoughton, 1966, London), p.192-193.
17. Powell, op.cit., p.141. *Brigadier Hackett's description of the swiftness and violence of German troops against his 4th Parachute Brigade.*
18. Ibid., p.339.
19. Kershaw, op.cit. , p.126.
20. Stephen Badsey, *Arnhem 1944: Operation Market Garden* (London: Osprey Publishing Ltd., 1993), p.56.
21. Kershaw, op.cit., p.40.
22. Ibid., p.43.
23. Geoffrey Powell, op.cit., p.144.
24. Ibid., p.110.
25. Kershaw, op cit., p.112.
26. Robert Jackson, op.cit. ,p.86. *The assaulting tank company was a II SS Panzer Corps reserve composed of six 32 Ton French Renault Char B's mounting a 47mm and 75mm gun. All six were knocked out immediately near DZ/LZ X by the 1st Airlanding Brigade's a six and seventeen pound anti-tank gun.*
27. *The Borders included Companies: A, B, D, and Headquarters.*
28. Bauer, op.cit. , pp.111-112.
29. Ibid., p.86.
30. Kershaw, op.cit., pp.339-340.
31. Ibid., p.340. *Total estimates vary from low 6,000 to as high as 9,000.*
32. *Some estimates based upon information provided in Robert Kershaw's It Never Snows in September, (pp. 323 - 340) and Colin Rumford, RAPID FIRE - Operation Market Garden (Raventhorp Retail, Wiberfoss, 1999), (pp.62-65). Some estimates were adjusted based upon the author's interpretation of units present. The intent of this table is to allow the reader to better appreciate the formidable strength of German Forces present near Arnhem.*

9

Stalemate and Withdrawal: "Der Hexenkessel"[1]

"Just a few minutes ago the fighter cover showed up and right behind them came those lovely supply planes which you can hear up above us right now. Yesterday and this morning our supplies came and they were dropped in the wrong place. The enemy got them but now these planes have come over and dropped them right over us. Everybody is cheering and clapping. They just can't give vent to their feelings about what a wonderful site this is. All those bundles and heavy parachute packages are coming down all around us through the trees and bouncing on the ground. The men are running out to get them and you have no idea what this means to us to see this ammunition and this food coming down here where the men can get them."

"They're such fighters if they could only get the stuff to fight with..."

- Stanley Maxted, BBC
Oosterbeek, September 20, 1944[2]

September 19-25

Within forty-eight hours of arrival, only two thirds of the British First Airborne Division remained following a series of continual but unsuccessful attacks eastwards along the Utrechtseweg and Amsterdamseweg by the 1st and 4th Parachute Brigades. Nearly every battalion had sustained heavy losses in men and equipment, except for the 1st Borders defending the western perimeter. Many senior commanders and NCOs were killed, wounded, or missing, and brigade integrity severely strained. Major General Urquhart was missing until Tuesday; Brigadier Lathbury lay wounded somewhere in Arnhem; and Brigadiers Hicks and Hackett quarreled amongst themselves while the disintegrating battalions were pounded hopelessly against an impregnable enemy at key junctures leading into Arnhem. Division von Tettau's unceasing attacks compressed Brigadier Hackett's 4th Parachute Brigade from the direction of Wolfheze and the Dreijenseweg into the British defensive pocket anchored by the Hartenstein Hotel. Following the Tuesday morning destruction of the 1st Parachute Brigade, Hohenstaufen armor and infantry pursued the four exhausted British battalions along the Oosterbeek Laag. Despite previous Dutch warnings of enemy roadblocks and domination of the high ground leading to Arnhem, acting Divisional Commander Hicks followed orders to march seven of nine available airborne battalions into the teeth of an overwhelming enemy.

The original airborne plan of seizing and holding Arnhem was no longer tenable, as Lt.-Colonel Frost's command of the northern ramp ended late Wednesday evening. Major General Urquhart, an eyewitness to the destruction of the 1st Parachute Brigade, would regain command of his shattered division following an enforced absence of nearly thirty-six hours.

Destruction of the Airborne Relief Battalions

By Late Tuesday afternoon, enemy firepower and seemingly unlimited reserves routed the four-battalion relief force attempting to reach Frost's troops at Arnhem. Of the nearly 2,000 airborne attackers, only a fistful of South Staffords completed the bloody trek along the Utrechtseweg, culminating in a last stand within the shell scarred walls of the Municipal Museum.

The final British thrust towards the Arnhem had ended, and the now exhausted groups, whose many officers and NCOs were killed or wounded, retreated westward along the lower road into the Oosterbeek defensive perimeter. As small bands of leaderless troops arrived, Lt.-Colonel W.F.K. Thompson, Commander of the 1st Airlanding Light Regiment, began collecting and repositioning them several hundred yards east of his artillery positions near the Oosterbeek-Laag Church.[3] Brigadier Hicks later sent Major Richard Londsdale, deputy commander of the 11th Battalion, to assume tactical command of the returning 2nd South Staffords' 1st, 3rd, and 11th Battalions, naming the new command "Londsdale Force."[4]

"Der Hexenkessel." Airborne troops dig in around the once pristine Hartenstein, now damaged by incoming artillery, mortar, and sniper fire.

XXX Corps' guns were now protecting the British airborne perimeter.

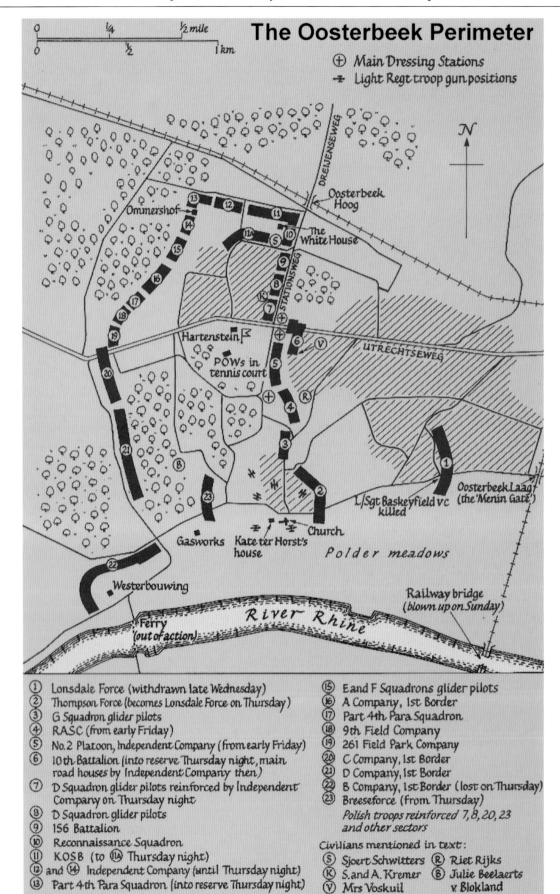

The Oosterbeek Perimeter

⊕ Main Dressing Stations
⌁ Light Regt troop gun positions

① Lonsdale Force (withdrawn late Wednesday)
② Thompson Force (becomes Lonsdale Force on Thursday)
③ G Squadron glider pilots
④ R.A.S.C (from early Friday)
⑤ No.2 Platoon, Independent Company (from early Friday)
⑥ 10th Battalion (into reserve Thursday night, main road houses by Independent Company then)
⑦ D Squadron glider pilots reinforced by Independent Company on Thursday night
⑧ D Squadron glider pilots
⑨ 156 Battalion
⑩ Reconnaissance Squadron
⑪ K.O.S.B (to ⑭ Thursday night)
⑫ and ⑭ Independent Company (until Thursday night)
⑬ Part 4th Para Squadron (into reserve Thursday night)
⑮ E and F Squadrons glider pilots
⑯ A Company, 1st Border
⑰ Part 4th Para Squadron
⑱ 9th Field Company
⑲ 261 Field Park Company
⑳ C Company, 1st Border
㉑ D Company, 1st Border
㉒ B Company, 1st Border (lost on Thursday)
㉓ Breeseforce (from Thursday)
Polish troops reinforced 7, 8, 20, 23 and other sectors

Civilians mentioned in text:
Ⓢ Sjoert Schwitters   Ⓡ Riet Rijks
Ⓚ S. and A. Kremer   Ⓑ Julie Beelaerts
Ⓥ Mrs Voskuil   v Blokland

The returning strength of the 1ˢᵗ Parachute Brigade to Oosterbeek [5]:

2ⁿᵈ South Staffords:	100 troops
1ˢᵗ Parachute Battalion:	120 troops
3ʳᵈ Parachute Battalion:	46 troops
11ᵗʰ Parachute Battalion:	150 troops

Destruction of the 4ᵗʰ Parachute Brigade

According to the original airborne plan, Brigadier J.W. Hackett's 4ᵗʰ Parachute Brigade, which included the 156ᵗʰ and 10ᵗʰ Parachute Battalions and the recently attached 7ᵗʰ KOSB, would advance northeast along the Ede-Arnhem railroad towards the high ground near a bisecting road called the Dreijenseweg. Brigadier Hackett ordered the 156ᵗʰ Parachute Battalion to capture the high ground near a rise called the Koepel while the 10ᵗʰ Battalion protected its flank by holding the junction near the Ede-Arnhem road and the northern end of the Dreijenseweg. Meanwhile, the 7ᵗʰ KOSB would protect Landing Zone L near Johannahoeve Farm until the safe arrival of the 1ˢᵗ Polish Independent Parachute Brigade Group's anti-tank guns and support troops.[6] The Polish gliders would arrive hours behind schedule because of poor weather in England. Unfortunately, the additional time required to defend the landing zone from heavy

enemy counterattacks sapped the remaining strength of the 7ᵗʰ KOSB.

After advancing eastwards to within a half-mile of the Dreijenseweg, the 10ᵗʰ and 156ᵗʰ Parachute Battalions encountered heavy arms fire from SS-Kampfgruppe Spindler's augmented forces. Almost simultaneously General von Tettau's three infantry battalions, supported by armor, attacked the rear of Hackett's advance from Wolfheze and Renkum. After quickly recognizing the impossibility of piercing the now formidable defensive barrier in the east while von Tettau's forces threatened his rear, the recently returned Urquhart ordered Hackett to disengage and withdraw southwards across the Ede-Arnhem railroad and take positions inside the Airborne Division perimeter at Oosterbeek. Major General Urquhart had expected the repositioned 4ᵗʰ Parachute Brigade to eventually move eastwards and break through to the Arnhem Bridge.

By early afternoon the 10ᵗʰ Parachute Battalion disengaged from heavy fighting along the Dreijenseweg and retreated across Landing Zone L, protected by the 7ᵗʰ KOSB. Shortly later the rumble of oncoming aircraft was heard, and within minutes dozens of Horsas circled and began descending onto the landing areas carrying Polish troops and anti-tank guns. The defenseless gliders were suddenly attacked by scores of enemy Messerschmitt Me 109s, and surviving gliders landed in a maelstrom of heavy weapons fire and

Early Tuesday morning the reinforced 1st Parachute Brigade conducted a two pronged advance along the Utrechtseweg and the exposed river road.

burning fields, resulting in heavy casualties and considerable loss of equipment. Confusion reigned as two British battalions and Hackett's 4th Brigade Headquarters became intermingled with the recently arrived Poles and SS Captain Sepp Krafft's companies swarming across the landing zone. At the southeast corner of the landing zone tragedy occurred as British soldiers mistook the Poles for the enemy and opened fire. The surviving but shocked Poles returned "frenzied fire" in every direction, even at a platoon of 7th KOSB. Difficulties in identifying friends from foes were further compounded by the language barrier among the Allied airborne troops.[7]

As the debacle at Landing Zone L unfolded, the 4th Parachute Brigade fighting withdrawal devolved into a rout of several British companies with large-scale surrenderings and loss of heavy equipment. Companies A and B of the 7th KOSBs became isolated in the surrounding heavy woods and eventually surrendered after exhausting all ammunition and sustaining heavy losses among commanding officers and NCOs.

Surviving companies of the 10th Battalion and 156th Battalion struggled to reach the Wolfheze crossing, holding defensive positions until a number of transports and guns had crossed the railway.

Other airborne troops crowded through a tunnel under the Ede-Arnhem railway embankment a half-mile east of the Wolfheze crossing. Less than 100 troops of the original 10th Parachute Battalion escaped into the Hartenstein perimeter by late Wednesday evening. After defending the Wolfheze crossing, troops of the 156th Parachute Battalion and 4th Parachute Brigade Headquarters attempted to reach the Hartenstein perimeter, but heavy fire by Kampgruppe Lippert's forces in the west and Eberwein and Krafft's reinforced battalions from the east inflicted a heavy toll on the diminishing forces.[8] Only a handful of troops reached the Hartenstein perimeter following a desperate charge, and by late evening the 4th Parachute Brigade mustered less than 300 troops.[9]

The 1st Airlanding Brigade
The 1st Airlanding Brigade—previously stripped of the 2nd South Staffordshires and 7th KOSBs—now retained only the 1st Border Battalion, but the unit retreated in good order eastward towards the Oosterbeek perimeter. The 1st Borders eventually held nearly the entire western Oosterbeek perimeter, which stretched one and a half miles towards the Lower Rhine, reinforced with troops of the 4th Parachute Squadron and Royal Engineers.

The battalions immediately became entangled between the heavy crossfire of SS Kampfgruppe Spindler on the upper road and surviving 9th SS Recce vehicles hidden between the brickworks on the southern banks of the Neder Rhine

Consolidating the Pocket

The British First Airborne Division was now isolated against the Lower Rhine at Oosterbeek. The defensive pocket was anchored by the 1st Airlanding Light Regiment near the Oosterbeek Laag Church in the southeast, the Westerbouwing in the southwest, and positions several hundred yards north and east of the Division Headquarters at the Hartenstein. The Heveadorp Ferry was located only several hundred yards to the southwest, where the 1st Polish Airborne Brigade was expected to arrive. Urquhart's decision to establish this static pocket sealed the fate of Frost's troops at the Arnhem Bridge and ended any further offensive operations.[10]

By Wednesday, September 20, Major General Urquhart concluded that the only reserves capable of stopping Kampfgruppe Lippert's armor and infantry attacks from the east were Lt.-Colonel Sheriff Thompson's Light Regiment, some reconnaissance troops, and sections from the Glider Pilots Regiment dug in near the Oosterbeek Laag Church. Urquhart reorganized his remaining command of 3,000 officers and men into two forces: the northwest and western perimeter commanded by Brigadier Hicks; and northeast and east commanded by Brigadier Hackett.[11]

Brigadier Hackett's new front included troops from three companies of the 7th KOSB facing north towards the Oosterbeek Station, flanked on its right by two troops of Recce Squadron and on the left by the 21st Independent Company, Royal Engineers, and three glider pilot squadrons. The depleted 156th and 10th Parachute Battalions were repositioned, along with several other glider pilot detachments, north and east of the Utrechtseweg-Stationsweg crossroads. The 4th Parachute Brigade Headquarters, along with survivors of the 1st, 3rd, 11th, and 2nd South Staffordshire Battalions, were placed under the command of Major R.T.H Lonsdale. This southernmost "Lonsdale Force" assembled 300 yards east of the Oosterbeek Laag Church and was supported by the PAK 75mm guns of the 1st Airlanding Light Regiment. Brigadier Hackett's new command numbered 500 troops, many of whom were exhausted and low on ammunition.[12] Brigadier Hackett was later wounded and replaced by Lt.-Colonel Ian Murray, Commander of No.1 Wing of the Glider Pilot Regiment.[13] Hackett's forces fought Kampfgruppe Bruhns, Battalion Junghan, and SS Kampfgruppe Krafft in the north, and troops from Hohenstaufen positioned along the Oosterbeek crossroads on the eastern side of the perimeter.[14]

"They're such fighters...if they could only get the stuff to fight with."

The western perimeter, now commanded by Brigadier Hicks, was defended by the relatively intact 1st Borders, which held an almost continuous defensive frontage stretching nearly one and a half miles to the Lower Rhine. Companies from the 4th Parachute Squadron, Royal Engineers, Glider Regiment, and late arriving elements of the Polish Parachute Brigade reinforced Hicks' command. Hicks' forces faced Division von Tettau positioned several hundred yards west along the Valkenberglaan.[15]

The trapped British and Polish forces in Oosterbeek placed little reliance on tactical air support and aerial resupply. The 2nd TAF support remained almost nonexistent because of improperly used or destroyed radio equipment. The continual lack of coordination between the First Allied Airborne Army Headquarters and support bases located in Belgium further compounded communication difficulties. Major General Urquhart repeatedly transmitted requests to FAAA Headquarters to alter supply drops onto the Hartenstein Perimeter, but numerous messages arrived either too late or were never received. However, RAF transport pilots valiantly, yet unknowingly, sallied through the deadly heavy flak, only to deliver several hundred tons of supplies onto enemy held drop zones. Less than ten percent of the desperately needed stores and ammunition reached the shrinking airborne perimeter. The Germans had named the surrounded Red Devil redoubt *Der Hexenkessel*, or "Witches Cauldron."[16]

The Closing Battle of the Oosterbeek Pocket

By early Thursday morning, September 21, the sounds of British guns were no longer heard in the direction of the Arnhem Bridge, making it apparent that the full fury of the 9th SS Panzers could be expected within the next few hours. At 9:00 a.m. General von Tettau's infantry from the NCO school of the Herman Göring Division and Tiger II heavy tanks of the 506th Heavy Tank Battalion launched an attack against the base of the Oosterbeek perimeter near the Heavesdorp Ferry. A platoon of 1st Borders valiantly defending the area were driven nearly 800 meters from the Westerbouwing Hill into the Oosterbeek perimeter, but von Tettau's attack lost momentum following the immobilization of three Tigers with PIATs. At the southeastern base of the Oosterbeek perimeter, Harzer's forces also attempted to dislodge the British from the banks of the Rhine using Panzergrenadiers and armor, but Lonsdale Force held firm supported by airborne artillery firing "open sights" at attacking armor.

Every enemy assault included a company of infantry supported by medium or heavy tanks probing for weakness along the perimeter. The attacks continued throughout the day, but the perimeter held at the cost of every remaining officer of the 1st KOSBs and 10th Parachute Battalion. The exhausted airborne troops remained well organized despite suffering heavy casualties, and counterattacked every German foray with a company of 1st Parachute Brigade re-

The enemy was within several hundred yards of the heavy 3-inch mortars.

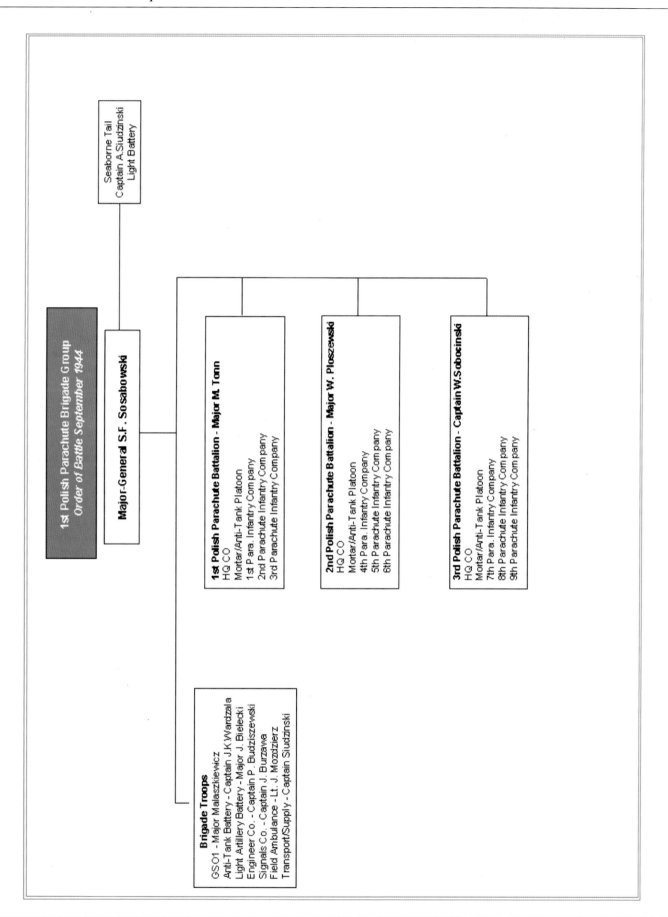

serves. Ironically, the shrinking defensive radius gave the British the advantage of solid interior lines. The limited perimeter allowed concentration of firepower, the reserves did not have to travel far to counter enemy attacks from any direction, and the consolidation improved battalion communications and even allowed the laying of field telephone lines.[17]

The perimeter was inundated with artillery, mortar, and Nebelwerfer rocket fire; this pattern was best described by the British as the "morning hate." Some of the nearly 200 German prisoners incarcerated in the Hartenstein tennis courts fell victim to shell and mortar blasts. Fog and rain in England delayed the arrival of much needed food and ammunition. With the exception of intermittent communications through the Phantom sets, communications between Division Headquarters and First Allied Airborne Headquarters remained poor. Urquhart eventually succeeded in utilizing the one surviving Phantom radio to inform FAAA headquarters via BBC to reroute several supply drops closer to the Hartenstein perimeter.[18]

Enemy sniper fire and small unit infiltration harassed British troops attempting to move around the Oosterbeek perimeter. Casualties mounted hourly, including the wounding of Sheriff Thompson and Brigadier Hackett. The main dressing station (MDS), situated several hundred yards east of the Hartenstein, eventually surrendered to save hundreds of German and British wounded. Resigned to the inevitable, even the brave Dutch "Orange" Battalion" of the PAN (Dutch Underground) disbanded the following day.[19]

"Link-up" with XXX Corps

News finally arrived at Urquhart's Headquarters that XXX Corps had crossed the Waal and elements of the 43rd Wessex Division had reached the town of Driel. British First Airborne Headquarters finally established firm radio contact with the Royal Artillery 64th Medium Regiment near Nijmegen on Thursday, resulting in the additional support of 4.5 and 5.5 inch artillery support around the perimeter. This vital link replaced the cumbersome and indirect connection with FAAA Headquarters in England and the BBC in London via the Phantom units. The 64th Medium Artillery Regiment immediately began firing from nearly eleven miles away, breaking up numerous enemy attacks within several hundred yards of forward airborne troop positions.

The much-needed air support of British 2nd TAF remained nonexistent because of Lt.-General Brereton's restrictions on close support aircraft during airborne lift operations. This decision, combined with unfavorable weather conditions over fighter-bomber airfields, limited the number of sorties to very short periods, usually in the evenings.[20] Direct communications with 2nd TAF were never

As the Oosterbeek perimeter contracted the ferocity and defiance of Urquhart's troops intensified.

One of the few remaining Heavy Vickers machine guns await another attack from the east.

Any enemy attempt to enter the British perimeter was met with deadly counterattacks.

A British tank hunting team using a PIAT to defend the lower road as enemy armor attempts to penetrate lower Oosterbeek.

established because of Brereton's decision to coordinate ground-to-air support through his headquarters in England and 2nd TAF Headquarters on the continent.[21]

The Arrival of the Poles

Late Thursday evening Urquhart received news that the Polish lift had finally arrived, albeit three days late. Only 60 of 114 troop carriers arrived safely at a landing zone east of the town of Driel across from the Heveadorp Ferry. Of 144 Dakotas sent from England forty-one turned back, and the resurgent Luftwaffe shot down another thirteen transports. As a result, less than 800 troops were delivered. Division von Tettau had destroyed most of the Poles' heavy equipment on Tuesday following their arrival on LZL near Johannahoeve.

Final Siege

For the next several days Bittrich's II SS Panzer Corps poured continuous mortar, heavy artillery, and sniper fire onto the perimeter, while overcast skies and increasingly heavy anti-aircraft fire limited the resupply missions. When the skies cleared the British Airborne troops watched helplessly from their slit trenches and barricaded buildings as RAF Dakotas, Sterlings, and American B-24s dropped desperately needed medical supplies and ammunition onto captured drop zones. During one mission nearly half of the trans-port aircraft were destroyed or damaged by the flak and Luftwaffe Fw190 fighters, and less than 15% of the supplies and ammunition reached the airborne perimeter.[22]

Enemy attempts to penetrate the Oosterbeek Pocket continued, with infantry and heavy armor attacks supported by mortaring, shelling, and sniper fire. Large caliber nebelwerfers and phosphorous bombs continued to devastate the perimeter. The once attractive Oosterbeek suburbs deteriorated into twisted and charred buildings, foliage, and casualties. It was estimated that over fifty mortar bombs per minute landed into the perimeter. German infantry, however, were terrified of entering the perimeter because the airborne troops excelled at utilizing mortars, anti-tank guns, and sharpshooters. One final attempt to dislodge the recalcitrant Red Devils[a] occurred on Friday September 22, but was routed following a bayonet charge by the 1st Borders and KOSB.

Despite continual heavy fog shrouding resupply bases in England, Lt.-General Horrocks planned to relieve the British First Airborne at Oosterbeek. XXX Corps resumed attacks northwards in the Betuwe, the name given to the land between the Nijmegen

---

[a]British Airborne forces wore a maroon beret designed by Lt.-General FAM Browning, the founder of the British First Airborne. The Germans mistook the maroon for red, hence the name "Red Devils."

Casualties continued to mount near the Hartenstein.

Left: The Oosterbeek Lagg Church, despite heavy damage, became the rallying point for the decimated battalions returning from Tuesday's attempts to relieve Frost.

Below: The remnants of four battalions attempting to reach Frost filter back to Oosterbeek. As they retreated westwards Lt-Colonel W.F.K. Thompson, commanding the 1st Airlanding Light Regiment, ordered the troops to assume defensive positions in the vicinity of his artillery.

Formation of Lonsdale Force: Major Richard Lonsdale, deputy commander of the 11th Battalion, now assumed command of nearly 500 hundred survivors despite being wounded in the face.

Weary airborne troops near the Oosterbeek Laag Church hear the distant thunder of battle to the south as XXX Corps attacks Nijmegen.

and Arnhem. By Friday morning the 214th Infantry Brigade of the 43rd Wessex Division attacked Harzer's forces towards the town of Driel, while the 129th Infantry Brigade and the Irish Guards continued attacks northeast towards Elst. The assault gained little ground, with the exception of several armored cars of the Household Cavalry reaching the Poles at Driel. By late afternoon the Driel perimeter was reinforced by the arrival of the 5th Duke of Cornwall's Light infantry Battalion and 4th/7th Dragoon Guards. However, the overall timetable was further delayed an entire day, as the 7th Somerset Light Infantry remained stuck in traffic jams and later devastating flanking attacks by German armor and infantry near the town of Oosterhout.[23]

After reaching Driel, Major General Thomas' assault battalions were unable to cross the Rhine with DUKW amphibious vehicles in sufficient numbers to relieve the First Airborne. Although a significant number of amphibious DUKWs were collected on the banks of the Rhine, including those of the just-arrived 1st Worcestershire Battalion, the vehicles experienced difficulty maneuvering across the soft Dutch polderland. Major General Sosabowski would make a final attempt to reach the Heveadorp Ferry with a handful of two-man rubber boats, resulting in thirty-five troops reaching the Oosterbeek perimeter.[24]

Compounding difficulties to reach Arnhem were continuous counterattacks by Brigadeführer Heinz Harmel's 10th SS Panzer Division in the Betwue, and further down the corridor General Student's attacks against XXX Corps' outstretched columns. General Student's forces occupied both sides of the narrow Allied Corridor and severed XXX Corps at Veghel. Kampfgruppes Huber and Walther constantly harassed the British columns along the left flank of the corridor, and on the right flank by the seemingly ubiquitous 107th Panzer Brigade, along with many artillery guns.

On Saturday, September 23, the 2nd TAC finally appeared over the skies of Arnhem, augmented by XXX Corps artillery. Attempts to cut off the base of the airborne perimeter were again repulsed by the 2nd South Staffords and XXX Corps artillery fire. General Bittrich had earlier ordered the II SS Panzer Corps, which now included all German forces in the west, to eliminate the airborne pocket with additional reinforcements arriving from Germany.

XXX Corps attempted to break through the now-formidable Betuwe defensive barrier of the 10th SS Frundesburg, but could not achieve sufficient strength in troops and armor. Major General Sosabowski would send another 200 men across the Rhine with boats provided by the 130th Brigade, 43rd Wessex Division, but these forces suffered heavy casualties within hours.

Lt.-Colonel Thompson's guns prevented enemy tanks from penetrating the southern perimeter.

Throughout the Oosterbeek siege, the First Airborne Division staff continued to issue orders, allocate food, and distribute diminishing ammunition reserves from the candlelit basement of the Hartenstein. Major General Urquhart finally sent Lt.-Col. C.B. Mackenzie and several of his staff officers across the Lower Rhine to report the deteriorating situation to Lt.-General Horrocks at XXX Corps Headquarters. By Sunday, September 24, the exhausted airborne troops inside the pocket were extremely low on ammunition after more than seven days of continuous fighting. At 3:00 p.m. a medical truce was called, and nearly 1,200 troops were transferred through the German lines, leaving less than 3,000 troops inside the pocket.

At the same time Generals Horrocks, Thomas, Sosabowski, Browning, and Gavin met to discuss the fate of the British First Airborne. Major General Thomas departed the meeting with the understanding that Urquhart's troops were to be evacuated the following day. However, an early morning river assault by the 4th Battalion of Dorsetshire, 43rd Wessex, resulted in the destruction of two companies. Many of the Dorsets were captured by General von Tettau's troops on the western side of the perimeter near the Westerbouwing heights.[25] Seeing the futility of further attempts to augment his forces, coupled with increasingly powerful attacks by

SS-Kampfgruppe von Alloworden with Tiger II tanks on the eastern perimeter, Major General Urquhart signaled Major General Thomas his intention to evacuate the division that evening. The codename for the evacuation of the British First Airborne Division was "Operation Berlin."

The following day Major General Urquhart received a message from Major General Thomas explaining that relief forces would not cross the Rhine to reinforce the besieged airborne division. Horrocks' XXX Corps could not sustain any momentum from the south because of continual flanking pressure applied by enemy forces along the Club Route. On Monday evening, 25 September, British and Canadian sappers began withdrawing the remaining airborne forces across the Lower Rhine. This operation was ironically code named "Operation Berlin."

Operation Berlin

At 9:00 p.m. during the Monday evening rains, Operation Berlin began with a heavy bombardment by XXX Corps medium artillery that lasted until the early morning hours of Tuesday. Two companies of the Royal Canadian Engineers with twenty-one storm boats began ferrying operations across the 700-meter wide Lower Rhine. The airborne defensive perimeter would slowly collapse in paper

By early Thursday morning only the sounds of enemy armor were heard in the direction of Arnhem.

VICTORIA CROSS: Captain Robert Henry Cain, The Royal Northumberland Fusiliers/South Staffordshires. "In Holland on 19th of September, 1944 Major Cain was commanding a rifle company of the South Staffordshire Regiment during the battle of Arnhem when his company was cut off from the rest of the battalion and during the next six days was closely engaged with enemy tanks, self-propelled guns and infantry. On September 20th a Tiger tank approached the area held by his company and Major Cain went out and dealt with it armed with a PIAT. The next morning the officer drove off three more tanks by the fearless use of his PIAT, on each occasion taking up position in open ground with complete disregard for his own safety."

Student's forces constantly counterattacked XXX Corps' corridor.

VICTORIA CROSS: Lance-Sergeant J.D. Bakeyfield, South Staffordshire Regiment. "On 20th September, 1944, during the battle of Arnhem, Lance-Sergeant Bakeyfield was the NCO in charge of a six-pounder anti-tank gun at Oosterbeek. The enemy developed a major attack on this sector with infantry, tanks, and self-propelled guns with the obvious intent to break into and over-run the battalion. Bakeyfield's crew had previously destroyed two Tiger tanks and at least one self propelled gun.... With complete disregard for his own safety he allowed each tank to come well within 100 yards of his gun before opening fire."

In the course of the engagement, Bakeyfield was badly wounded but continued to fire his gun and a previously knocked out gun single handed until felled by a shell from a German tank.

bag like fashion, preempting any enemy suspicion that a withdrawal was imminent. By 1:30 a.m. airborne troops north of the Hartenstein were withdrawn, by 2:00 a.m. the remaining ammunition supplies were destroyed, and by 5:00 a.m. nearly 2,600 troops had either escaped by boat or were swimming across the river. Bittrich's forces did not enter the Oosterbeek pocket until mid-afternoon Tuesday,

only to find abandoned equipment, severely wounded, medical and religious personnel, and hundreds of unburied dead.

Out of 10,000 airborne troops that landed, over 7,500 men were wounded, killed, captured, or missing. The defeat of the British and their American and Polish allies would be the last Wermacht victory in the Western European Theater.

Colonel Tucker's 504th PIR waited impatiently alongside the road south of Elst while the Grenadier Guards "stopped for tea."

Operation Berlin: On September 25 at 9:40 pm the 1st Airborne began to withdraw from the Oosterbeek Pocket.

Two companies of Royal Canadian Engineers with twenty-one stormboats and two companies of Royal Engineer companies with sixteen assault boats reached the northern shore.

Notes:

1 Robert J. Kershaw, *"It Never Snows in September"* (Ramsbury: The Crowood Press, 1990), p.239.
2 "They're such fighters", BBC Radio Collection, BBC Enterprises, 1989.
3 Robert Jackson, *Arnhem: The Battle Remembered* (Shrewsbury: Airlife Publishing, 1994), p.111.
4 Stephen Badsey, *Arnhem 1944* (London: Osprey, 1993), p.66.
5 Martin Middlebrook, *Arnhem 1944* (Boulder: Westview Press, 1994), p.326.
6 Powell, op.cit, p.124. *Cloud and fog in England delayed the arrival of the Poles and only 62% of the expected 1,086 transports and gliders would arrive. Air transport planners had over confidently decided to airland the artillery and support vehicles of the 1st Polish Parachute Brigade north of the Rhine while the infantry landed across the river near the southern end of the Arnhem Bridge.*
7 Kershaw, ibid., pp.202-207.
8 *Now reinforced with the 642nd Marine Regiment, 1st Marine Cadre regiment, and 10th Company of the 3rd Police Regiment.* Robert Jackson, *Arnhem, The Battle Remembered* (London: Airlife, 1994), p. 122.
9 Geoffrey Powell, *The Devil's Birthday* (London: Leo Cooper, 1992), p.127.
10 John MacDonald, *Great Battlefields of the World* (New York: Macmillan Publishing Company, 1984), p.180.
11 Powell, op.cit., p.165.
12 Ibid., p.168.
13 By Air To Battle, op.cit., p.118.
14 Kershaw, op.cit., p.263.
15 Powell, op.cit., p.167.
16 Kershaw, op.cit., p.239.
17 Ibid., p.169.
18 Badsey, op.cit., p.59.
19 Ibid., p.60.
20 Powell, ibid., p. 171.
21 *1944 provided air-support signaler detachments to work with ground units and transmit requirements for air support and direct pilots towards the targets. Prior to the implementation of Market Garden, two American air-support units were allocated to each airborne division and one to Browning's Airborne Corps Headquarters. However, the airborne support units were destroyed and remaining failed to use the equipment properly.*
22 Ibid., pp.69-71.
23 Powell, op. cit., p.191.
24 Ibid., p.73.
25 Ibid., p.80

10

"The Hollow Victory"

"After all they had endured, they held high their pride."
- General Sir John Hackett

Operation Market Garden was *nearly* successful. Five major bridgeheads were captured, including the crossings of the Waal and the Maas Rivers. The bridgehead over the Maas eventually served as the springboard for the 21ˢᵗ Army Group's dash over the Rhine into Germany in February 1945. The Allies had succeeded in liberating large areas of Holland, gained valuable airfields, and drew several large enemy formations from the center of the Western Front. The operation, however, failed to retain a bridgehead across the Lower Rhine, turn the northern flank of the West Wall, and initiate a collapse of German forces prior to the end of 1944. Furthermore, the German Fifteenth Army escaped, and a large portion of Holland remained German occupied until the spring of 1945. The greatest toll, however, was the displacement of 100,000 and deaths of nearly 18,000 Dutch civilians following the German halt of rail transportation throughout the winter of 1945.

Allied Losses Though September 25, 1944[1]

	Killed	Wounded	Missing	Total
Hdqtrs. Br. Airborne Corps	4	-	8	12
1st British Airborne	286	135	6,041	6,462
82nd Airborne	215	790	427	1,432
101st Airborne	315	1,248	547	2,110
1st Polish Parachute Brigade	47	158	173	378
Glider Pilot Regt.	59	35	644	738
US Glider Pilots	12	36	74	122
38 Group	6	23	184	213
46 Group	8	11	62	81
30 Corps*	370	740	370	1,480
VII/XII Corps*	962	1,924	962	3,847
IX US Troop Carrier	16	204	82	302
	2,300	**5,304**	**9,574**	**17,177**

*Author's estimates
Tanks lost – 88*
Allied Aircraft Lost – 144
Many of the missing were captured.

Summary of Failures

It was quite unreasonable to assume that a single British airborne division could sustain an airhead across the Lower Rhine until XXX Corps advanced sixty-four miles along a narrow two-tank front in three days. Though quite audacious, Market Garden was a complex and risky endeavor incorporating nearly every military branch and requiring an extraordinary degree of command and control. Despite the tremendous energies and military resources dedicated to the strategic application of "vertical envelopment," the operation failed to achieve a strategic end during September 1944. Market Garden was, however, a rare example of a battle planned and fought on the concept which, in the future, would be referred to as combined operations.

Poor Distribution of Intelligence Findings

"...It is reported that one of the broken Panzer Divisions has been sent back to the area North of Arnhem to rest and refit; this might produce some 50 tanks.... There seems little doubt that our operational area will contain a fair quota of Germans, and the previous estimate of one division may prove not far from the mark...."[2]

Allied Intelligence grossly underestimated the resiliency of German forces late in 1944, and failed to communicate the whereabouts of General von Zangen's Fifteenth Army, Bittrich's II SS Panzer Corps, and the presence of Field Marshal Walther Model to tactical commanders. Because of the paramount need to protect ULTRA, detailed findings were not passed below the equivalent of army group headquarters, and any information reaching a corps or divisional headquarters arrived disguised as operational orders, intelligence summaries, reports, or instructions.[3]

British 21ˢᵗ Army Group intelligence possessed access to ULTRA decrypts, and by September 10 remained well aware of sizeable enemy forces in proximity to the proposed airborne landings and ground attack axis. ULTRA decrypts had revealed that the II

SS Panzer Corps, despite losing nearly two-thirds of its armor, had been ordered to refit three panzer divisions, including the 9th and 10th SS Panzer Divisions, in the vicinity of Venlo-Arnhem's Hertogenbosch. While lacking sufficient heavy armor assets, SS General Bittrich retained organic support, a significant number of lightly armored fighting vehicles, artillery, and a defensive tenacity instilled by battle-hardened officers and NCOs.

Later, ULTRA decrypts on September 14-15 revealed that Model's headquarters had previously concluded that the Allies' intentions were directed towards Eindhoven and Arnhem. The messages also indicated that Model's headquarters was located somewhere near Oosterbeek, and that a significant number of General von Zangen's 15th Army troops and vehicles had escaped eastwards through the Beveland isthmus in the direction of the left flank of the British Second Army. Dutch Resistance later confirmed these findings. By mid-September, the Dutch Resistance also confirmed the presence of the 9th SS Panzer Division in the area of Arnhem-Zutphen and Apeldoorm. Brigadier E.T. Williams, Chief of Intelligence 21st Army Group, had informed Field Marshal Montgomery of these findings, but failed to influence any change in plans.[4] Several days prior to Market Garden, Field Marshal Montgomery received additional warnings from Eisenhower's Chief of Staff, General Bedell Smith, but the Field Marshal ridiculed any suggestions to further adjust Operation Market Garden.[5]

Was Capturing the Groesbeek Heights Necessary?

SHAEF commanders incorrectly concluded that enemy ground resistance would be significant east of the Groesbeek Heights and anti-aircraft fire heavy near Nijmegen. These concerns influenced Brigadier General Gavin's decision to commit nearly half of the 82nd Airborne Division to defending the heights and landing six miles southeast of the Nijmegen Bridge. Gavin's forces were too weak and thinly spread to both defend the Groesbeek Heights and capture the time critical Nijmegen Bridge from the south. Ensuing confusion between Gavin and one of his regimental commanders during the first twenty-four hours delayed the capturing of the Nijmegen Bridge and allowed enemy forces sufficient time to strengthen defenses near the southern end of the ramp and key traffic circles. In Gavin's memoirs he states that:

"When we look back on the situation years later, we realized that it should have been obvious that Tucker's 504th (PIR) was much better prepared to spare a battalion."[6]

The Browning Controversy

On September 15, senior intelligence officer Major Brian Urquhart[a] warned Lt.-General F.A.M. Browning, Deputy Commander of the First Allied Airborne Army, that Dutch underground reports and later air reconnaissance photographs supported Urquhart's concern that enemy armor was located dangerously near the proposed drop

The Hollow Victory.

and landing zones. Browning waved these concerns aside and eventually sent his intelligence officer on sick leave. Another puzzling episode was the intelligence summaries used by the FAAA on September 7 for the canceled Operation Comet, which included specific references to panzer forces refitting near Arnhem and the relocation of SS training units to Nijmegen. These findings were mysteriously missing in Browning's intelligence summary for Operation Market Garden.[7]

Major General Robert Urquhart, Commander of the First British Airborne Division, would later comment that Browning informed him on September 15 that the First British Airborne Division was "not likely to encounter more than a German brigade group supported by a few tanks."[8]

The Possibility of Two Sorties on Market Garden D-Day

Surprise, the trump card of airborne operations, was sacrificed over concerns for insufficient aircraft maintenance and pilot fatigue. Air Vice-Marshal Leslie N. Hollinghurst, Commander of both the 38th and 46th RAF Group, requested a two-sortie flight to Arnhem by departing in the morning darkness from England. However, Major General Paul Williams, Commander of the larger IX Troop Carrier Command USAAF and overall commander of all FAAA transports, disagreed with this proposal on the basis of insufficient ground support personnel to sustain a two-sortie operation, and out of concerns for potential pilot fatigue. Another issue was the lack of American night formation experience and concern for scattering of airborne troops. Both the Sicily and Normandy operations were conducted at night, resulting in both heavy casualties and scattering of troops. As a result, only one operation was scheduled each day, with a maximum lift of 16,500 troops or heavy supply equivalent per flight.[9]

A Landing Too Far

Both Air Vice-Marshal Hollinghurst and Major General Williams agreed that landing close to the Arnhem Bridge was a difficult task due to heavy flak concentrations near the Deelen airfield and soft polderland unsuitable for glider landings. Major General Urquhart was compelled to land the British First Airborne between four and nine miles west of the main objectives. Brigadier General Gavin's 82nd Airborne Division would land nearly six miles southeast of Nijmegen, spreading the unit too thinly to capture all key objectives. Ironically, "Operation Comet," the precursor to Market-Garden, had included a plan to land glider borne troops close to all three major spans, akin to the seizure of the Orne River Bridge on June 5, 1944.[10]

A Battalion Too Few

Despite Major General Urquhart's misgivings of the first lift size, he elected to transport a large number of divisional support in lieu of assault infantry. The American 82nd and 101st Airborne Divisions, however, elected to drop eighteen assault parachute battalions on D-Day in comparison with Urquhart's three parachutes and two and a half glider battalions. The commander of the British First Airborne Division could have landed the 4th Parachute Brigade on D-Day in place of his administrative and support units. Further com-

pounding the transport issue was Lt.-General Browning's decision to extravagantly utilize thirty-six aircraft to carry his advanced British Airborne Corps Headquarters, which included a portion of his wine collection. These gliders could have carried two additional companies of much needed British assault troops to Arnhem.

Number of Transport Aircraft September 17, 1944:

British 1st Airborne	480
82nd Airborne	520
101st Airborne	590

Cumulative Battalion build-up and German Counter Measures:

	American	British	German[11]
September 17	18	6	11
September 18		9	37
September 19			46

One of the key factors leading to the defeat of the British forces at Arnhem was the rapidity of the German buildup and close proximity of powerful armored forces. The presence of the II SS Panzer Corps rendered the operation untenable even before Major Gough's specially equipped assault jeeps departed Wolfheze for Arnhem.

SS Captain Sepp Krafft's companies initially delayed the British Airborne within several hours of arriving until reinforced by SS Kampfgruppe Spindler. The German forces quickly expanded from two companies of former artillery troops to nearly 1,000 troops and thirty armored vehicles. Spindler's blocking line (*Sperrlinie*) effectively sealed off Urquhart's forces within thirty-six hours by forming a critical defensive barrier between the landing sites and Arnhem Bridge. The rest of the battle became a buildup of fresh German reinforcements thrown swiftly and aggressively against the trapped British Airborne Division and the overextended British XXX Corps. German troop movements were relatively unhampered due to General Brereton's insistence that 2nd and IX TAC concentrate on protecting the airborne fleet instead of engaging in ground interdiction.

Parceling the 1st Parachute Brigade

The distance of more then six and a half miles between the British 1st First Airborne Division landings and the objective at Arnhem eliminated surprise, but the error was further compounded by Brigadier Lathbury's decision to parcel the 1st Parachute Brigade into three oversized assault battalions. With the exception of Frost's 2nd Battalion, Lathbury's units were too weak to push through individually and were out of communication with one another within hours of departing the landing areas. A concerted brigade front assault along a single axis may have improved any chance of reaching the Arnhem Bridge in force by the evening of September 17.

Tactical Air Support

Air to Ground support was a critical factor throughout Market Garden, yet it was totally inadequate at Arnhem. Lt.-General Brereton had grounded all Allied fighter-bombers during the air transport

---

[a]No relation to Major General Robert Urquhart.

phase, and compounded difficulties by earlier exclusion of effective liaison between the First Allied Airborne Army and the 2nd and IX TAF in early September.

Without effective forward air control it was difficult to allocate sufficient TACS over Arnhem, and by D+2 nearly impossible to support the First British Airborne Division. A forward air control link with the 2nd TAC and IX Tactical Air Command unit was eventually added to each airborne division prior to the operation, and each Allied airborne division possessed two air support parties, including an SCR-193 and VHF SCR-522 unit. The SCR unit directed requests for TACS support to Second Army, while the VHF unit direct ground-to-air communications with tactical support. However, these units failed to fulfill their roles due to limited range of the SCR unit and the destruction of the VHF units on the ground. The 2nd TAF, however, experienced greater success below the Neder Rhine, flying over 3,500 sorties between September 17 and 26.[12]

Failure to Effectively Utilize the Dutch Underground
In short, the British distrusted Dutch Intelligence. At the end of 1943, the SOE discovered that the Germans had penetrated secret operations in Holland, leading to the capture of fifty agents. When German agents realized British discovery of their counter-spy ring, they sent a final message "in the clear" (unencrypted) to London bragging about their success. Perhaps as a result, British intelligence and ground commanders were loath to employ either intelligence or direct assistance from the Dutch Underground. On the other hand, the Americans made extensive use of the Dutch Underground throughout the course of the battle, including vital Dutch assistance in capturing the Nijmegen Bridge.

Adverse Weather
Weather delayed the 1st Polish Parachute Brigade Group's arrival until D+4 and the 82nd Airborne's 325th Glider Infantry Regiment until D+6. Field Marshal Montgomery concluded that had these units arrived on schedule, they could have provided the much-needed infantry required in achieving both objectives. While the weather did indeed contribute to Market Garden's failure, it was not the real culprit. A two-sortie air operation on D-Day could have mitigated the risk of adverse weather conditions. After D-Day, weather conditions at key tactical airfield and combat zones remained poor throughout the operation, worsening the already deteriorating situation.

Slow Progress of XXX Corps
The XXX Corps assault relied on roads running atop dykes surrounded by wide ditches, silhouetting the British and providing easy targets for German gunners. The two tank wide column was continually harassed by fresh enemy formations. The rigidity of the regimental command structure and an insufficient number of transports compounded British problems in dealing with this situation.

The Hartenstein Hotel.

In his autobiography "A Full Life," Lt.-General Horrocks admits that a number of tactical errors compounded difficulties, including his failure to swing left with the 43rd Wessex Infantry Division and cross the Neder Rhine further west of Oosterbeek.[13]

Within three days the Market-Garden corridor devolved into a struggle to protect the flanks of XXX Corps, with the momentum shifting to the swiftly counterattacking German formations. Rather than rely on such a deep and narrow assault, it may have been better to clear both sides of the Scheldt and establish stronger lines of supply and communication.

Would Different Commanders Have Changed the Outcome?
An interesting question arises in the genre of "after the fact speculation." Could the outcome have been different if Hoyt S. Vandenberg, Matthew Ridgway, and Richard Gale were selected in place of Lt.-General Lewis Brereton, Lt.-General F.A.M. Browning, and Major General Urquhart?

Lt.-General Lewis Brereton considered his new appointment as FAAA Commander a disappointment in comparison with commanding the illustrious Ninth American Air Force. Brereton struggled to overcome his reputation as a querulous and difficult commander, somewhat unprepared for command of an inter-Allied operation. Brereton's focus was training and delivery of airborne forces, but he appeared to misunderstand the importance of communications between FAAA headquarters based in England and the 2nd British Army, as well as IX Tactical Support located across the English Channel. In short, Brereton did not support a proposed D-Day double lift, approved landing sites distant from the bridge objectives, and grounded TACS support throughout the first day of air transport operations. On D+2, Brereton and Ridgway flew to the battlefront near Eindhoven, only to experience the medium range bombing attack by over a hundred Luftwaffe bombers. By prematurely departing England Brereton effectively severed his command, along with any chance to influence or alter the air plans as the battle unfolded.

Lt.-General F.A.M. "Boy" Browning, the founder of the First British Airborne Division, possessed an extensive background in airborne warfare, yet he was quite inexperienced commanding large formations in combat.[14] Browning was well respected by his troops, but was similar to Brereton in delegating critical details to subordinates.

During the critical fourth day of the battle, the commander of the British 52nd (air transportable) Lowland Division, Major General Hakewill-Smith, had requested permission to airland his troops across the Neder Rhine to reinforce the British First Parachute Division. Lt.-General Browning rejected his subordinate's offer without fully understanding the severity of Major General Urquhart's difficulties at Arnhem. Browning's response was simply "Thanks for your message but offer not repeat not required as situation better than you think…."[15]

On the other hand, Lt.-General Matthew Ridgway had successfully commanded the 82nd Airborne Division in Italy and France and was a pioneer of airborne warfare. Ridgway's later successes throughout the Korean War several years later would clearly demonstrate his capabilities as a senior combat commander. During Market Garden Ridgway was assigned a strictly administrative post as commander of the American XVIII Airborne Corps. Ridgway would stand idly aside while Brigadier General Gavin counter attacked enemy probes near the Groesbeek Heights.

Major General Robert Urquhart had commanded a brigade in the Sicilian and Italian campaigns with great success, but he was inexperienced with airborne operations. Despite exhibiting tremendous leadership at Arnhem, Urquhart's limited experience with airborne operations may have influenced him during the planning phase. With more experience he could have strongly opposed plans to use drop and landing zones so far from his objectives. Urquhart could have pressed for a change in the landing mix by including more infantry, or possibly stage a small glider borne *coup de main* akin to the Orne River operations, as well as improve the quality of TACS liaison support. When the question of why the radio sets were so unsatisfactory was put to Urquhart some time after the battle he said, "Everybody got used to the fact that wireless sets hardly ever worked."[16] Ironically, Urquhart's counterpart, Major General Orde Wingate in the Burma Campaigns, was quite keen that insufficient wireless communications would doom an airborne operation. Though Urquhart proved a strong leader in the field, one ponders the outcome if Major General Richard Gale, the former commander of the British 6th Airborne Division, was given command of British First Airborne.

…But despite these ruminations it was certainly a bridge too far.

Notes:

1. Charles B. MacDonald, *The Siegfried Line Campaign* (Washington D.C: Center of Military History, US Army, 1993), p.199.
2. Geoffrey Powell, *The Devil's Birthday* (London: Leo Cooper, 1992), p.40. *Excerpt from 1st Airborne Planning Intelligence Summary No.2, dated September 7, 1944.*
3. Ibid., p.43.
4. *A number of authors believe that had Freddie de Guingand, Montgomery's Chief of Staff, not taken ill, may have persuaded the Field Marshal to relent.*
5. Ibid., pp.42-43.
6. James M. Gavin, *On to Berlin: Battles of an Airborne Commander 1943-46* (New York: Viking Press, 1978), p.162.
7. Powell, op.cit., pp.46-47.
8. Ibid., p.45.
9. Powell, op.cit., p.34. *This was based on the assumption that ground flak was expected to inflict over 40% casualties.*
10. Ibid., pp.36-37. *Allied and Dutch Intelligence erred in determining that the land south of the Arnhem Bridge was unsuitable for glider borne troops.*
11. Robert J. Kershaw, *It Never Snows in September* (Ramsbury: The Crowood Press, 1990), p.304-305.
12. Robert Jackson, *Arnhem: The Battle Remembered* (Shrewsbury: Airlife Publishing, 1994), p.161.
13. Lt.-General Brian Horrocks, *A Full Life* (London: St. James Place, 1960), p.231.
14. Geoffrey Powell, *The Devil's Birthday* (London: Leo Cooper, 1984), p.38.
15. Lewis Brereton, *The Brereton Diaries* (New York: DaCapo Press, 1976), p.354.
16. Major Victor Dover, *The Sky Generals* (London: Cassell, Ltd., 1981), p.135

Bibliography

Ambrose, Stephen E. *The Supreme Commander: The War Years of General Dwight D. Eisenhower*, Garden City, Double-Day & Company, Inc., 1970.

Badsey, Stephen. *Arnhem 1944: Operation Market Garden*, London: Osprey Publishing, 1993.

Bando, Mark. *The 101ˢᵗ Airborne: From Holland to Hitler's Eagle's Nest*, Osceola, Motorbooks, 1995.

Bauer, Cornelius. *The Battle of Arnhem: The Betrayal Myth Refuted*, London: Hodder and Stoughton, 1963.

Bekker, Cajus. *The Luftwaffe War Diaries*, London: MacDonald and Company, 1966.

Blair, Clay (and Omar Bradley). *A General's Life*, New York: Simon and Shuster, 1983.

Blair, Clay. *Ridgway's Paratroopers: The American Airborne in World War II*, New York: William Morrow, 1985.

Barnett, Correlli. *Hitler's Generals*, New York: Quill/William Morrow, 1989.

Brereton, Lieutenant General Lewis Hyde. *The Brereton Diaries: The War in the Air in the Pacific, Middle East and Europe 3 October 1941-8 May 1945*, New York: Da Capo Press, 1946.

Bryant, Arthur. *Triumph in the West, Completing the War Diaries of Field Marshal Viscount Alanbrooke*, London: Collins, 1959.

By Air to Battle, The Official Account of the British Airborne Divisions, London: HMSO, 1945.

Chandler, Alfred D., ed., Stephen E. Ambrose, assoc. ed., et al.. *The Papers of Dwight David Eisenhower: The War Years (5 vols.)*, Baltimore: Johns Hopkins Press, 1970.

Chappell, Mike. *The Guards Divisions 1914-45*, London: Osprey, 1995.

Cholewczynski, George F, *Poles Apart: The Polish Airborne at the Battle of Arnhem*, New York, Sarpedon, 1993.

Davis, Brian (editor), *The British Army in World War II: A Handbook on the Organization, Armament, Equipment, Ranks, Uniform, etc. 1942*, London, Greenhill Books, 1990.

Devlin, Gerard M. *Paratrooper!*, New York: St. Martins, 1979.

Dixon, Norman F. *On the Psychology of Military Incompetence*, London: Ebenezer Baylis and Son, Ltd., 1976.

Dunn, Bill Newton. *Big Wing, The biography of Air Chief Marshall Sir Trafford Leigh-Mallory*, Shrewsbury, Airlife, 1992.

Dutyts W.J.M, and A. Groeneweg editors. *De oogst van tien jaar (The Harvest of Ten Years)*, Oosterbeek, Linders-Adremo BV, 1988.

Eastwood, Stuart. *When Dragons Flew: An Illustrated history of the 1ˢᵗ Battalion The Border Regiment 1939-45*, Wadenhoe: Silver Link Publishing Ltd., 1994.

Essame, Major-General H. *The 43rd Wessex at War 1944-1945*, London: Williams Clowes and Sons Limited, 1952.

Farrar-Hockley, Anthony, Airborne Carpet: *Operation Market Garden*, New York: Ballantine Books, 1969.

Farwell, Byron. *Queen Vicoria's Little Wars*, New York: W.W.Norton & Company, 1972.

Farwell, Byron. *Mr. Kipling's Army*, New York: W.W.Norton & Company, 1981.

Featherstone, Donald. *Wargaming Airborne Operations*, New York: A.S. Barnes and Company, 1979.

Frost, Major General John. *A Drop Too Many*, London: Leo Cooper Ltd., 1994

Gavin, James M. *On To Berlin: Battles of an Airborne Commander, 1943-45*, New York: Viking Press, 1978.

Green, Alan T. *1ˢᵗ Battalion The Border Regiment*, Kendal: Titus Wilson & Sons, 1991.

Gregory, Barry. *British Airborne Troops 1940-45*, Garden City: Doubleday and Company, 1974.

Hamilton, Nigel. Monty, *The Battles of Field Marshal Bernard, Montgomery*, New York: Random House, 1994.

Hinsley, F.H., ed., *British Intelligence in the Second War World, Volume III, Part Two*, London: HMSO, 1988.

Horrocks, Lt. General Sir Brian Horrocks, *A Full Life*, London: Collins, 1960.

Horne, Allistar. *Monty, The Lonely Leader 1944-45*, London: Macmillan, 1994.

Huston, James A. *Out of the Blue: U.S. Army Airborne Operations in World War II*, Nashville: The Battery Press, 1972.

Jackson, Robert. Arnhem, *The Battle Remembered*, Shresbury: Airlife Publishing, 1994.

Kershaw, Robert J. *It Never Snows in September: The German View of Market Garden and The Battle of Arnhem September 1944*, Ramsbury: Crowood Press, 1990.

Liddell-Hart, B.H. *Strategy*, New York: Henry Holt & Company, 1991.

Liddell-Hart, B.H. *The Other Side of the Hill*, London: Cassell and Company Ltd., 1951.

Liddell-Hart, B.H. *History of the Second World War*, New York: G.P. Putnam's Sons, 1970.

Linsay, Oliver. *A Guards' General, The Memoirs of Major General Sir Allan Adair*, London: Hamish Hamilton, 1986.

Maxted, Stanley. *"They're Such* Fighters…." , London, BBC Radio Collection, 1989.

Macdonald, Charles B. . *The Siegfreid Line Campaign*, Washington DC: US Military Institute, 1993.

MacDonald, John. *Great Battlefields of the World*, New York: Macmillan Publishing Company, 1984.

Middlebrook, Martin. *Arnhem 1944*, Boulder: Westview Press, 1994.

Murrow, Edwin R. Account of Airborne Landings September 17, 1944, (tape and transcript), New York: Columbia Broadcasting System, 1944.

Powell, Geoffrey. *The Devil's Birthday: The Bridges to Arnhem 1944*, London: Leo Copper, 1992.

Ryan, Cornelius. *A Bridge Too Far*, New York: Simon and Shuster, 1974.

Ramsey, Winston, ed. *"Prelude to Market Garden", The Battle of Arnhem*, London: Battle of Britain Prints Ltd., After the Battle Magazine, 1986.

Sigmond, Robert. *Off at Last: An Illustrated History of the 7th (Galloway) Battalion The Kings Own Scottish Borders*, Ede: Veenman Drukkers, 1997.

Swiecicki, Marek. *With The Red Devils at Arnhem*, London: Love & Co. Limited., 1945.

Tedder, Lord. *With Prejudice: The War Memoirs of Marshal of the Royal Air Force*, London: Cassell, 1966.

Tieke, Wilhelm. *In the Firestorm of the last years of the War, II SS Panzerkorps with the 9th and 10th SS Hohenstaufen and Frundsberg*, Winnipeg: J.J. Fedorowicz Publishing, 1999

Urquhart, Major General R.E. . *Arnhem, The Epic Story of the Greatest Airborne Assault of World War II*, Derby: Monarch Books, 1960.

Waddy, John, *A Tour of the Arnhem Battlefields*, London: Leo Cooper, 1999.

Warlimont, Walter. *Inside Hitler's Headquarters 1939-45*, Novato, Presidio Press, 1964.

Weigley, Russell F. *Eisenhower's Lieutenants*, Indiana: Indiana University Press, 1981.

Index

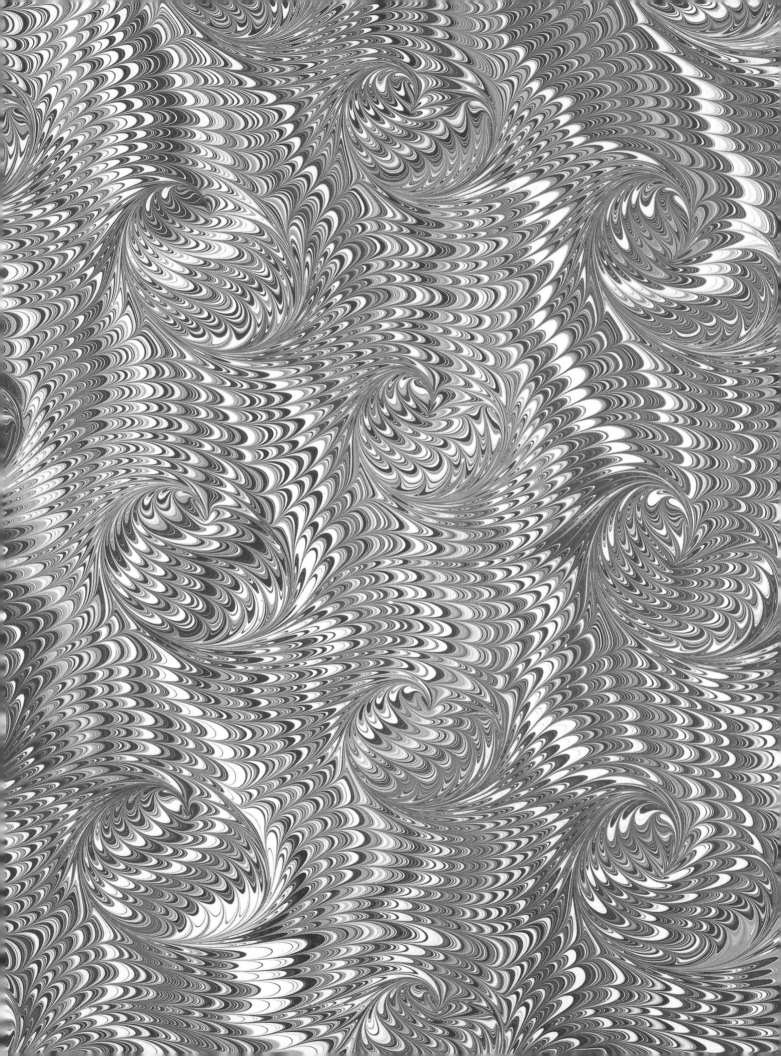